Towards an Urban Renaissance

MISSION STATEMENT

The Urban Task Force will identify causes of urban decline in England and recommend practical solutions to bring people back into our cities, towns and urban neighbourhoods. It will establish a new vision for urban regeneration founded on the principles of design excellence, social well-being and environmental responsibility within a viable economic and legislative framework.

Design by Draught.

Typesetting, artwork and origination by Tempo Graphic Design Ltd.

Technical and architectural illustrations by Andrew Wright Associates
– Master Planning and Architecture, with the assistance of
Grant Associates – Landscape Architects.

Department of the Environment, Transport and the Regions
Eland House
Bressenden Place
London SW1E 5DU
Telephone: 0171 890 3000
Internet service: http://www.detr.gov.uk/

Distributed by E & FN Spon (Taylor & Francis Group plc),
11 New Fetter Lane, London EC4P 4EE.

ISBN 1 85112 165 X
Reprinted July 1999
Printed in Great Britain. Printed on material containing
75% post-consumer waste and 25% ECF pulp.

PREFACE

THE RT. HON. JOHN PRESCOTT, DEPUTY PRIME MINISTER

Over the past few decades many of our urban areas have suffered neglect and decline with an exodus from inner cities, driven by a lack of confidence in schools, fear of crime, an unhealthy environment, and poor housing. This is bad for our people, bad for quality of life, bad for our economy, and bad for society. One of the key political challenges of the new Century is to make Britain's towns and cities not just fit to live in, but thriving centres of human activity. There is no single solution and we need co-ordinated action based on the joint principles of design excellence, economic strength, environmental responsibility, good governance and social well-being.

In April last year I asked Lord Rogers to set up the Urban Task Force. Lord Rogers is not only an architect of global reputation, but an evangelist of urban renaissance, and he has certainly brought experience, intelligence, and inspiration to the Task Force. The Members were chosen for their expertise in the many key elements which are necessary for an urban renaissance, including social exclusion, sustainable development, urban design, and urban regeneration. The Task Force was asked to find out what has caused urban decline in England and to recommend practical solutions to turn our cities, towns and urban neighbourhoods into places where people actively want to live, work and play.

We have already taken a number of steps. We have started the modernisation of our planning system, including setting a 60% target for new homes to be built on previously developed land or by converting existing buildings and consulting on new planning guidance on housing. We have launched a comprehensive package to revive our urban areas and tackle social exclusion, including the New Deal for Communities to transform our most deprived estates, crime prevention measures to make our communities safer and Health Action Zones to tackle poor health in deprived areas. We have released £5 billion of capital receipts for social housing and regeneration and increased and improved the targeting of the Single Regeneration Budget. We have reformed local democracy to ensure that we get best value in our local services and we have put in place an integrated transport policy designed to make our urban and rural areas work. These are just a few of the initiatives under way but still more can be done.

I welcome the thrust of this report – it provides a wide range of interesting and forward-thinking recommendations to feed into ongoing work across Government and beyond. The Government will now be considering the recommendations in detail. It will inform us in preparing our White Paper on urban policy – the first in over 20 years. It will also inform the complementary Rural White Paper, because reviving our towns and cities is key to relieving pressures in rural areas. The Urban Policy White Paper will set out the framework which the Government is committed to developing to ensure that towns and cities are not only competitive and prosperous, but offer a good quality of life for everyone who lives there.

As Lord Rogers says, cities make citizens, and citizens make cities. We can all make a difference, and I welcome views on this report.

The Rt. Hon. John Prescott M.P.

FOREWORD

PASQUAL MARAGALL, FORMER MAYOR OF BARCELONA

I feel privileged to be asked to say some words to preface an attempt to describe ways and means to improve English cities.

If the experience of Barcelona has helped in any measure to influence this report, I would feel more than happy; not only as a former mayor of Barcelona, but also as a European citizen. Defending local in a global world takes courage. And this report demonstrates that this is being done in England today.

The best way to solve some of our global problems is breaking them down analytically into local ones. Not because local is easier; not at all. But because the roots of disenfranchisement, hate and misery always have local roots. It is in making safe and healthy neighbourhoods, towns and cities, that Europe will become what it was decided in 1945 that it should be, a land of peace and justice.

It is also by relating in a clever and efficient manner the well-being of cities to that of countryside, or more properly, it is by understanding human space as a network of centres of different size and density, that we will approach the goal of finding fitting solutions to real problems. It is critical to understand that improving public space is relevant to solving social and economic problems.

The renaissance of Barcelona has a lot to do with the fact that this is a city which is not a national state capital, but still a capital, a nodal city, a cultural stronghold. In Europe today you have chances to succeed if you are centrally placed, along the urban stream flowing from South East England, into the Rhine, and then either towards the Danube or towards the Rhone; or else if you are a state capital.

Barcelona did not have these chances. Therefore she has sought her fortune in two directions: through a rather well-perceived, moderately nationalistic project as the Catalan capital, and by way of improvement of her urban quality and international prestige.

The trick in Barcelona was quality first, quantity after. At the heart of our renaissance, the marriage between City Hall and the School of Architecture has been a happy and strong one. In fact, it is difficult to believe that the outstanding role of the city authorities throughout the process would have been accepted by other public and private actors, without this alliance.

The 1992 Olympics were not the cause of Barcelona's design fame. For example, the prestigious Harvard University Prize was specifically given for the quality of urban design up to 1987. A commitment to develop networks of new plazas, parks and buildings was the cause of our success. The Olympics helped to multiply the good works. And this year the Royal Institute of British Architects awarded the city the most prestigious Medal in recognition of its achievements. Previously, this award had always gone to an individual.

A further factor in our success has been the importance of consensus building. The fact that Barcelona didn't start with great works, (no money was available), created the base of the solid complicity between City Hall and the city at large when it came to engaging in the bigger works.

The projects in Barcelona came thick and fast, and were of the same quality whether at the centre or in the working class peripheral districts. This is another key to social acceptability of urban change.

I wish English towns and cities all the best in seeking to translate the important principles contained in this report to reflect your own circumstances. It will require strong leadership and a commitment to participatory democracy. It will require boldness and foresight. It will require risks to be taken but the lesson of Barcelona is that the rewards can be great.

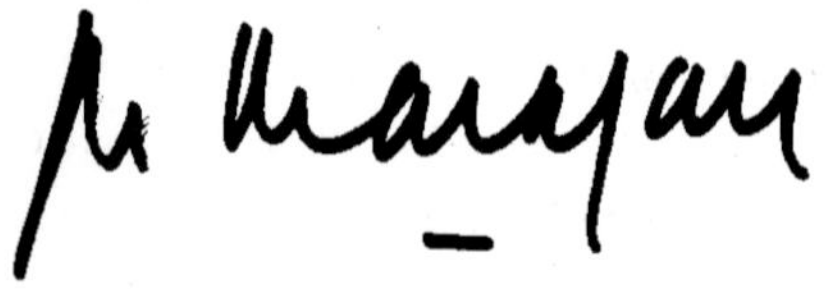

Pasqual Maragall

INTRODUCTION

LORD ROGERS OF RIVERSIDE, CHAIRMAN

How can we improve the quality of both our towns and countryside while at the same time providing homes for almost 4 million additional households in England over a 25 year period?

This report is our response to that question.

We calculate that, on current policy assumptions, the Government is unlikely to meet its own target that 60% of new dwellings should be built on previously developed land. Achieving this target is fundamental to the health of society. Building more than 40% of new housing on greenfield sites is both unsustainable and unacceptable. It will lead to further erosion of the countryside. It will also increase traffic congestion and air pollution, accelerate the depletion of natural resources, damage biodiversity and increase social deprivation within our towns and cities.

But achieving an urban renaissance is not only about numbers and percentages. It is about creating the quality of life and vitality that makes urban living desirable. To stem a long period of decline and decay, pessimism and under-investment, we must bring about a change in urban attitudes so that towns and cities once again become attractive places in which to live, work and socialise.

The report marks the end of a year's intensive effort. We have gathered evidence from many organisations and places. We visited projects in all parts of England and considered the experience of Germany, the Netherlands, Spain and the United States. In the quality of our urban design and strategic planning, we are probably 20 years behind places like Amsterdam and Barcelona.

What we learnt from these visits is that regeneration has to be design-led. But to be sustainable, regeneration also has to be placed within its economic and social context. There are essential issues – education, health, welfare and security – which fall outside the remit of this report. It is important that through the forthcoming Urban White Paper and into the future, government departments and institutions combine policies, powers and resources to achieve an integrated approach in meeting the needs of urban communities.

The report contains over 100 recommendations for change. They cover design, transport, management, regeneration, skills, planning and investment. Inevitably, we have not always been able to reflect within the report the full extent of the discussion and analysis which informed every recommendation. For that reason, we are also publishing a number of supporting reports covering skills, fiscal issues, planning guidance and planning obligations. We have also handed across to the Government the many working papers produced by the Task Force and others over the last 12 months.

The strength of the Task Force's work has been in its diverse membership, reflecting the breadth of the urban agenda. It is testament to our sense of common cause that we are able to promote a clear and unambiguous set of recommendations which have been agreed by all members of the Task Force.

Some 90% of us live in urban areas. We recognise there is a need for a wide variety of solutions to affect every street in every town, from the deprived inner-city council estate to the suburban neighbourhood. The complexity of the report and its recommendations reflect the complexity of the urban condition in England.

Since the industrial revolution we have lost ownership of our towns and cities, allowing them to become spoilt by poor design, economic dispersal and social polarisation. The beginning of the 21st century is a moment of change. There are three main drivers:

- the technical revolution – centred on information technology and exchange;
- the ecological threat – based on greater understanding of the implications of our rapid consumption of natural resources and the importance of sustainable development;
- the social transformation – flowing from increased life-expectancy and new lifestyle choices.

We need a vision that will drive the urban renaissance. We believe that cities should be well designed, be more compact and connected, and support a range of diverse uses – allowing people to live, work and enjoy themselves at close quarters – within a sustainable urban environment which is well integrated with public transport and adaptable to change.

Urban neighbourhoods must become places where people of all ages and circumstances want to live. We have to increase investment in our urban areas, using public finance and incentives to steer the market towards opportunities for lasting regeneration. And we must all take responsibility for the process of change, combining strengthened democratic local leadership with an increased commitment to public participation.

To be effective, our recommendations require a transformation in the quality of urban government. There is a need to re-think the role, the responsibilities and structure of local government in our urban areas. Our cities and towns need strong leadership and democratic structures which are meaningful and accessible to citizens. Local authorities must be empowered to lead the urban renaissance.

We are indebted to hundreds of people who have dedicated their time and expertise in helping us to produce this report. In particular, I would like to thank Jon Rouse, Miffa Salter and the other members of the Secretariat for their work.

An urban renaissance is desirable, necessary, achievable and long overdue.

Lord Rogers of Riverside

THE KEY PROPOSALS

THE KEY PROPOSALS

The report is organised into the following five sections:

PART ONE: THE SUSTAINABLE CITY

Establishes the importance of developing a higher quality urban product by creating compact urban developments, based upon a commitment to excellence in urban design and the creation of integrated urban transport systems that prioritise the needs of pedestrians, cyclists and public transport passengers.

- Create a national urban design framework, disseminating key design principles through land use planning and public funding guidance.
- Undertake area demonstration projects which illustrate the benefits of a design-led approach to the urban regeneration process.
- Make public funding and planning permissions for area regeneration schemes conditional upon the production of an integrated spatial masterplan.
- Commit a minimum 65% of transport public expenditure to programmes and projects which prioritise walking, cycling and public transport, over the next ten years.
- Place local transport plans on a statutory footing. They should include explicit targets for reducing car journeys, and increasing year on year the proportion of trips made on foot, bicycle and by public transport.
- Introduce Home Zones, in partnership with local communities, which give residential areas special legal status in controlling traffic movement through the neighbourhood.

PART TWO: MAKING TOWNS AND CITIES WORK

Improve the management of the urban environment, targeting resources on the regeneration of areas of economic and social decline, and investing in skills and innovative capacity.

- Give local authorities a strategic role in managing the whole urban environment, with powers to ensure that other property owners maintain their land and premises to an acceptable standard.
- Create designated Urban Priority Areas, where special regeneration measures will apply, including a streamlined planning process, accelerated compulsory purchase powers and fiscal incentives.
- Develop a network of Regional Resource Centres for Urban Development, promoting regional innovation and good practice, co-ordinating urban development training and encouraging community involvement in the regeneration process.

PART THREE: MAKING THE MOST OF OUR URBAN ASSETS

Developing on brownfield land and recycling existing buildings must become more attractive than building on greenfield land. The priority is to make the planning system operate more strategically and flexibly in securing urban renaissance objectives in partnership with local people.

- Make statutory development plans more strategic and flexible in scope, and devolve detailed planning policies for neighbourhood regeneration into targeted area plans.

- Produce dedicated Planning Policy Guidance to support the drive for an urban renaissance.
- Adopt a sequential approach to the release of land and buildings for housing, so that previously developed land and buildings get used first.
- Require local authorities to remove allocations of greenfield land for housing from development plans where the allocations are no longer consistent with planning policy objectives.
- Establish a national framework for dealing with the risks that arise throughout the assessment, treatment and after-care of contaminated sites.
- Require every local authority to maintain an empty property strategy that sets clear targets for reducing levels of vacant stock.
- Establish a Renaissance Fund whereby community groups and voluntary organisations can access the resources needed to tackle derelict buildings and other eyesores spoiling their urban neighbourhood.

PART FOUR: MAKING THE INVESTMENT

Sufficient public investment and fiscal measures must be used to lever in greater amounts of private investment into urban regeneration projects.

- Establish national public-private investment funds and regional investment companies, to attract additional funding for area regeneration projects.
- Introduce a new financial instrument for attracting institutional investment into the residential private rented sector.
- Introduce a package of tax measures, providing incentives for developers, investors, small landlords, owner-occupiers and tenants to contribute to the regeneration of urban land and buildings.
- Include the objective of an urban renaissance in the Government's spending review which will determine public expenditure priorities for the early years of the new millennium.
- Review the local government spending formula, which determines the allocation of central government resources, so that it reflects the financial needs of urban authorities in managing and maintaining their areas.

PART FIVE: SUSTAINING THE RENAISSANCE

New apparatus will be required to ensure that the goal of an urban renaissance remains a political priority over the 25 year period of the household projections.

- Publish an ambitious Urban White Paper, which addresses economic, social and environmental policy requirements, tying in all relevant government departments and institutions.
- Establish an Urban Policy Board which combines national, regional and local leadership in driving the renaissance at all levels of government.
- Introduce an annual 'State of the Towns and Cities' report to assess progress against key indicators.
- Create a special Parliamentary Scrutiny Committee to ensure government accountability for the delivery of urban policy objectives.

CONTENTS

CONTENTS

PART ONE: THE SUSTAINABLE CITY

PART THREE: MAKING THE MOST OF OUR URBAN ASSETS

PART ONE

THE SUSTAINABLE CITY

1

A TIME FOR CHANGE

In presenting this report, the Urban Task Force establishes a framework to deliver a new future for urban England; to use a projected increase of 3.8 million households over a 25 year period as an opportunity to revitalise our towns and cities.

The report sets out a commitment to urban communities and establishes a vision for our towns and cities in which an image of failure and decline is replaced by one of opportunity and sustainable growth.

An urban renaissance should be founded on principles of design excellence, economic strength, environmental responsibility, good governance and social well-being.

To be successful, the renaissance should affect every street in every town. It will have to address economic and social disparity as well as the more physical manifestations of urban decline, and it will need to ensure that the policy mechanisms, the skills and the investment are available to deliver results.

There can be no single solution. Instead, this report proposes a framework for change which offers different places the opportunity to define and interpret their own priorities. For many inner-urban areas this will require a radical improvement in the quality of life they offer if they are to outweigh the attractions of suburban living.

In this first Chapter we set out the main features of our urban legacy and describe how the impact of information technology, a greater appreciation of the implications of consuming finite natural resources, and changing life patterns are now driving towns and cities in new directions. It is our collective ability to harness these forces which will determine the future success of English towns and cities.

THE URBAN LEGACY

From Hellenic Athens and classical Rome, to renaissance Florence and Georgian London, history is rich with examples of towns and cities which embodied the best of urban tradition. These were the places which stimulated new ideas and transacted knowledge. They inspired generations in terms of their design, their economic strength and their cultural diversity. They live on as a reminder of the vital links which can be forged between city and citizen.

By contrast, more recent urban history has been dominated by a severance in the relationship between people and place. In England, we have paid a particularly heavy price for our leading role in the industrial revolution. The industrial age was a period of phenomenal urban growth which made a lasting and indelible mark on the British attitude towards the role and function of the city. It marked a point of departure from the Continental attitude towards urban development and urban living. The industrial city, with its pollution, its slums and its short term vision, destroyed our confidence in the ability of the city to provide a framework for humane civic life.

The realities of Victorian urban life

It is therefore not surprising that so many of the visionaries of the 19th and 20th centuries – from Ebenezer Howard to Le Corbusier – have sought to provide us with an escape from the city. At the same time, the writings and the influence of William Morris, John Ruskin and a host of successors have cherished a romantic vision of a lost pre-industrial order and innocence, which still affects attitudes towards our towns and cities today.

Our attempts to escape the city have had mixed results. At their best, the garden cities and new towns have provided a form of suburban living where the relationship between urbanity and country; of public transport and walkability; of work and residence, continues to hold significant implications for sustainable planning today. Such places represented, however, only a small fraction of a general process of urban decline at the centre, and expansion at the periphery, of our towns and cities, which began at the turn of the century and continues to this day.

Suburbs and peripheral council estates sprang up on the outskirts of all our major towns and cities, pushed along by comprehensive slum clearance programmes and the growth in car ownership. The planning system has increasingly submitted to market forces. Edge-of-town and out-of-town housing estates, business parks and retail centres have merged into one – both literally and psychologically. Large tracts of our countryside have been eroded and the need to sustain life and livelihood in nearby towns and villages has been largely ignored. Meanwhile, many of our towns and cities continue to decay. The residue of the industrial age, together with more recent changes in economic history, has left an urban landscape littered with under-utilised buildings and empty sites.

The city is, first and foremost, a meeting place for people. It is the framework that holds together the many institutions – schools, hospitals, workplaces etc. – which form part of our everyday lives. As the city fragments, it damages the potential of these institutions to play their part in the city's unifying civic role. As a result, urban communities are severely weakened as people and activities are dispersed over ever greater distances. From the worst of our social housing estates to the swathes of industrial dereliction, we have increasingly lost ownership of the places and spaces which were once deemed to be the heart of civilised society.

Despite this bleak picture, there are encouraging signs of change. The success of cities as diverse as Barcelona, Stockholm, Portland and Amsterdam as places where people want to live, shows that we can take ownership of our cities once again, and turn an unwanted urban legacy into an opportunity for renewal. In England we are starting to see people move back into city centres, drawn by a lifestyle where home, work and leisure are interwoven within a single neighbourhood. These achievements are small but they can be built upon. To do so, we first have to understand what is driving the process of urban change at the turn of the 21st century.

THE DRIVERS OF CHANGE

In the post-industrial age, powerful drivers are already at work, transforming our towns and cities beyond recognition. It is our ability to harness and direct these drivers which will affect the future of urban areas.

Three main factors have emerged as central to this process of change:

- the technical revolution: centred on information technology and the establishment of new networks connecting people from the local to the global level;
- the ecological threat: greater understanding of the global implication of mankind's consumption of natural resources and the importance of sustainable development; and,
- the social transformation: changing life patterns reflecting increasing life expectancy and the development of new lifestyle choices.

Together, these forces are changing the way we think about cities. To bring about change on the ground, we need a combination of leadership – local, regional and national – and action from below. The combined effect of these three drivers is to create new conditions for empowerment and inclusion of the citizen in civic life. This has the potential of transforming the decision-making process from the top-down, paternalistic model of governance which has characterised most of the 20th century to a less confrontational, more open and flexible democratic political framework, based upon participation.

The information age

The transition from a carbon-based economy to one driven by cleaner knowledge-based industries is a catalyst for change. The decline of the most traditional of our heavy industries has seen the emergence of large tracts of wasteland as well as growing concentrations of unemployment and social deprivation. Contrary to initial predictions, the growth of this new breed of industries has not led to a mass migration to rural cottages linked by an electronic superhighway. Inevitably, information technology does allow for a greater flexibility in terms of location, particularly for back office functions, but it is also resulting in new urban concentrations for face-to-face activity. Thus, the main hubs of economic activity, particularly the head office functions, will remain within larger towns and cities – 'command and control centres' – where good linkages will make communication easy.[1]

The growing emphasis on clean technologies also means that we can once more re-capture an urban environment which offers the best quality of life for the majority and in which people themselves actively want to live. The historic separation of work and home is no longer an imperative,

1 'The Information Age: Economy, society and culture'; Maurice Castells (1996)

and closer links can be forged between the different components of city life. Increasingly, residential, commercial and leisure uses can be combined within a single building or in close proximity within a given area, allowing a new synergy to develop between uses and users. The most sustainable development option for the start of the 21st century is to concentrate people, homes and jobs at the hearts of our urban areas, thus reducing energy consumption and avoiding the further depletion of the countryside.

The ecological imperative

The last 100 years have seen global population increase from just over 1 billion to just under 6 billion inhabitants. This rate of growth is set to continue with a current projection of 8.5 billion inhabitants by 2025. At the start of the century, 10% of the population lived in towns and cities; now we are moving quickly to a situation where over 50% of the world's people will live in urban settlements. The combined effect of population growth and urbanisation is placing a tremendous strain on resources and the environment.[2]

As economic trends point to new patterns of growth and decline, there is an increasing recognition of the need for a more environmentally responsible approach to development. Already, 75% of all pollution arises from urban environments, roughly 45% from buildings and 30% from transport.[3]

Moreover, cities are themselves extremely vulnerable organisms which rely heavily on a delicate balance of inputs, in terms of physical resources, as well as generating a significant number of outputs in terms of waste products. The importance of achieving higher environmental standards in the places we build, as well as protecting existing natural environments from damage, is one of the greatest challenges of the next century. The need to respond to current demands without compromising those of future generations is already driving the adoption of new technology in building, transport, water management and energy recycling. These innovations provide new opportunities for further improving the performance of our urban areas by reducing the consumption of raw materials and the production of waste products, as well as serving to preserve and promote the natural world within the built environment. Nowhere is the implementation of sustainable products and processes more important than within cities.

Changing lifestyles

Changing life patterns associated with increasing life expectancy and the development of new lifestyle choices also point to a different set of demands on our urban environments. Today, the 80 hour working week which typified the last century has been practically halved. In the same period life expectancy has doubled and it is expected to increase further still. Family units have shrunk dramatically, both in absolute terms, as the number of births has declined, and as a proportion of all households. At the same time, new trends, in particular the increase in the number of one-person households, point to a diverse and growing consumer group.

As life patterns change, free time increases

2 'An Urbanising World'; UNHCS (1996)
3 'Cities for a Small Planet'; Richard Rogers (1995)

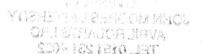

Figure 1.1: Changing life patterns

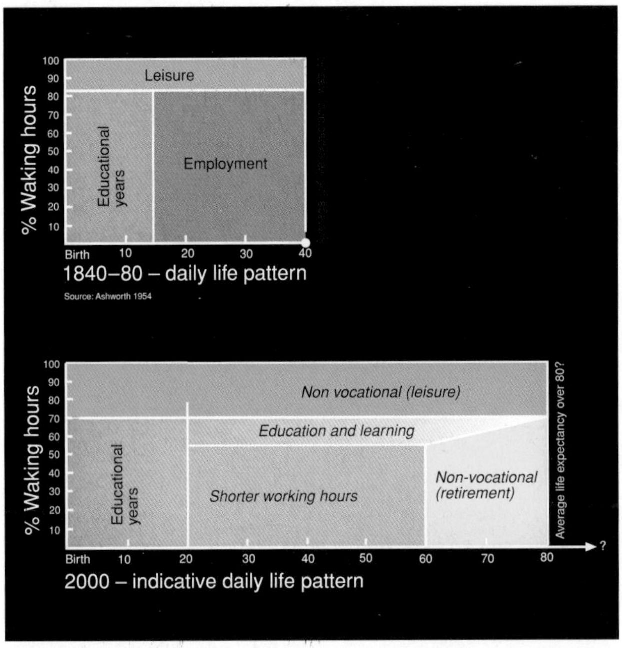

(Andrew Wright Associates)

As lifespans lengthen, and working and parenting are taking up smaller proportions of people's lives, the amount of time to devote to leisure, culture and education is increasing. On the one hand this points to a more mobile population, able to move more freely between residences with reduced ties to work or family. On the other hand, it suggests that for people to remain in situ, homes will have to become increasingly adaptable to changing requirements. Either way, people will require access to life-long learning, emphasising the need for ever stronger ties between academic institutions and the work-place. Employees will also tend to work more flexible hours and many of them will retire younger than the statutory retirement age.

UNDERSTANDING THE ENGLISH CONTEXT

In England – one of the most densely populated countries in Europe – these driving forces take on a particular significance. In 1991, 90% of a total population of 47 million lived in urban areas.[4] The extent to which our towns and cities respond to these pressures for change will impact upon the quality of life for the vast majority of the population.

If the urban framework fails we lose much more than the physical structures. As a nation, our economy relies on the productivity of our urban areas. The cohesion of our communities depends upon an urban form which supports core institutions. The quality of our natural environment demands that development decisions respect the direct relationship between man and nature.

Figure 1.2: English urban areas 1991: over 80% of the English population live in towns and cities of over 10,000 people

Population of urban area	Total population (million)	Cumulative percentage of population (%)	Area covered (hectares)
250,000 +	21.8	46.3	509,000
100,000 – 250,000	5.4	57.7	139,000
50,000 – 100,000	4.1	66.5	109,000
20,000 – 50,000	3.8	74.5	105,000
10,000 – 20,000	2.7	80.3	78,000
5,000 – 10,000	2.1	84.8	61,000
3,000 – 5,000	1.2	87.3	39,000
< 3,000 and rural areas	5.9	100	12,002,000
TOTAL ENGLAND	**47.1**	**100**	**13,042,000**

Source: DoE, OPCS 1991.

4 Source: 1991 Census. NB. In this context, an urban area is defined as an area with land use which is irreversibly urban in character. Pre-requisites for inclusion of settlements are a continuous area of urban land extending for 20 hectares or more, and a minimum population of approximately 1,000 persons

East Manchester: Land going to waste (English Partnerships)

The diversity of urban neighbourhoods means that different places will respond to the pressure for change in different ways. This means that there is no blueprint for success. In this respect the terms 'town' and 'city' which we use throughout this report are deceptively simple: each encompasses a range of different circumstances according to size, location, history and culture. This diversity reflects the full richness of the English urban tradition, from the capital city and the large industrial conurbations, to the medieval market towns and Victorian seaside resorts; from the naval ports and dockyards, to the coal-mining villages and the more recent examples of commuter towns. Similarly, terms such as 'suburb' or 'town centre' describe a range of different places, each with a different capacity to respond to change.

It is clear that if we are to work with the drivers for change we need to understand how they are already affecting English towns and cities to produce a new urban geography.

Figure 1.3: The city provides the framework for core institutions

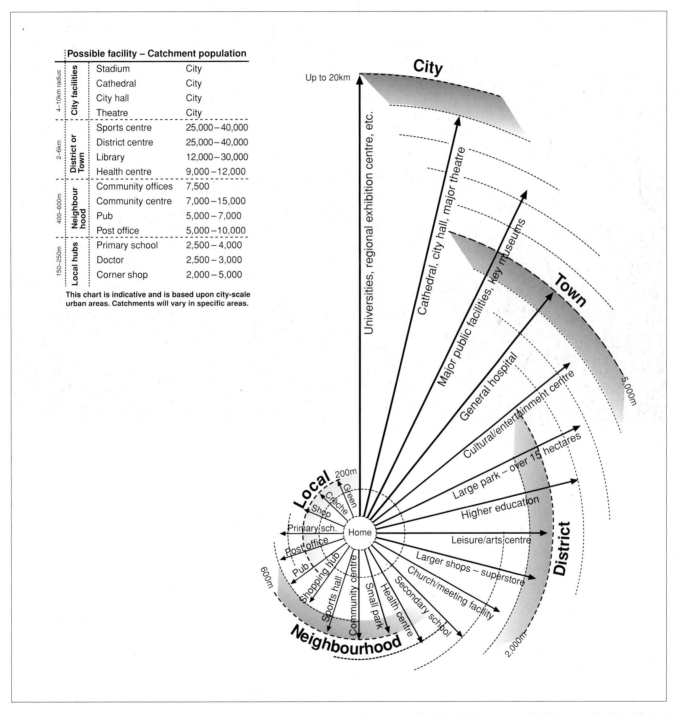

Radius	Group	Possible facility	Catchment population
4–10km radius	City facilities	Stadium	City
		Cathedral	City
		City hall	City
		Theatre	City
2–6km	District or Town	Sports centre	25,000–40,000
		District centre	25,000–40,000
		Library	12,000–30,000
		Health centre	9,000–12,000
400–600m	Neighbour hood	Community offices	7,500
		Community centre	7,000–15,000
		Pub	5,000–7,000
		Post office	5,000–10,000
150–250m	Local hubs	Primary school	2,500–4,000
		Doctor	2,500–3,000
		Corner shop	2,000–5,000

This chart is indicative and is based upon city-scale urban areas. Catchments will vary in specific areas.

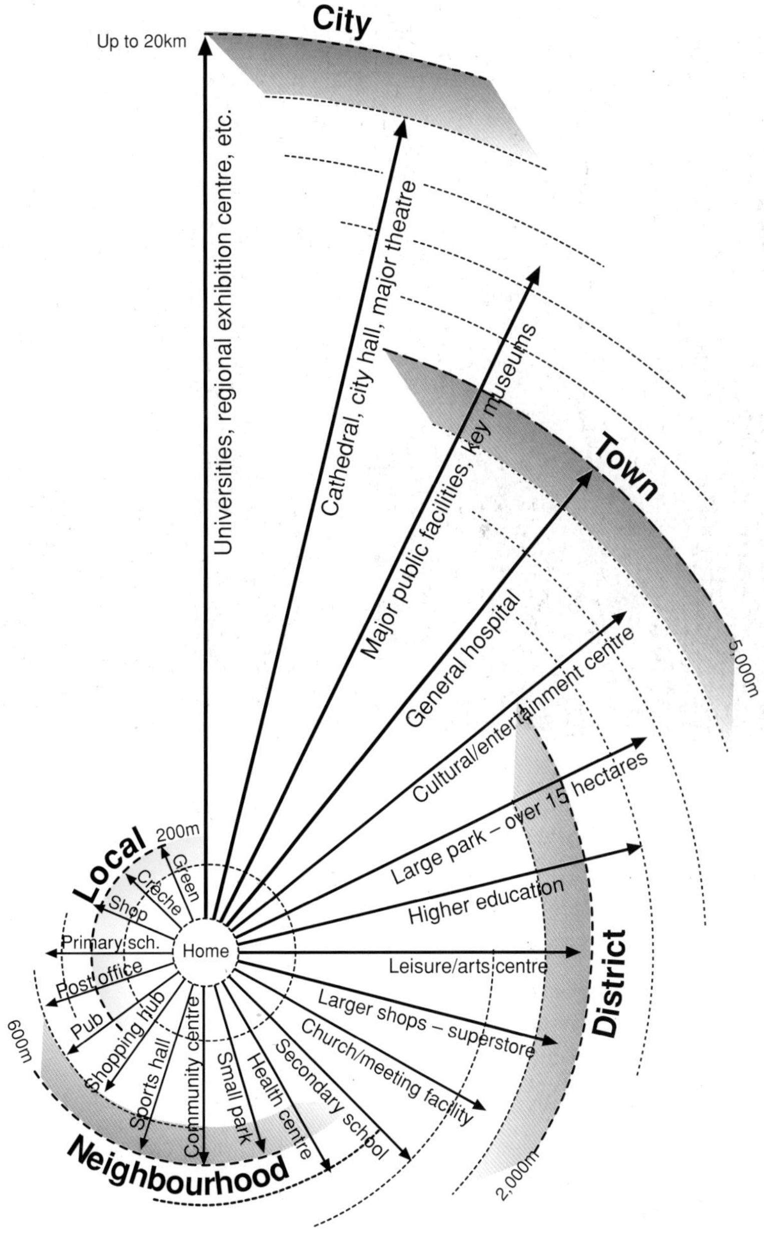

(Andrew Wright Associates)

Source: Adapted from 'Sustainable settlements guide'; University of the West of England

Night-time satellite image of Europe, showing a continent of cities and city regions (WT Sullivan & Hansen, Planetarium Science Photo Library)

The economic context

In England, urban areas provide for 91% of the total economic output and 89% of all the jobs.[5] Maintaining and improving the economic strength of our towns and cities is therefore critical to the competitive performance of the country as a whole. The future economic success of urban areas is itself dependent upon their ability to carve out a competitive role within the knowledge-based economy. This means providing an attractive location for investment.

While the first signs of industrial decline were discernible at the start of the century,[6] the last 30 years have seen an accelerated decline in traditional heavy industries, such as the manufacturing, mining and mechanical engineering sectors, across Britain. This has been coupled with a growth in high technology industries, a significant increase in self-employment, and a steady growth in the service sector. Employment losses in certain sectors have served to isolate whole communities alongside abandoned factories, mines and shipyards. The result has been growing pressure for urban regeneration as well as renewed interest in urban management as a critical component in the re-creation of economically competitive environments.

Inevitably, the impact of changing economic fortunes has had a disproportionate impact on different places. Global cities such as London, Tokyo and New York have become

5 Source: UNCHS Habitat II conference documentation
6 'A Social History of Britain'; Asa Briggs; Cambridge (1990)

more prominent as business and finance centres, sharing the 24 hour business day between them to provide 'command and control' functions which affect entire continents. Other towns and cities are already providing a similar economic function on behalf of their hinterlands and wider regions. But the success stories are far from universal.

Within our city areas, there is a disproportionate share of older and less productive manufacturing plants, as well as a local workforce often lacking the requisite skills to take advantage of the changing economic and technological conditions. This has meant that the employment base within these areas has shrunk dramatically. In 1997 unemployment was 9.5% in inner-city areas while averaging 3.9% in all other areas.[7] Inner-city residents are now almost twice as likely to be restricted to low paid, insecure employment compared to those in non-inner city areas. Even within inner-city areas, there is huge inequality of employment and unemployment, so that a city as prosperous as London still contains almost 20% of all the unemployed people in Britain.[8]

It is not only the inner city which has suffered. The English suburban experience continues to be characterised by heavy dependence on separate zones for different uses, undermining its economic and social cohesion as well as impacting negatively upon the natural environment.

This trend has been fuelled by private property investment activity over the last 20 years which has tended towards a pattern of dispersal. Housebuilders have responded to the demand for suburban housing by providing new estates in peripheral locations. Retailers have developed larger and larger edge-of-town shopping centres for a predominantly car-borne public. Industrialists have moved out of congested urban centres to peripheral sites to take advantage of good motorway access.

The size of the property market highlights the need for the full involvement of the private sector in securing a sea change in investment decisions and in attitudes to urban living. The total value of property transactions in 1996 in the residential and commercial sectors was estimated at £75.7 billion and £17.6 billion respectively. This value was generated through just over 1,100,000 residential and 68,000 commercial transactions.[9] Residential property values in our town and city centres have generally performed close to the national average over the last 20 years.[10] This performance could improve – and, as importantly, extend to less popular, under-performing inner-urban areas.

There is also clear regional inequality. A review of comparative incomes for the different regions shows that only London and the South East exceed the average income per head in the UK. In 1995 London income levels were 140% of the average GDP per head, in contrast with other regions such as Merseyside, with incomes as low as 75% of the average. With the exception of London and the South East, all the other seven regions in England are below the average national and EU GDP per head.[11]

Figure 1.4: Gross Domestic Product per head: workplace based. Index (UK=100)

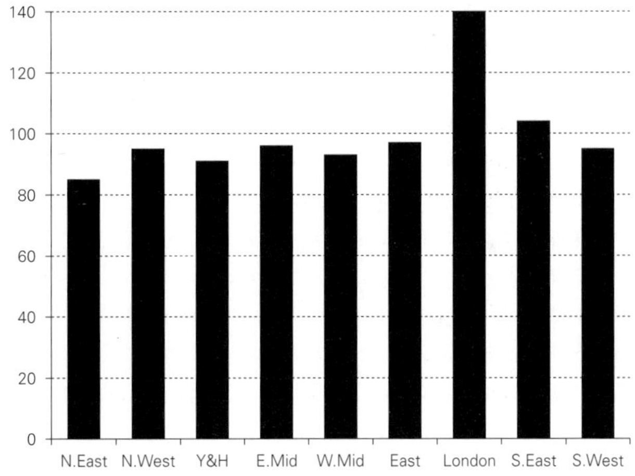

Source: Regional Accounts, ONS (1995)

7 UK Employment Statistics
8 Labour Force Survey (Dec 98 – Feb 99)

9 Source: Royal Institution of Chartered Surveyors
10 Source: Duncan Maclennan, Department of Urban Studies, University of Glasgow (1999)
11 Eurostat (1999)

Even London's position disguises a more complex trend: it is generating increased wealth on the basis of a lower employment base, causing increased income differentials within the capital, particularly between the east and west of the city.

Regional inequality is accentuated by regional migration of population and businesses. The loss of economic activity and the closure of industries have left large amounts of derelict and vacant land and buildings in northern towns and cities, while London and much of southern England is facing a shortage of space to accommodate all the people who wish to live there. A renaissance in the economic performance of our secondary towns and cities in the north of the country may well be vital not only for their own future, but also to ease some of the pressures in the southern regions.

The process of economic change has created other disparities in our urban geography. For example, there is much debate about potential loss of greenfield land in the south east of the country to cope with housing demand, but there is also a problem of too much greenfield land being released in the northern regions, where there is a large stock of brownfield sites. This further exacerbates the loss of population from the urban heartlands in those regions.

A further complexity is in the demand for social housing. There are pockets of the country, particularly in areas with high land values in London and the south east, where it is very difficult for low income households to access affordable housing. This places considerable pressure on social housing providers to meet demand. In contrast, in other parts of the country there are inner-urban areas where there is now more social housing stock than is strictly needed. A significant minority of the projected new households likely to form in the next 20 years or so will not be able to afford their own housing. If we are going to provide these homes in the right places, there will need to be a greater focus on regeneration investment to make the existing stock more attractive in the midlands and the north, and investment in additional housing in regions such as London and the South East.

The social context

Following the rapid expansion associated with the industrial revolution, the urban population in England has stayed relatively stable throughout most of the 20th century. However, this broad overview hides a much more complex story of loss of population from larger urban settlements.

Outward migration, fuelled by housing and economic policies spanning most of this century, has seen significant transfers of population from the city centre cores to outer suburban rings, and to smaller towns within a widening commuter hinterland. Alongside this trend has been significant inward migration, so that, for example, the minority ethnic population in London boroughs such as Newham and Tower Hamlets almost doubled between 1981 and 1991, and minority ethnic groups now represent over a quarter of the total population of Leicester.[12] These changes have transformed the character of many inner-city areas, bringing a rich racial and cultural diversity, as well as challenges to race relations.

Figure 1.5: Population change in the urban areas of England 1961–1994

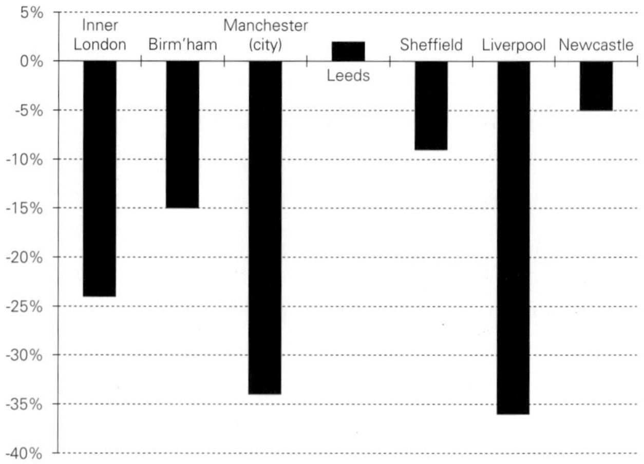

Source: Office for National Statistics, Regional Trends 32, 1997, HMSO

12 'Urban Trends 2'; Policy Studies Institute (1994)

It is only in the last few years that population growth in urban centres has picked up. After decades of decline, some of the central and inner London boroughs are now showing increases in population, fuelled by international migration.[13] Intense urban regeneration activity has also served to create renewed market confidence in certain areas outside the M25. Leeds, Newcastle, Manchester and Glasgow, as well as a number of other cities are, as a result, enjoying an influx of new residents into their centres, attracted by both homes and neighbourhoods which have begun to offer a competitive package of 'goods'. Employment opportunities within the city cores are also growing. The degree to which these trends can be both sustained and encouraged is critical, but is heavily dependent on how we respond to future housing demands.

The 3.8 million additional households projected to form between 1996 and 2021 represent an increase of approximately 19% on the number of households in England at the start of the period.[14] Even though these figures represent a slight slowing down of household growth when compared to previous projections, the critical issue is that we are still facing a sizeable growth in the number of households expected to form over the next couple of decades.

There are probably three main differences to the situation which faced previous generations. First, the current projections are against a back-drop of growing opposition to further development of the English countryside. Second, there is the unique expectation that as many as 80% of these newly formed households will be single-person households – a mix of young people living alone, an increase in people who are divorced or unmarried, and a growing proportion of older people. Third, a significant proportion of the new households are expected to be from minority ethnic groups.

Figure 1.6: Projected breakdown of households by household types, England (1991 and 2016)

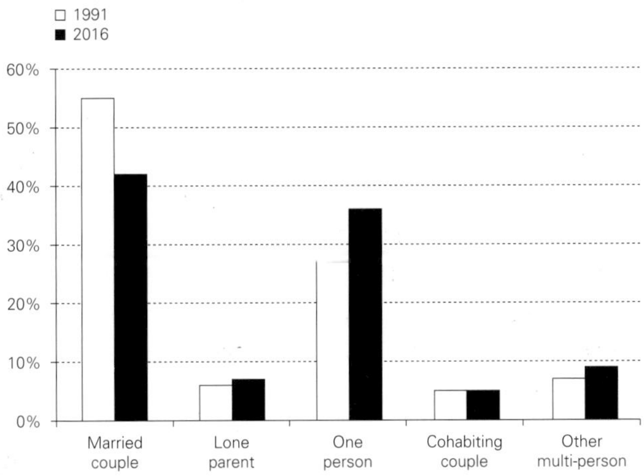

Source: 'Home Alone'; The Housing Research Foundation (1998)

Fuelled by labour mobility and increasing personal wealth, many households will have a growing choice as to where they live. In judging an area, people will continue to focus on low crime rates, good transport links, good health facilities, low levels of pollution, a low cost of living, good shopping facilities, good schools and good race relations. There are urban areas which exhibit these qualities. However, there are many more which consistently under-perform; including many inner-city estates. We should also not lose sight of the fact that in many towns and cities, there are people so disenfranchised from society that they do not have a home at all.

In persuading people to re-consider urban living, we have to recognise that needs will change throughout an individual's lifetime. For many people, the crunch comes with having children. An urban environment, previously perceived as diverse and stimulating, starts to appear unsafe. Schools and health services become more important. While it is therefore accepted that, at this stage in their life cycle, many people will continue to move to more suburban or small town environments, we must look to persuade more families to stay. This means looking beyond the design,

13 'Focus on London 98'; ONS (1998)
14 DETR Press Release (29/3/99)

planning and building of the urban environment at the role played by health, education, security and social services, amongst others.

Just as we need to look at how we persuade people to stay, we need to understand how we can encourage people to move back to our urban heartlands once children have left home. As well as ease of access to work and a good mix of leisure attractions, childless households will want high quality living accommodation and space for guests, including visiting children and grandchildren. We cannot therefore make a direct translation between smaller households and smaller living spaces. In fact evidence suggests that single households with economic choice exhibit many of the same characteristics in terms of their preferred homes and neighbourhoods as larger households. We need to look more closely at where trade-offs can be made in terms of the demand for private space and the benefits of an urban living environment.

The environmental context

At the heart of the environmental agenda is the relationship between city and countryside. The qualities which we all associate with the countryside – wildlife, tranquillity and beauty – are becoming seriously eroded. The map opposite – produced by the Countryside Commission and the Council for the Protection of Rural England – shows that, in just 30 years, we have already destroyed these qualities in many parts of the country. The countryside can only retain its intrinsic qualities if the city adheres to a more compact urban form which contains urban sprawl.

Counter-urbanisation is one of several factors that have contributed directly to energy consumption by households in England having increased by 20% in the 25 years to 1995.[15] Although falling real fuel prices and rising household incomes are also important factors, there is a proven link between urban densities and energy consumption. Urban sprawl contributes significantly to energy consumption due to the increased dependency on car use.

Over the past 25 years, fuel use for road transport in England has risen by nearly 90%. There has been a 63% increase in motor vehicle traffic between 1980 and 1996. Almost all of this was increased car traffic, which accounted for nearly 82% of all road traffic in 1996.[16] This mounting dependence on the motor car has led to increased pollution, noise and congestion, as well as the isolation of individuals without access to a car.

British towns and cities also under-perform in respect of waste management. They currently recycle only 5–7% of their household waste, compared to 30–50% across Europe and the USA.[17] In Germany, the introduction of the 'circular economy law' has led to a significant reduction of packaging of consumer goods as well as the wider use of 'materials labelling' to make recycling easier. In England, we are still landfilling and incinerating almost all of our waste, placing an unfair burden on the surrounding hinterland by contaminating land with waste deposits and polluting air with emissions.

Figure 1.7: The city as consumer

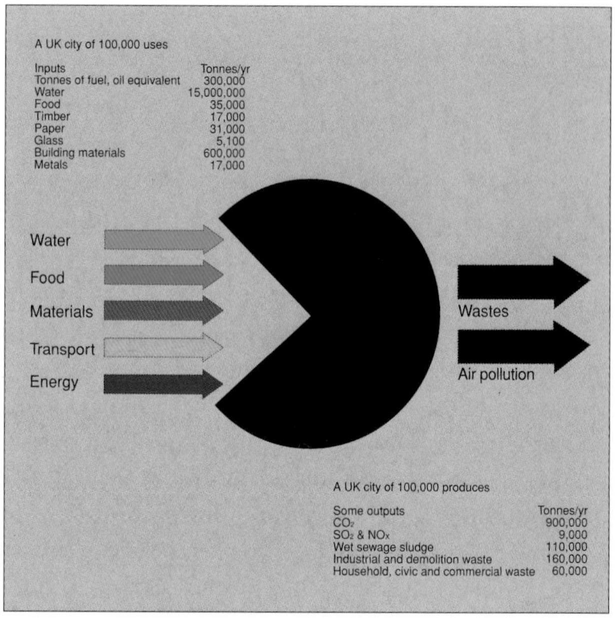

(Andrew Wright and Herbert Giradet)

15 'Digest of UK Energy Statistics'; DTI and 'Indicators of Sustainable Development for the United Kingdom'; DETR (1996)

16 'A New Deal for Transport'; DETR (1998)

17 Source: Urban Futures (1999)

Figure 1.8: The steady erosion of our tranquil countryside

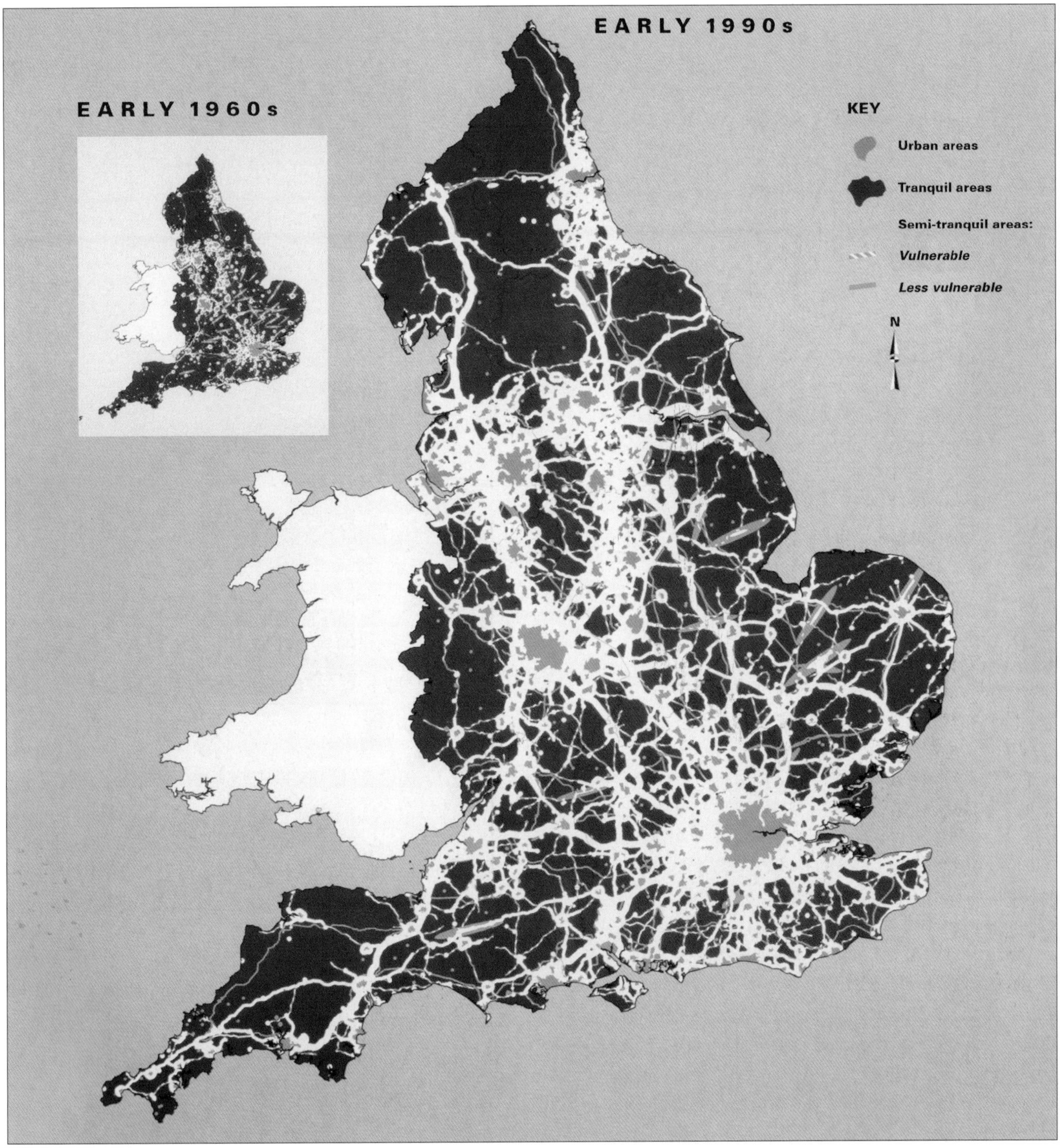

Source: Countryside Commission and CPRE (1994)

Non-sustainable patterns of suburban development: Phoenix, Arizona

Ultimately, town and country are interdependent. The welfare of one cannot be secured at the expense of the other. The guiding principle must be, therefore, that we focus maximum efforts on using available building land within our existing urban fabric. This does not mean that there will be no new greenfield development or that some of that development will not intrude upon the existing green belts. What is important is that where such development has to take place, it is based upon strong principles of sustainable urban design, and that it minimises its impact upon the surrounding countryside.

CREATING THE CONDITIONS FOR CHANGE

Our visits to successful towns and cities show that there are a number of core conditions which underwrite the sustained success of urban areas. English towns and cities will need to appropriate the very best of national and international experience to respond to the range of economic, social and environmental challenges set out above. Success will be predicated upon five central principles.

Warwick town centre: a compact urban form (Skyscan Photolibrary)

Achieving design excellence

A commitment to quality and creativity in the way in which we design buildings, public spaces and transport networks will form the basis for the sustainable city of the future. We will need to rekindle a strong national interest in design and architecture, so that both the public and the professional work together in the provision of a high quality urban environment. This will need to be guided by a new national framework for promoting urban design which sets out principles, ideas and tools to be interpreted flexibly at the local level. Today, participation and local involvement are as important to achieving success in urban regeneration as government policy.

In this report, 'design' is defined as a product and a process. Design is a core problem-solving activity that not only determines the quality of the built environment – the buildings, public spaces, landscape and infrastructure – but also delivers many of the instruments for the implementation of an urban renaissance.

The poor quality of the urban environment has contributed to the exodus from English towns and cities. To redress this balance, we must re-establish the quality of urban design and architecture as part of our everyday urban culture, as it is in the Netherlands, Spain and the towns and cities of many of our other European neighbours.

This is not a question of regulation. We must use the skills and talents of good designers, rather than depend heavily on manuals and controls which have often failed to deliver a quality product. We also have to regard good design as adding to the long term sustainability of the city. This means seeing design as a long term investment.

Excellence in the design of buildings and spaces cannot exist in isolation from a clear understanding of what makes for the most sustainable urban form. In this report we argue that the compact, many-centred city of mixed uses which favours walking, cycling and public transport, is the most sustainable urban form. While different places will be able to appropriate this model to differing degrees, in every case it is the neighbourhood which forms the basic building block of the town and the city. The way in which we define relationships within a neighbourhood, and between neighbourhoods, determines whether or not the city functions efficiently and harmoniously.

The city of easy contact: Covent Garden, London (Martin Bond Environmental Images)

Urban neighbourhoods need a critical mass of people before they feel safe, and before they engender a strong sense of belonging and vitality. This does not, however, mean placing artificial pressures on people to accept housing which does not meet their basic desires in terms of space and privacy. Instead, we have to provide homes which reflect private needs and aspirations but not at the expense of broader social, economic and environmental imperatives.

By itself, housing does not make a neighbourhood. Neighbourhoods need to comprise a mix of uses which work together to encourage formal and informal transactions, sustaining activity throughout the day. The mixing of different activities within an area should serve to strengthen social integration and civic life. To do this will mean concentrating a range of public facilities and commercial uses in neighbourhood and district centres and maximising the use of buildings which are currently not being put to optimal use.

In some areas this is easier to envisage than others. All our towns and cities – whatever their size – include large residential suburban areas. Well-designed suburbs, such as those in Stockholm or the German town of Freiburg, provide a high quality living environment with a mix of uses, good local services and excellent public transport connections to the city centre. Suburbs can provide us with opportunities to strengthen and integrate our towns and cities. While major restructuring of the built form is impractical and likely to meet with local resistance, small scale intervention will mean that suburban areas can function as entities in their own right with places for people to meet, shop and enjoy leisure facilities. At the same time, efficient public transport networks will allow them to be well connected with surrounding urban areas.

The compact urban form highlights the value placed upon proximity and ease of contact between people. It gives priority to the provision of public areas for people to meet and interact, to learn from one another and to join in the diversity of urban life. At its best, the sustainable city therefore operates as a series of interconnected networks of places and spaces devoted to making the most of human interaction.

To do this most effectively means putting the pedestrian first, and ensuring that walking is the preferred option in accessing different facilities within an area. This does not mean outlawing the car as a means of transport because it can offer exceptional personal mobility and freedom of movement. However, provided that the transport linkages between the different urban neighbourhoods are in place, then the bus, the train or, better still, cycling or walking, can become the easiest and quickest way of getting around. In cities with shops, schools and work in close proximity, use of the car can be reduced significantly. At the same time we must give priority to investment in public transport to the point where our public transport system becomes more efficient and cost effective than the car. This will mean a combination of more reliable, more attractive and quicker bus services, cheaper train travel, more innovative and safer forms of urban transport, and better service information across the board.

In achieving design excellence, there is a need both to embrace innovation, and to work to protect and preserve the best of our past. The future development of urban neighbourhoods

Living on the edge in Stockton, Warwickshire (Martin Bond Environmental Images)

must therefore be based on an understanding of their historic character. Within this context, it is then possible to appreciate the relative value of different buildings and spaces. The presumption throughout should be to preserve and adapt historic buildings to accommodate new uses and provide a focus for urban communities.

Creating economic strength

Cities, towns and urban neighbourhoods need to develop clear economic identities which promote and foster clusters of specialist businesses that can work together and compete together within a global market-place.

An attractive, well-designed environment can help create a framework for promoting economic identity and growth. It can fulfil a role at a strategic level by providing the city with the mix of cultural, commercial and infrastructure facilities which it will require to compete on the global economic map. But perhaps more importantly, it can ensure that the city does not stagnate, by continually recycling buildings and spaces to perform new economic functions compatible with the city's business needs. In the 21st century, it is the skilled worker, as well as the global company, who will be footloose. Cities must work hard to attract and retain both.

Sustained investment will underpin economic growth. We estimate that, each year, some £200 billion of public expenditure flows into our towns and cities, into health, education, policing, social security etc., as well as the physical realm. This represents some two thirds of all public expenditure. An enormous amount of national wealth is therefore locked into our towns and cities.

Urban regeneration should be one of the nation's most important drivers of wealth creation. The Council for the Protection of Rural England recently calculated that the urban regeneration sector contributes £12.5 billion each year to the economy and that over 750,000 jobs are reliant on urban regeneration activity, directly or indirectly, including one in four construction jobs.[18]

In this respect, a task of government should be to provide the market with sound commercial reasons for directing private resources toward urban revitalisation; using a combination of regulation and economic instruments for this purpose. Over the next 30 years, the public sector must invest more strategically in towns and cities, targeting regeneration expenditure on three priorities:

- areas which have been in long term economic decline but where, over time, there is a good chance that the market will be able to sustain recovery;
- areas of long-standing social exclusion where careful planning is needed to ensure sufficient public capital and revenue investment over the long term;
- other inner-urban areas and areas within the first inner ring of suburbs to be found in all our major towns and cities, which are starting to go into long term decline[19] and need remedial action now to stem the process of decline.

Taking environmental responsibility

If, as a nation, we are to contribute to alleviating the increasing global ecological pressures, our towns and cities will need to be more resource efficient. We must adopt the principle of sustainable development, which recognises the global environmental impacts of our urban settlements, and the implications both for current and future generations. We should operate on a strict basis of reducing the use of natural resources, and then recycling and re-using those resources wherever possible. Creating environmentally responsible cities means recognising the value of clean air, clean earth and clean water. This includes seeking to minimise air pollution from industrial and transport uses; avoiding the contamination of land and, where contamination does occur, investing in remediation.

18 'Renaissance Pays: Counting the Benefits of Urban Regeneration'; Council for the Protection of Rural England (1999)

19 'Sustainable renewal of suburban areas'; Gwilliam et al.; Joseph Rowntree Foundation (1999)

Hyde Park: the great metropolitan parks are part of our urban legacy and must be protected, enhanced and augmented (Skyscan Photolibrary/Pitkin Unichrome Limited)

To achieve these objectives, we should give priority to energy efficiency. Sustainable transport systems play a key role in reducing energy consumption. Improvements in energy performance in new and old buildings alike can be achieved through the use of new neighbourhood and district-wide energy supply systems such as combined heat-and-power generation. Building efficiency will be enhanced through the wider use of fuel cells and photo-voltaic modules, as well as improved insulation levels.

We also need to promote the idea of the ecologically sensitive city in which humans recognise that they cohabit with nature. Trees, woodland and other open space are all important in fostering biodiversity, in enhancing human health and well-being, and in reducing noise and pollution. We can use some of our previously developed land to create new areas of urban green space.

A strong national commitment to redress the plight of our towns and cities will not succeed without taking account of the needs of our countryside. As we set out in detail in Chapter 7 of the report, current policies are unlikely to deliver more than 55% of new housing on previously developed land. It should be possible to accommodate at least 60% of new housing on recycled land, but as this report demonstrates, this will require significant changes in policy and attitude.

Investing in urban government

In a well-governed city, urban living and civic pride go hand in hand. Excellence in urban management is expected, but also rewarded, and anti-social behaviour is minimised. Research and innovation are encouraged, and the responsibilities of government are constantly reviewed in response to changing circumstances. Most importantly, the well-governed city must establish a clear vision, where all policies and programmes contribute to high quality urban development. In partnership with its citizens and its business leaders, the city authorities have a flexible city-wide strategy which brings together core economic, social and environmental objectives. It is a city which is therefore characterised by strong political leadership, a proactive approach to spatial planning, effective management, and commitment to improve its skills-base.

In this context, local government should be based upon principles of subsidiarity, mediation and partnership. It must combine strong strategic local government, which can provide long term vision and which can consider in a holistic way all the major needs and opportunities of a town or city, with the engagement of its people. The full application of such a model is a long way from where we are now, where decision-making powers still very much reside within national government departments, driven by service-based policies, rather than the multi-faceted needs of local urban communities.

An active participatory democracy will mean investing in and promoting the open exchange and sharing of knowledge. By tapping into people's knowledge, expertise and experience on a wide range of local issues, this investment can provide better end results, while also saving time and money. The process of negotiation, mediation and joint learning can also help foster a sense of ownership and care within a neighbourhood which will reap dividends beyond the parameters of the immediate decision-making requirements.

We hope that the Government's modernisation agenda will go some way towards regaining confidence and public support for local government. The four White Papers issued to date and the ensuing legislative programme contain a far-reaching programme centred on a new duty on local authorities to promote the social, economic and environmental well-being of their area. New forms of governance will be required, with options for elected mayors, local cabinets, scrutiny committees and extensive public involvement. Nolan-type standards of public office will be enforced. Best Value will replace the previous Compulsory Competitive Tendering system. It will challenge traditional patterns and providers of services within local government, and must ensure

Woolwich Town Hall: strong strategic local authorities must lead the urban renaissance (Lisa Woollett)

that local people get the best quality services at a price they are prepared to pay. Better performing authorities will be rewarded with more financial freedoms.

At the heart of local government's responsibilities, we need a planning system which is strategic, flexible and accountable. A strategic planning system regards land use planning as a positive mechanism for achieving change, particularly urban regeneration objectives, rather than, primarily, a reactive means of controlling development. This includes managing the land supply to enable previously developed land and buildings to be put to new uses, and ensuring that greenfield land is not released before it is required. A flexible planning system responds to the needs of different places in different ways, and rewards higher quality development with faster and less conditional permissions. An accountable planning system renders those making or advising on planning decisions responsible for the quality of the decisions they take.

In focusing on strategic leadership, we must not lose sight of the importance of the day-to-day management of our existing assets. More than 90% of our urban fabric of 30 years time already exists. Much of it is in difficulty, particularly many of the large public estates. The state in which we hand our urban areas on to the next generation depends entirely on how we manage our existing assets between now and then. We need to provide a level of care for the urban environment that signals to people a long term commitment to their personal well-being and quality of life.

Prioritising social well-being

To succeed, the urban environment of the future must foster and protect the diversity of its inhabitants while ensuring that all enjoy access to the range of services and activities which constitute the best of urban life. Without a commitment to social integration, our towns and cities will fail. We can, however, establish certain principles to ensure that wealth and opportunity are spread more evenly among urban neighbourhoods.

At the heart of our vision for a culturally diverse and socially equitable city is a commitment to positive community relations and ethnic diversity. Alongside the globalising economy comes a far greater movement of goods and people, with the result that prosperous cities are taking on a more cosmopolitan character. This diversity of cultures attracts many people to city living. However, discrimination against and exclusion of different communities – in particular ethnic and other minorities – will undermine the sustainable city. While we should celebrate the cosmopolitan nature of our towns and cities, we must not gloss over the serious marginalisation which many ethnic communities actually face.

Nightingale Estate, Stoke Newington, London 1998: the realities of a social divide (David Hoffman)

In responding to social problems we must avoid repeating the mistakes of the past. Developing large amounts of social housing in one location does not work. Many existing social housing estates have a strong sense of community – often more so than many wealthier neighbourhoods – but there is not the economic capacity to make these neighbourhoods work over the long term. As a result, jobs and investment go elsewhere, exacerbating the physical isolation of many of these estates. In future, we must develop on the basis of a mix of tenures and income groups. Indeed, our objective should be that a visitor to an urban neighbourhood is unable to tell the difference between social and market housing. The way that affordable housing is developed and allocated needs to reflect the desire for mixed communities. In short, there should be greater integration, quality and choice.

We must also work to reconnect isolated deprived areas to other parts of the city. Too often, social and physical isolation and degradation go hand in hand. In many of these areas, levels of car ownership are low, placing an even greater priority on the provision of adequate public transport at prices which are affordable. We can also give priority to creating jobs within the neighbourhoods themselves.

Social integration should extend to all members of society, including older people, the sick and the disabled. One critical aspect of this integration is to make adequate provision for people with reduced mobility. The 1991 Census and the General Household Survey of the same year suggest that the incidence of disability amongst adults in the United Kingdom is at the very least 11% but is more likely to be 15–16%. Many of these people experience mobility problems. Given an aging population, it is clear that the overall incidence of disability will rise. We need to respond sensitively to this distinct set of needs so that everyone can participate fully in urban life.

In overall terms, we must recognise that the urban renaissance is going to involve many trade-offs. If we are to accommodate many more households in existing urban areas, while still giving priority to social equity and environmental responsibility, this will encroach on the desires and aspirations of individuals and existing urban communities. We also know, however, that to be successful, the process of urban revitalisation has to be owned by the people whom it will affect most: existing residents. People living in urban areas are often strongly committed to their neighbourhoods and are sceptical of change. We therefore need to promote consultation alongside more proactive mechanisms for active participation, linking people with the decision-making processes which affect their own neighbourhood. That is why, with strong local government, we wish to see more decisions which concern neighbourhoods devolved down to that level.

IN SUMMARY

The projection that 3.8 million additional households will form over the period to 2021 raises serious questions about how we use our land and buildings. If we were to build 3.8 million new dwellings at prevailing average density levels for new development, they would cover an area of land larger than the size of Greater London. If we did only develop 55% of the new dwellings on brownfield land, and were to build 45% of dwellings on greenfield land at prevailing average densities for greenfield development, they alone would cover an area of countryside bigger than the size of Exmoor.

It is, however, not just about loss of land. The implications of non-sustainable forms of development go much wider. It means more traffic on over-crowded roads, more energy use, further depletion of natural resources, fewer tranquil areas, loss of biodiversity, increased air pollution and intensified social polarisation. It is therefore for a combination of compelling reasons that we must give priority to creating higher-density, compact developments in existing urban areas, using recycled land and buildings.

As things stand, many urban neighbourhoods are not attractive places to live. Without radical policy intervention there is a real danger that, over the next 20 years, our towns and cities will be further undermined – socially, economically and environmentally – by a combination of deteriorating physical form, social polarisation, environmental degradation, loss of skills and investment, and widespread crime. The very best of urban experience may be denied to all but a wealthy minority if we do not act now. The Task Force's visits to a number of US cities highlighted scenarios in which city centres flourish only behind security gates and private armed police. The population that can afford to move out continues to do so, while the urban poor remains trapped within the decaying remnants of the inner city. Such a future is already in the making in some of our own urban heartlands.

The alternative, however, is also within our grasp – to create a political, professional and cultural framework which can respond to new economic, social and environmental drivers by giving priority to the development of compact, high quality urban neighbourhoods over the continued erosion of our countryside. We can use the opportunity of sustained household growth to repair the current tears in our urban fabric, to achieve more mixed and diverse urban areas, well designed and well connected with one another through a network of sustainable transport options and open space. We can create towns and cities that have enduring economic strength, founded upon new knowledge-based industries employing skilled local workforces. We can create beautiful places that are socially cohesive, avoiding disparity of opportunity and promoting equity and social solidarity.

The aim is to achieve a new equilibrium between cities, society and nature. We believe that such a goal is both realistic and achievable.

2

DESIGNING THE URBAN ENVIRONMENT

Successful urban regeneration is design-led. Promoting sustainable lifestyles and social inclusion in our towns and cities depends on the design of the physical environment. This does not mean that design alone will be sufficient. It must be accompanied by investment in health, education, social services, community safety and jobs. But design can help support the civic framework within which these institutions function successfully. This is why, together with the other key management, policy and financial instruments described in subsequent chapters, design features strongly in our recommendations to secure urban regeneration.

The Task Force's visits to Barcelona, Germany and the Netherlands confirmed the importance of urban design in turning cities round. Well-designed urban districts and neighbourhoods succeed because they recognise the primary importance of the public realm – the network of spaces between buildings that determine the layout, form and connectivity of the city. The shape of public spaces and they way they link together are essential to the cohesion of urban neighbourhoods and communities. When the framework is well designed and integrated – as in the traditional compact city – it plays a fundamental role in linking people and places together. When it is fragmented and unstructured – as in so many modern urban developments – it contributes to social segregation and alienation.

This Chapter therefore focuses on the ingredients of good urban design and the processes that are needed to produce it. It analyses the structure of English towns and cities, and discusses the importance of density, mix of uses, architecture, and, crucially, the layout of public spaces, in making successful urban neighbourhoods. It proposes a set of key design principles and a framework of policy implementation that can deliver sustainable urban development on greenfield, infill or larger previously developed sites.

The chapter draws the following main conclusions:

- in all future urban development, and, where possible in existing urban areas, we must strive for a much greater mix of building types and housing tenures, and seek to optimise development density in proximity to public transport hubs;
- we need to raise standards of urban development in England by improving the process of procurement and the quality of the design product;
- we must improve the quality of design and development briefs, use design competitions more effectively and introduce the benefits of integrated spatial masterplanning to new urban redevelopment schemes;
- to implement these objectives we need a national framework for urban design founded on a set of guiding principles which guarantees public participation at regional, local and community levels.

REGAINING OUR URBAN TRADITION

A process of fragmentation

In England, we seem to have lost the art of designing cities which was once part of our rich urban tradition. Before the industrial revolution we created urban areas of great beauty and lasting quality. Today, the cities and towns of Bath, Edinburgh, Harrogate and Oxford provide models of urban excellence with elegant buildings surrounded by generous open spaces, crescents, parks and squares. The pioneering 'garden suburbs' at Letchworth or Bedford Park, with their tree-lined avenues and spacious villas, provided similarly innovative solutions to the urban problems at the turn of this century. With a few notable exceptions, such as the post-war Roehampton Estate in London, the remainder of the 20th century has failed to deliver spaces and places of similar architectural and urban distinction.

For most of this century English towns and cities have become more fragmented. Recent development has not only been typified by a loosening of the urban form and a lower intensity of land use, but it has also featured a growing segregation between different uses and different users.

The landscape of the inner city has changed dramatically. Here, we have lost much of the quality of mix and variety, the 'fine urban grain' of the city that contributes to street life and vitality. The dense and varied rhythm of the traditional street is being replaced by larger residential and commercial developments, increasingly zoned into single-use ghettos.

At the same time the fringes of our towns and cities have similarly been transformed by free-standing enclaves, surrounded by car parks and access roads. While the design of residential developments in England has not reached the extreme forms of social isolation of many American suburbs, our housing layout is moving in the same direction. This growing separation has actively undermined sustainability in economic, social and environmental terms. For the less mobile resident isolated in a sea of houses, or the commuter forced to drive to work, single-use zoning detracts from the very qualities which make mixed urban areas work so well.

Many of the current problems in English towns and cities lie within the development professions and businesses, alongside those who regulate them. There has been an over-reliance on rigid planning standards and controls on zoning, parking and density which have stifled creativity. We have tolerated a lazy over-use of off-the-peg designs and layouts. We have allowed highway and traffic requirements to dominate urban layouts. And we have been willing to allow developments which undermine the coherence and viability of the towns that do 'work', without giving careful thought to the effects on the logical hierarchy and balance of the whole urban structure.

The redevelopment of recycled urban land can play a critical role in reversing this process of fragmentation. Due to their size, location and distribution, brownfield sites play a major role in the regeneration of our cities. They have the potential to link together parts of cities which for generations have remained divided by industrial activity and physical barriers.

Architecture and urban design

Our analysis of successful urban case studies emphasises how deeply quality of urban life is affected by good design. Urban design determines the very shape of the streets and public spaces which make up our urban areas. It influences how easy and pleasant it can be to move from one area to another; how much daylight, landscape and beauty we can enjoy. As a vital component within this framework, architecture determines the shape, function and aesthetic quality of the buildings that make up our collective urban experience. By weaving together the natural with the man-made, architecture, landscape and urban design establish a balance between people and their environment.

People respond to beauty in cities. They choose to walk from one destination to another along favoured routes.

Good design should provide a stimulus to the senses through choice of materials, architectural form and landscaping. Equally, areas showing signs of wear and tear or neglect can often be 'repaired' with modest investments in good landscaping, lighting and street furniture.

Improving the quality of design in English towns and cities is within our grasp. At the end of the 20th century British architecture is internationally celebrated. Yet we have not made the most of this professional skills-base in respect of our own urban planning and housing design. A concerted effort is required, through the education system and the professional design bodies, to involve emerging and established architects, urbanists and landscape designers in transforming the growth in housing demand and availability of recycled urban land into a major design opportunity to create sustainable urban environments.

This renewed commitment should not just be directed at brownfield sites in existing towns and cities. It is also applicable to greenfield sites and existing suburbs. Some English suburbs are amongst the most popular and successful urban forms of the 20th century. They exist in dozens of varieties, and have adapted and changed over time. Many suburbs, however, were never designed around the principles of sustainable development. They will particularly benefit from being analysed and re-thought in terms of the urban design principles set out in this report.

For some suburban areas this could involve 'retrofitting' or 'recycling' land and buildings to provide better local services at focal points, and improved public transport connections. It could also involve development densities and provision of facilities increasing in order to attract and integrate new residents within existing communities.

We now turn to the key physical aspects which impact on performance of successful urban neighbourhoods, towns and cities.

The English urban tradition: Notting Hill, London (Martin Jones/Arcaid)

The absence of urban design: Glastonbury (Martin Bond Environmental Images)

Figure 2.1: The urban structure of dispersed and compact cities

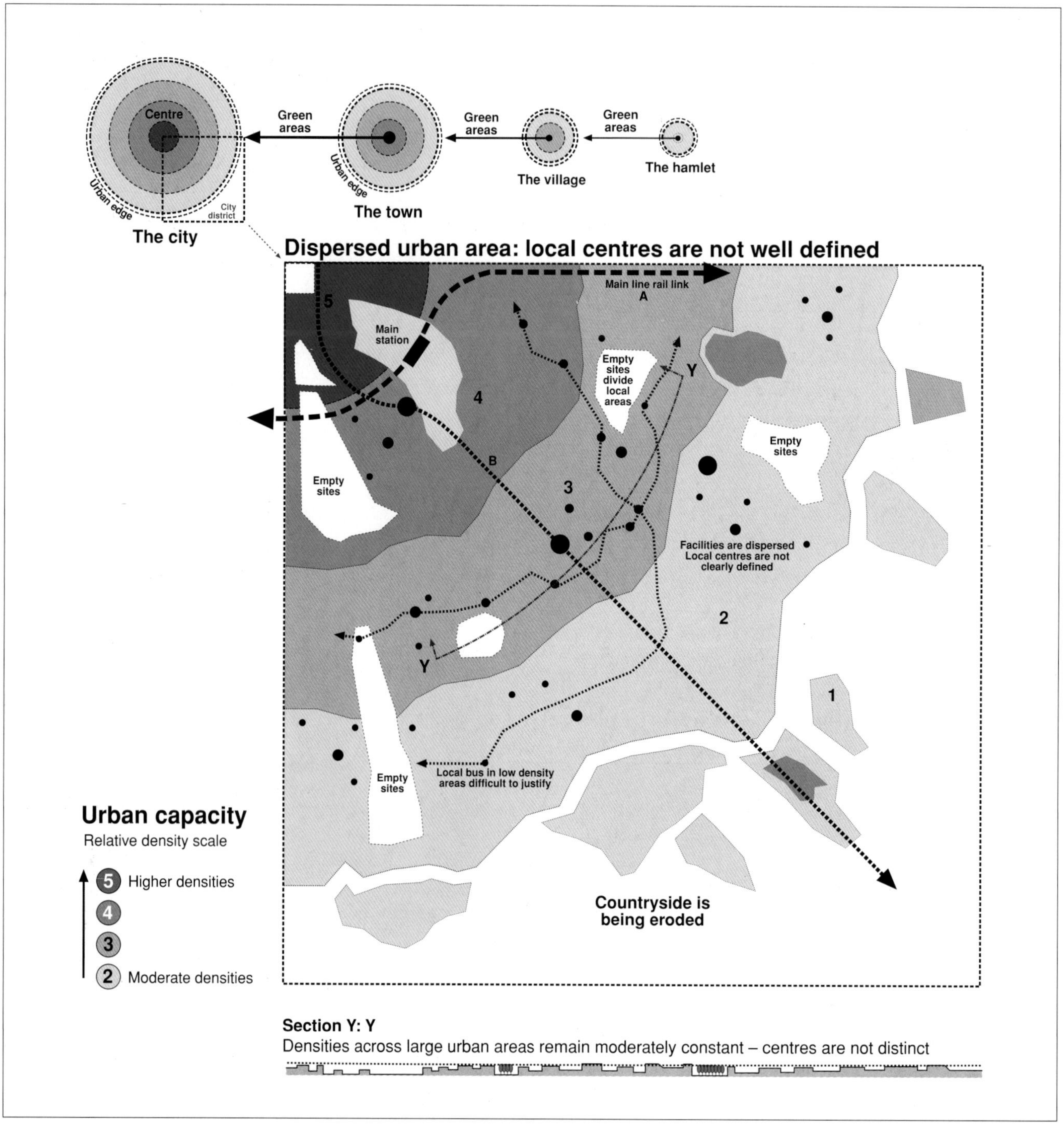

(Andrew Wright Associates)

A clear movement hierarchy from city centre to the home

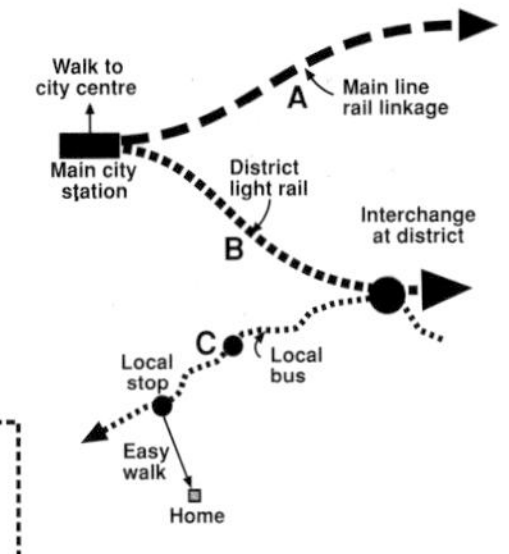

Compact urban area: clear urban districts and distinct neighbourhoods

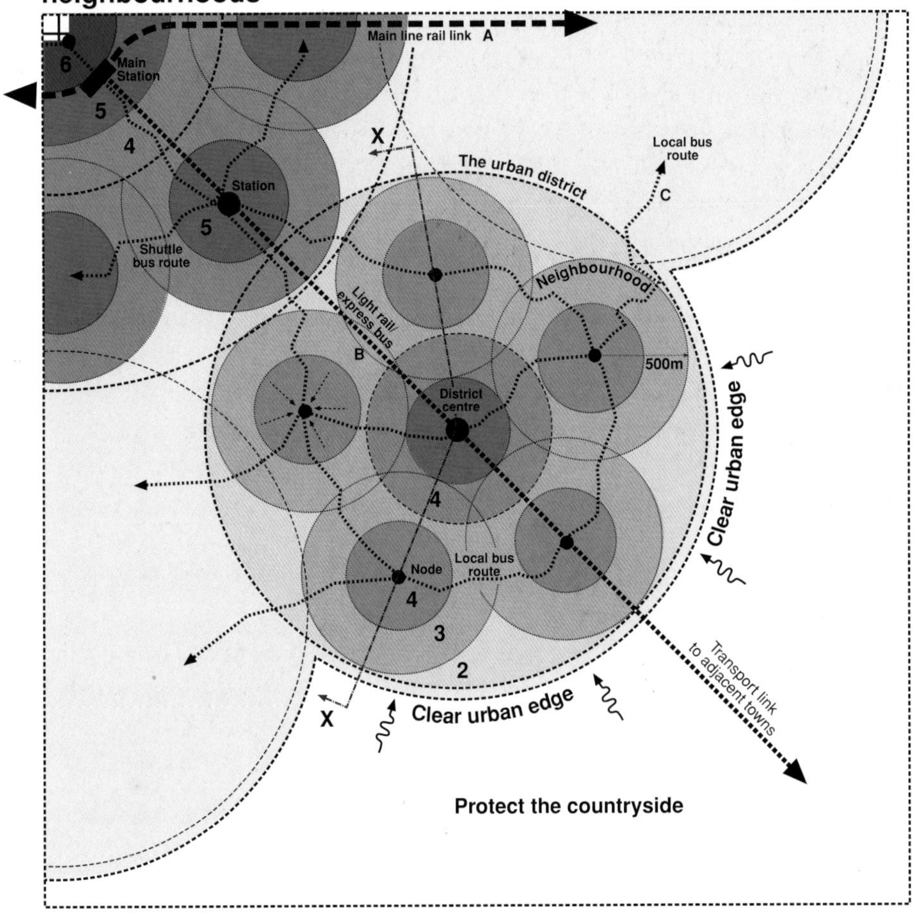

Urban capacity

Relative density scale

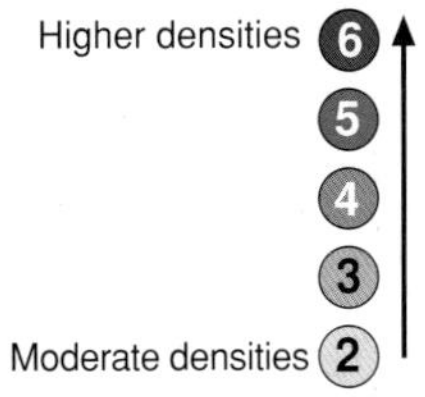

Section X: X

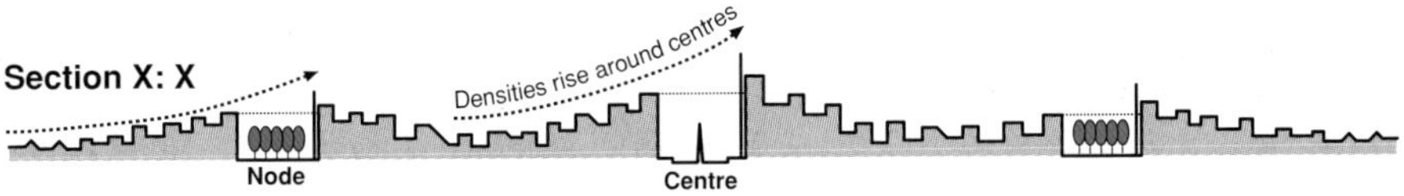

THE COMPACT AND WELL-CONNECTED CITY

A well-designed, compact and connected city is a flexible structure which relates the parts to the whole. A clear articulation of public space not only connects different quarters, neighbourhoods and communities to each other across the city, it also links people within localities to their homes, schools, work-places and basic social institutions.

Figure 2.1 illustrates the difference between a dispersed city and a compact city. This intentionally diagrammatic representation shows how a dispersed city has large areas of low density development which is quite remote from the urban 'hub' or centre. While the hub contains the core functions that support urban life – public transport, civic services, commercial and retail facilities – the lower density areas are mainly occupied by residential accommodation, with a limited mix of uses.

The diagram of the compact city reveals a contrasting structure. Urban areas are organised in concentric bands of density, with higher densities around public transport nodes, (rail, bus and underground stations), and lower densities in less connected areas. The effect of this compact layout is to establish a clear urban boundary, contain urban sprawl and reduce car use.

This pattern of compact urban development sustains appropriate levels of economic and social activity around urban centres and local 'hubs'. It also ensures that all parts of the city – even the more remote, quieter neighbourhoods – are within an acceptable distance from basic transport and social facilities. It is precisely this level of integrated development that is missing from much of the dispersed and fragmented urban developments of the post-war era.

The compact urban structure reflects the complex reality of everyday life in many successful towns and cities. It applies equally to radial cities and linear towns which have grown organically along historic communication routes, resisting the tendency towards urban sprawl. London is an example of integrated urban development, where the inhabitants of local district centres – whether they live in Ealing, Hampstead or Stratford – can benefit from local facilities on the high street and participate in the metropolitan scale of activities that take place in the central districts and the West End.

Figure 2.2 examines the structure of movement within urban neighbourhoods in greater detail. It describes how, to be truly sustainable, the different elements of the town or city – the local community, the neighbourhood and district – ought to be well connected to each other through a network of public routes and streets. The role of public transport in integrating communities is discussed more fully in Chapter 3, but it is important to stress that the structure of the city supports its patterns of movement and communication.

The diagram illustrates the distances which people are prepared to walk to reach the facilities within their local or metropolitan area. For example, most people would be prepared to walk five minutes to reach their neighbourhood shop, school or local bus stop before resorting to the car or other forms of transport. The wider urban district should sustain a range of commercial and social facilities, such as civic space, the leisure centre, college or park.

This family of design principles should inform the layout, distribution of facilities and transport arrangements in new developments – whether inner city or on greenfield sites. Significantly, they should also provide guidance to strengthen existing urban areas which lack these fundamental urban qualities.

Figure 2.2: Linking urban neighbourhoods and communities

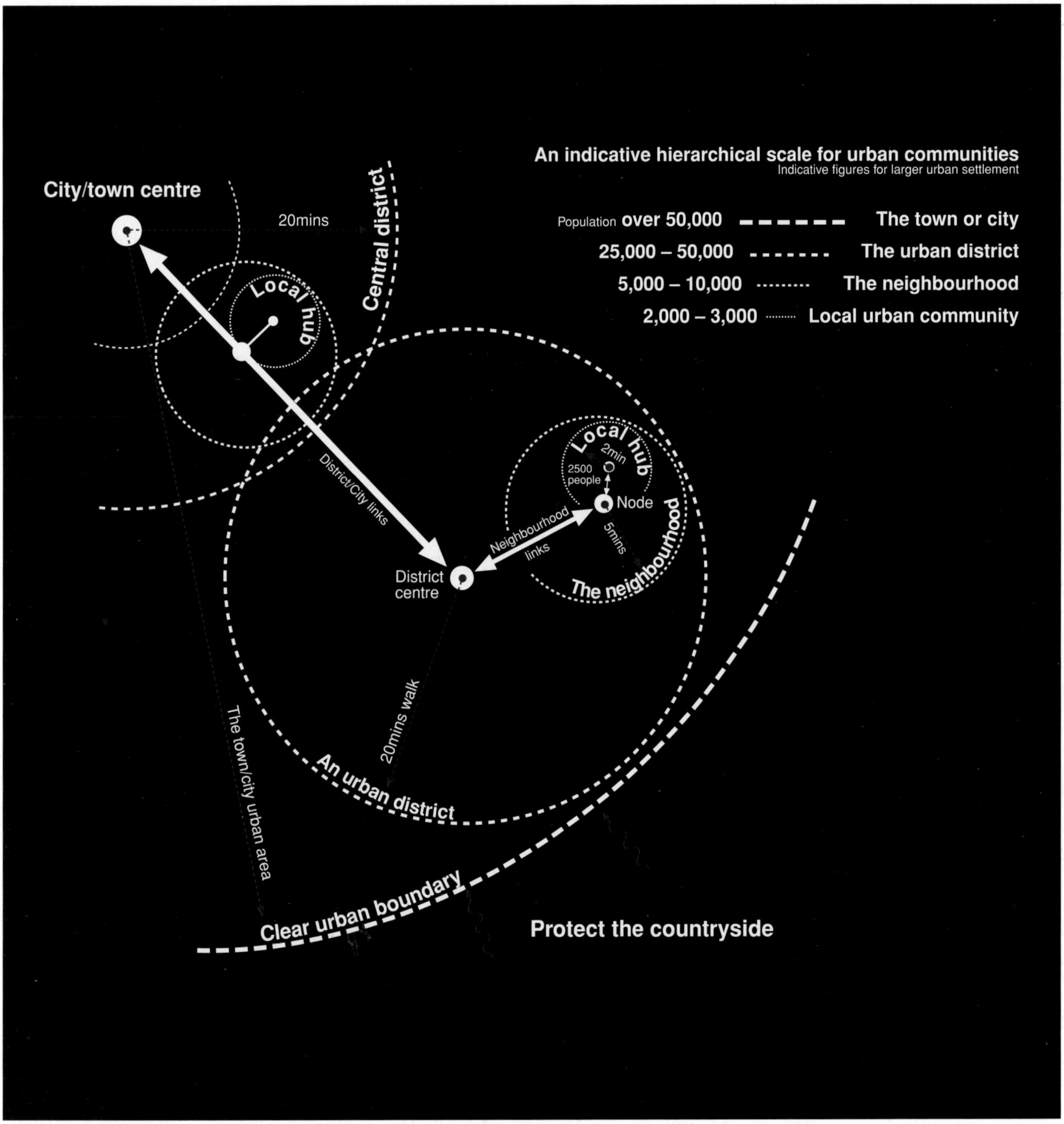

(Andrew Wright Associates)

PORTLAND, OREGON: PIONEERING SMART GROWTH

Instead of accepting ever-escalating levels of traffic, air pollution, sprawl and inner city decay, Portland has developed an effective urban policy of 'smart growth' that sets it apart from most American cities.

The first step towards a new urban development policy was taken in 1975 when Mayor Goldschmidt, responding to intense pressure from community groups in working-class south-east Portland, cancelled plans for the Mount Hood motorway, which would have ripped apart several neighbourhoods to accommodate suburban commuters. Instead, the East Side tram line was built to service commuter needs, and the city adopted an Urban Growth Boundary to contain the type of uncontrolled urban sprawl that has evolved in Southern California.

Since the inception of the Urban Growth Boundary and despite a sharp rise in population, the total area of the city has expanded by only five square miles. Downtown Portland has been revitalised and the number of jobs in the central city has doubled since the 1970s. The limits on the development of land have encouraged the maximum usage of existing facilities and services and have allowed for the preservation of open spaces and farms.

THE PUBLIC REALM: A PUBLIC RESPONSIBILITY

Creating a network of public spaces

In most urban settlements, public space, including streets, squares, parks and less well defined 'common areas' adds up to more than half the total area of land – the rest is occupied by buildings and infrastructure. In England, this valuable 'common good' is predominantly owned by public or quasi-public bodies and institutions. The public sector must act as the custodian of the public realm.

The network of public spaces provides a web of connections that offers people a range of choices when deciding to make local journeys in the course of their daily lives. Most compact and well-ordered cities are designed around a well-connected pattern of streets and public spaces. New urban developments – whether infill or new build sites – should do the same, with a clear hierarchy between the major through-routes and the more subtle structure of local streets and alley-ways.

While many contemporary residential developments in England are based on standard layouts which lack this level of urban integration, there are also excellent examples of towns that have successfully absorbed new neighbourhoods and communities over time, creating a seamless continuity between the old and the new. A popular example is Brighton and neighbouring Hove. Sandwiched between the Downs and the sea, the 18th and 19th centuries created these adjoining towns as unique, popular, multi-purpose places, and a robust and long-enduring form and fabric, which still house many different activities and a wide mixture of housing tenures.

Brighton: The Lanes (David Noble)

Achieving urban integration

To achieve urban integration means thinking of urban open space not as an isolated unit – be it a street, park or a square – but as a vital part of the urban landscape with its own specific set of functions. Public space should be conceived of as an outdoor room within a neighbourhood, somewhere to relax and enjoy the urban experience, a venue for a range of different activities, from outdoor eating to street entertainment; from sport and play areas to a venue for civic or political functions; and most importantly of all as a place for walking or sitting-out. Public spaces work best when they establish a direct relationship between the space and the people who live and work around it.

The traditional street plays a key role in the formation of community. It is where people of all ages come together and interact. The re-establishment of the street as an urban focus could make an immediate impact on people's lives. Streets with continuous active frontages, and overlooked from upper storeys, provide a natural form of self-policing. The continuous presence of passers-by as well as informal surveillance combine to create the blend of urban vitality and safety that is characteristic of many successful urban areas.

Safe, well maintained, attractive and uncluttered public spaces provide the vital 'glue' between buildings, and play a crucial role in strengthening communities. But not all public space in English towns and cities is like this. Some urban areas have too much public space, much of which is poorly designed, managed and maintained. Many 20th century residential developments have a public realm which is simply 'SLOAP' (Space Left Over After Planning) – soulless, undefined places, poorly landscaped, with no relationship to surrounding buildings. A key task in these areas is to re-configure public space so that all parts of the public realm contribute towards achieving a high quality environment.

Often, local authorities will need to work together in defining strategies in this respect. While one priority should be the creation of 'centre to edge' networks of public space which provide the basis for longer journeys for pedestrians and cyclists, a second should be the establishment of networks around cities – green inner rings that supplements the outer Green Belt by creating breathing space close to inner urban neighbourhoods.

It is not just human demands which need to be satisfied in the provision of open space. Networks of open space must also be considered in terms of wildlife requirements, with the aim of increasing the habitat range for other species. Parks and gardens cannot satisfy all these needs. Less formal areas such as greens and commons, local nature reserves, small woods and coppices, and multi-use wildlife corridors all need to be considered, as illustrated in Figure 2.4. Landscape design plays a critical role in establishing a balance between nature and the ecology, and the needs and requirements of contemporary urban life.

Figure 2.3: A computer-generated image of Newcastle, showing the integrated and well-connected pattern of streets and public spaces of a typical city

(Space Syntax Laboratory, University College London)

Figure 2.4: Cities and towns should be designed as networks that link together residential areas to public open spaces and natural green corridors with direct access to the countryside

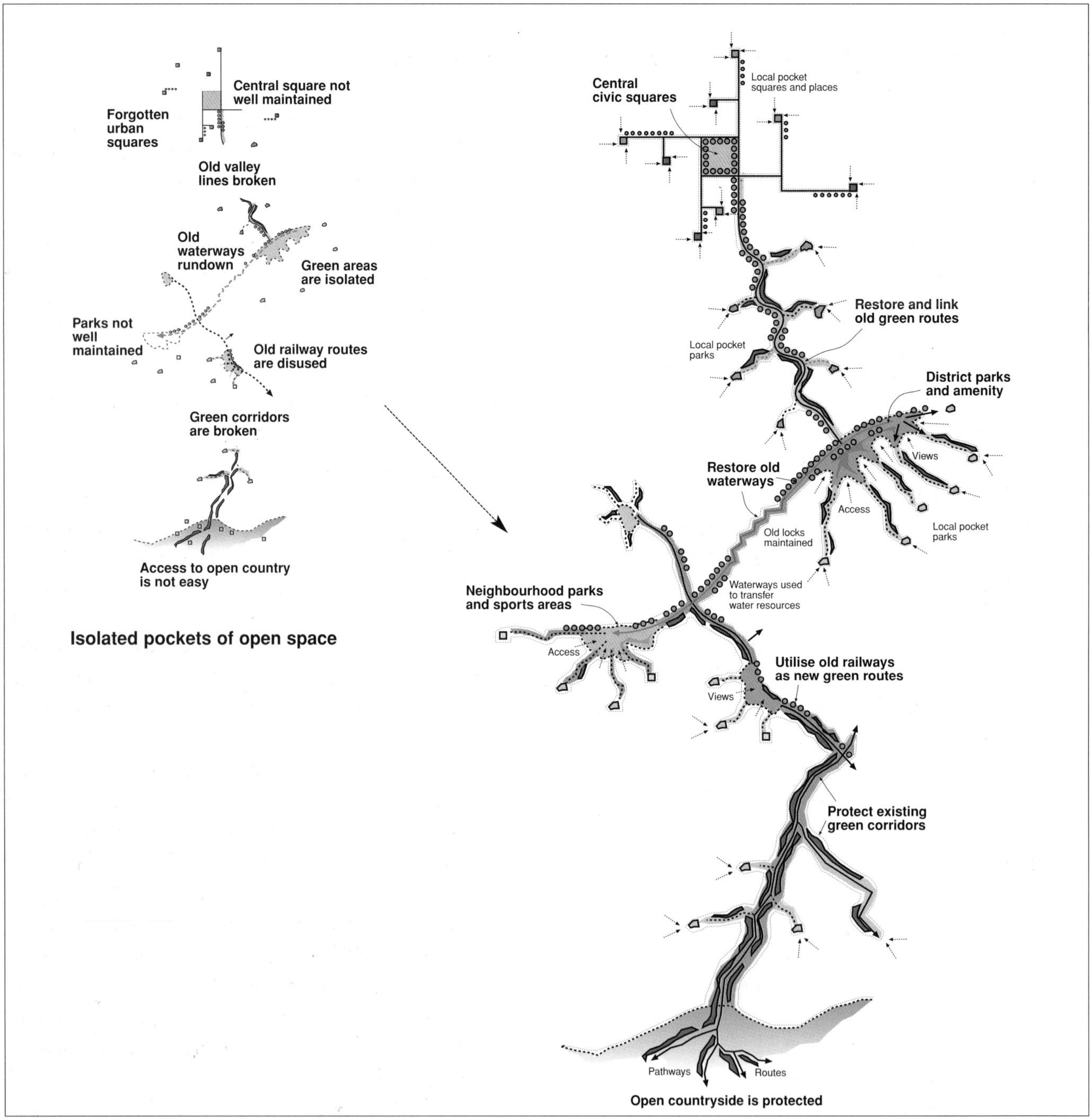

(Andrew Wright Associates)

LEE VALLEY REGIONAL PARK: A STRATEGIC OPEN SPACE

Lee Valley Regional Park stretches a total of 25 miles from East India Dock in London to Ware in Hertfordshire. Established by parliamentary statute in 1967, the park now covers an area of 10,000 acres, which includes a host of contrasting environments ranging from more formal recreational uses to wildlife habitats. Its management structure provides an excellent model that reinforces the links between the park and the surrounding city.

The regional park started life as a number of different sites occupied by mineral extractors and other industrial uses. As the industries declined and sites were left derelict it was recognised that a new resource could be created by linking areas to establish a coherent set of open spaces for both recreation and conservation.

The success of the park relies on a strong Park Plan which clearly articulates a vision for the area. This strikes a balance between conservation and the opening up of areas for public access. At the same time it focuses on the need to establish links between the different components of the park as well as with the neighbouring communities. The Park Plan is incorporated within the local development plans of the various authorities which administer areas along its length. A strong partnership between these authorities and the Park Authority, which owns a third of all the land, underpins the success of the regional park.

Towards a public realm strategy

To create a public realm with positive amenity value requires a comprehensive approach to planning, urban design and management which gets over the current fragmentation of statutory roles and responsibilities. A Public Realm Strategy, which requires local authorities to plan comprehensively for all aspects of the public realm, should either form part of the Local Plan or should have a clear relationship with it, possibly in the form of Supplementary Planning Guidance. The strategy should specify a clear network and hierarchy of open space provision based on a combination of nationally agreed standards and guidance and a careful interpretation of local need.

Recommendations:

- **Require local authorities to prepare a single strategy for their public realm and open space, dealing with provision, design, management, funding and maintenance. (1)**
- **Introduce a national programme to create comprehensive green pedestrian routes around and/or across each of our major towns and cities. (2)**

DENSITY AND INTENSIFICATION

Defining density

To achieve a more sustainable level of development and meet the Government's targets for housing on recycled urban land, we must change the way in which we respond to the concept of urban density. In this section we illustrate how it is possible, through good design, to create liveable urban neighbourhoods designed to higher densities than tends to be allowed by existing planning rules and regulations.

Urban densities vary enormously from city to city, and from one urban area to another. The most compact and vibrant European city, Barcelona, has an average density of about 400 dwellings per hectare. The density of some of the most lively inner city areas in English towns and cities, such as Bloomsbury and Islington in London, can rise as high as 100 – 200 dwellings per hectare. Similarly, towns such as Brighton and Harrogate include examples of sought-after residential locations, which exceed the level of density allowed by most current planning regulations. Most urban areas generally exhibit much lower densities, including dispersed suburban developments or high-rise blocks surrounded by vast expanses of open space with as few as five to ten dwellings per hectare.

A different take on high rise living: Kensington, London (Geoffrey Taunton)

Increasing the intensity of activities and people within an area is central to the idea of creating sustainable neighbourhoods. 'Intensity' and 'density' carry connotations of urban cramming: too many buildings and cramped living conditions. Perhaps because of this, the norm for post-war house-building in this country has often been translated as car dependent mono-cultures built down to standard densities of between 20–30 dwellings per hectare. The problem with parts of English towns and cities – particularly the rebuilt areas of the 1960s and the car-based suburbs of the 1980s and 1990s – is that the densities are just too low. What seems to be happening at the moment is that many quantitative planning measures – 'residential density', 'overlooking distances' and 'car parking' – are being used in an overly simplistic way to dictate design. The result is that insufficient attention is paid to how we can design quality urban environments – and hence promote a better quality of life – alongside a more intensive use of space and buildings.

Density and design

In analysing the performance and character of new urban developments in England and abroad, the Task Force has looked carefully at the relationship between density and design. Figure 2.5 illustrates the link between levels of density and land-take in a typical neighbourhood of 7,500 people. The message is clear: the lower the density, (say, 20 dwellings per hectare), the larger the amount of area that is occupied by buildings, roads and open space. A hypothetical low density neighbourhood could extend to nearly 1.5 kilometres in diameter, pushing over 60% of the houses beyond the acceptable 500-metre or five-minute walking limit. This form of layout promotes excessive car use and makes it difficult to justify a bus route. As density levels are increased – even to the moderate levels of 40 or 60 dwellings per hectare – the land-take diminishes rapidly. More people are close enough to communal facilities to walk, and an efficient bus service can be made viable. Moreover, the critical mass of development contributes to the informal vitality of the streets and public places that attracts people to city centres and urban neighbourhoods, as well as contributing to energy efficiency.

A mixed-use urban centre

Figure 2.5: Models of urban capacity

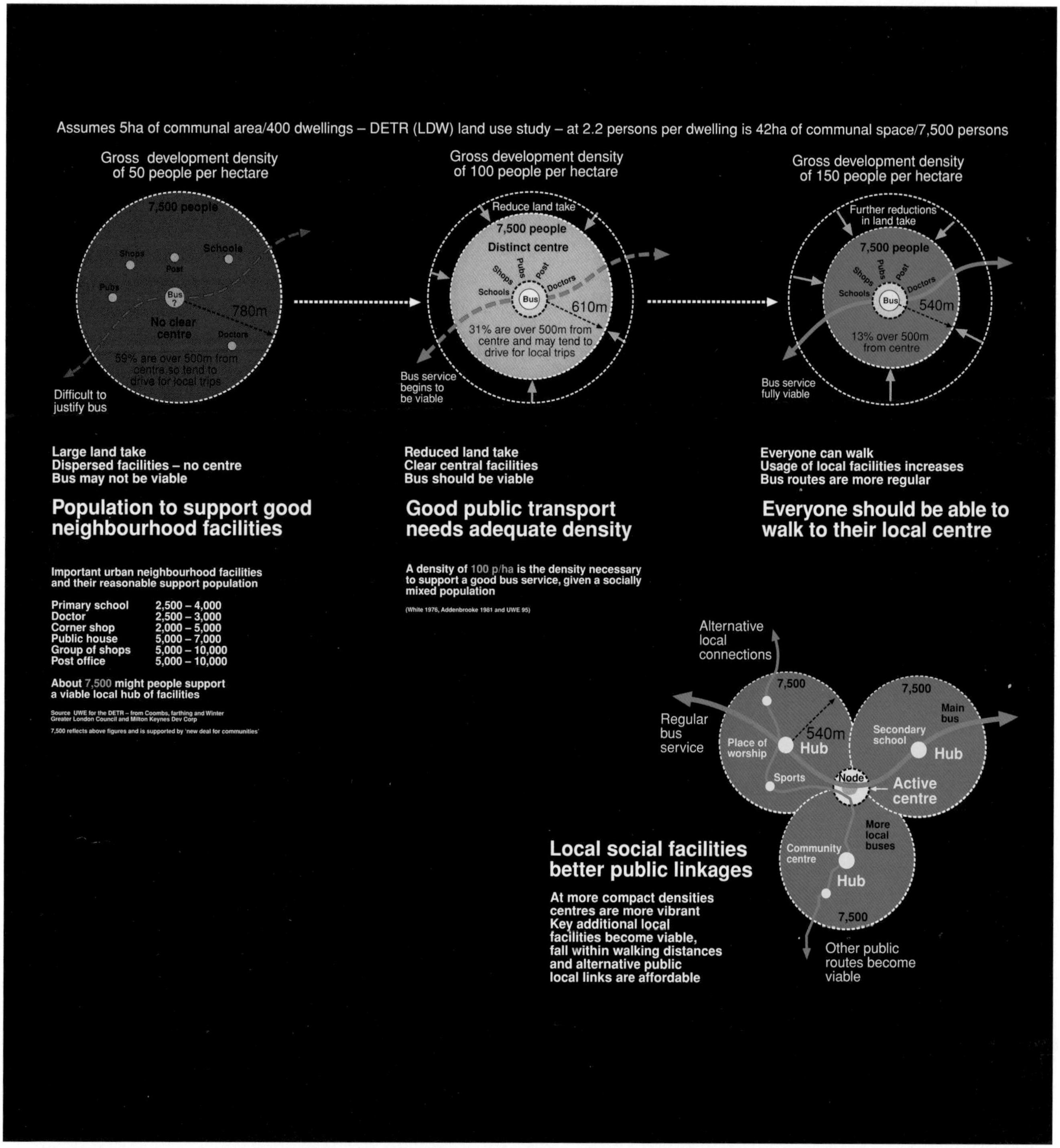

Assumes 5ha of communal area/400 dwellings – DETR (LDW) land use study – at 2.2 persons per dwelling is 42ha of communal space/7,500 persons
Gross development density of 50 people per hectare
7,500 people
Shops
Post
Schools
Pubs
Bus ?
780m
No clear centre
Doctors
59% are over 500m from centre so tend to drive for local trips
Difficult to justify bus
Gross development density of 100 people per hectare
Reduce land take
7,500 people
Distinct centre
Shops
Pubs
Post
Schools
Bus
Doctors
610m
31% are over 500m from centre and may tend to drive for local trips
Bus service begins to be viable
Gross development density of 150 people per hectare
Further reductions in land take
7,500 people
Shops
Pubs
Post
Schools
Bus
Doctors
540m
13% over 500m from centre
Bus service fully viable
Large land take
Dispersed facilities – no centre
Bus may not be viable
Population to support good neighbourhood facilities
Important urban neighbourhood facilities and their reasonable support population
Primary school 2,500 – 4,000
Doctor 2,500 – 3,000
Corner shop 2,000 – 5,000
Public house 5,000 – 7,000
Group of shops 5,000 – 10,000
Post office 5,000 – 10,000
About 7,500 might people support a viable local hub of facilities
Source UWE for the DETR – from Coombs, farthing and Winter Greater London Council and Milton Keynes Dev Corp
7,500 reflects above figures and is supported by 'new deal for communities'
Reduced land take
Clear central facilities
Bus should be viable
Good public transport needs adequate density
A density of 100 p/ha is the density necessary to support a good bus service, given a socially mixed population
(White 1976, Addenbrooke 1981 and UWE 95)
Everyone can walk
Usage of local facilities increases
Bus routes are more regular
Everyone should be able to walk to their local centre
Alternative local connections
Regular bus service
7,500
Place of worship
540m
Hub
Sports
Node
7,500
Main bus
Secondary school
Hub
Active centre
More local buses
Community centre
Hub
7,500
Other public routes become viable
Local social facilities better public linkages
At more compact densities centres are more vibrant
Key additional local facilities become viable,
fall within walking distances
and alternative public local links are affordable

(Andrew Wright Associates)

Figure 2.6: Relationship between density and urban form

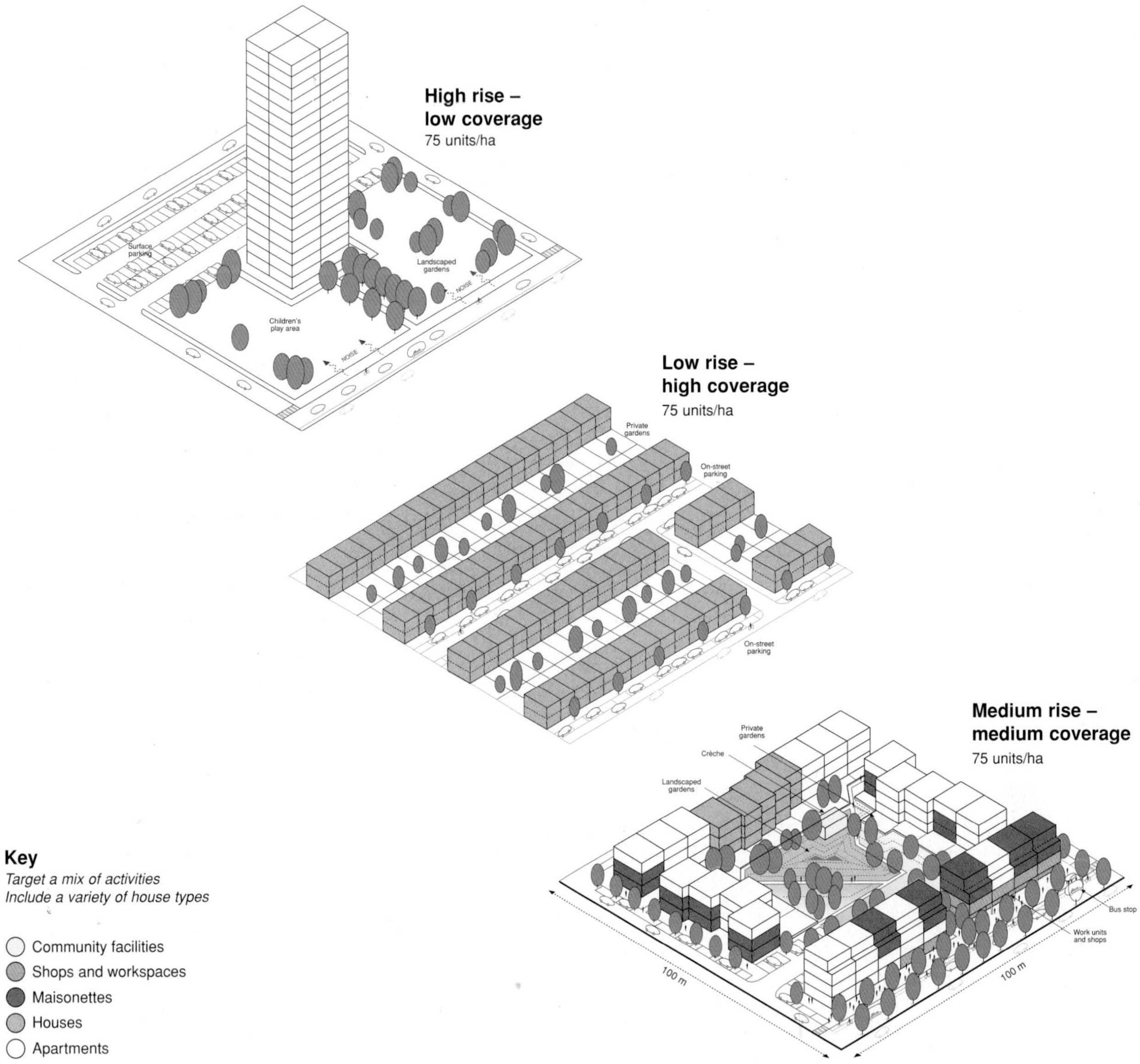

(Andrew Wright Associates)

Figure 2.6 illustrates that density per se is not an indicator of urban quality. The three sketches show how different forms of architecture – a single point block; a traditional street layout and a series of urban blocks enclosing an open space – can be built to the same density, in this case an inner-urban density of 75 dwellings per hectare, with surprisingly different results in terms of the type of private and public space they deliver.

The first example illustrates a high-rise development standing in open space. There are no private gardens or amenities directly available to the inhabitants. There is no direct relationship between the building and the surrounding streets. The large area of open space demands significant levels of investment to manage and maintain it at acceptable standards.

The second example is typical street layout with 2–3 storey houses with front and back gardens. Here, the public space is defined by continuous street frontages. The streets form a clear pattern of public space, but the high site coverage minimises the potential for communal spaces and a more varied urban landscape.

The third example shows how the same ingredients can be harnessed to create a strong urban focus to a residential community. The buildings, which can be of different heights and configuration, are arranged around a landscaped open space which contains a community-based facility, such as a community centre, crèche or playground. Commercial and public activities can be distributed along the ground floor, maintaining an active street frontage along the main through-routes. More space is available for rear private gardens, communal areas or a park.

These diagrams illustrate three different ways of relating public and private space. They confirm that there can be no hard and fast rules for establishing 'ideal' density levels. However, as things stand, over half of land for new housing in England is built at less than 20 dwellings per hectare, so that 25% of the new housing takes up 54% of the land used.

Figure 2.7: Cross-section through a residential district showing a tree-lined street enclosed by buildings with ground floor retail and commercial facilities and upper level apartments enjoying views in private and communal gardens

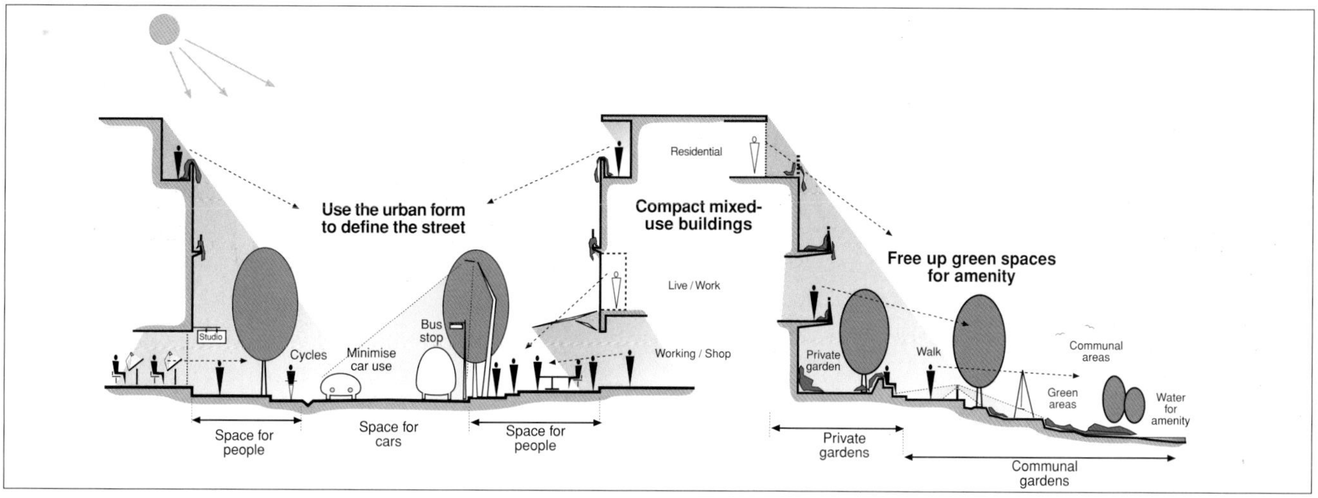

(Andrew Wright Associates)

We are faced with the unsustainable situation that those areas with the highest land pressures, the highest prices and the greatest supply constraints regionally, are where the lowest average densities are built. Research has shown that real land economy gains are being achieved from increasing densities from the current range of 20–25 dwellings per hectare (which characterises much new urban development) to a level of 35–40 dwellings per hectare. Though land use gains diminish above these levels, experience confirms that higher densities allow a greater number of public amenities and transport facilities to be located within walking distance, thus reducing the need for the car and contributing to urban sustainability.[1]

Creating pyramids of intensity

Developers, local planning authorities and planning inspectors all need clear guidance on the relationship between urban design, density and quality of life if we are to achieve the Government's targets in relation to development on brownfield land. Such guidance will need to be based on a range of values whose application would be directed by local circumstance. Imposing universal minimum standards is not the solution.

Location is a vital factor in creating a more flexible density policy. There are certain areas where the priority should be to increase the intensity with which space is used. Transport hubs and town centres both justify higher population densities and a more diverse mix of uses. There is, therefore, a strong case for promoting 'pyramids of intensification' in urban areas, subject to the provision of appropriate transport, social facilities and local amenities. Because of their location in our towns and cities, many brownfield sites are ideally suited to this form of intense and integrated development. Density bonuses could be employed by local authorities to reward developers who submit high quality designs compatible with a higher density solution, and who are also willing to contribute towards improving the public infrastructure to accommodate a higher density development.

1 'The Use of Density in Urban Planning'; Llewelyn-Davies & Bartlett School of Planning; DETR (1998)

Our recommendation is:

- **Revise planning and funding guidance to:**

- **discourage local authorities from using 'density' and 'over-development' as reasons for refusing planning permission;**

- **create a planning presumption against excessively low density urban development;**

- **provide advice on use of density standards linked to design quality. (3)**

GETTING THE RIGHT MIX

Mixing uses

One of the main attractions of city living is proximity to work, shops and basic social, educational and leisure uses. Whether we are talking about mixing uses in the same neighbourhood, a mix within a street or urban block, or the mixing of uses vertically within a building, good urban design should encourage more people to live near to those services which they require on a regular basis.

Many activities can – with careful design and good urban management – live harmoniously side by side. Except for certain industries or activities that attract very high traffic volumes or create noise at unsociable hours, most businesses and services can co-exist with housing. Figure 2.8 illustrates how successful urban neighbourhoods integrate a range of services near residential areas without creating single-use zones of shopping, business and housing. There is a greater concentration of public amenities – shops, schools, community and business facilities – around the streets and public spaces near the centre of the neighbourhood or district.

A small urban park or open space, with local facilities acting as the social focus for the surrounding community

For a growing number of residents, active urban locations – based on the principles illustrated in Figure 2.8 – such as Clerkenwell and Bloomsbury in London or parts of Central Manchester – present an attractive option. On a larger scale, Leeds is a city which has recognised the power of an attractive new mixed quarter. The Calls & Riverside district has become a lively mixed-use extension of the city centre, from the Corn Exchange through railway arches to the Aire & Calder Navigation and beyond, filled with entertainment, media and creative businesses, hotels, housing, shops and visitor attractions.

Naturally, some areas will never show the same potential for accommodating such diversity. It may remain very difficult, (and ultimately undesirable), to introduce significant non-residential uses to whole swathes of suburbia. But even here, well-located local shops, community facilities and a more flexible approach to live-work units can be encouraged. Since a growing proportion of urban residents will work in the neighbourhood in which they live, their requirements for local facilities will also change and adapt.

In both outer and inner urban areas, achieving more mixed and balanced communities, with convenient local services, will often require a readiness to restrict any further expansion of services that draw on a wider and predominantly car-borne catchment. Otherwise, there will be no market for the local services we want to mix within the neighbourhood or district.

A number of research studies are currently exploring the issues connected with mixing uses. This should provide a basis for new national guidance on the benefits, the practicalities, (such as separate access for homes and businesses), and the limitations of promoting mixed development.

Mixing households

The creation of mixed income neighbourhoods is a separate, although related issue. Whether we are talking about new settlements or expanding the capacity of existing urban areas a good mix of incomes and tenures is important for a number of reasons. By helping to bring about a more even distribution of wealth within a locality, it can work towards supporting viable neighbourhood facilities, with more possibility of spending being recycled through the purchase of local goods and services. For households, a mix of tenures provides options to change their tenure to meet changing circumstances, without necessarily having to leave the neighbourhood – a factor favouring community stability.

For such policies to work, they have to look beyond the development framework, at how we define 'social' or 'affordable' housing, and how we manage this element of the housing stock. The Task Force's visits to the Netherlands highlighted a very different definition of affordable housing compared to our own – in some cases including households on 80% of national average income. This means that many of the people occupying 'social' housing are working households in reasonably-paid jobs. In these circumstances, the exact tenure mix becomes a lot less important.

Figure 2.8: The key components of a mixed-use and integrated urban neighbourhood

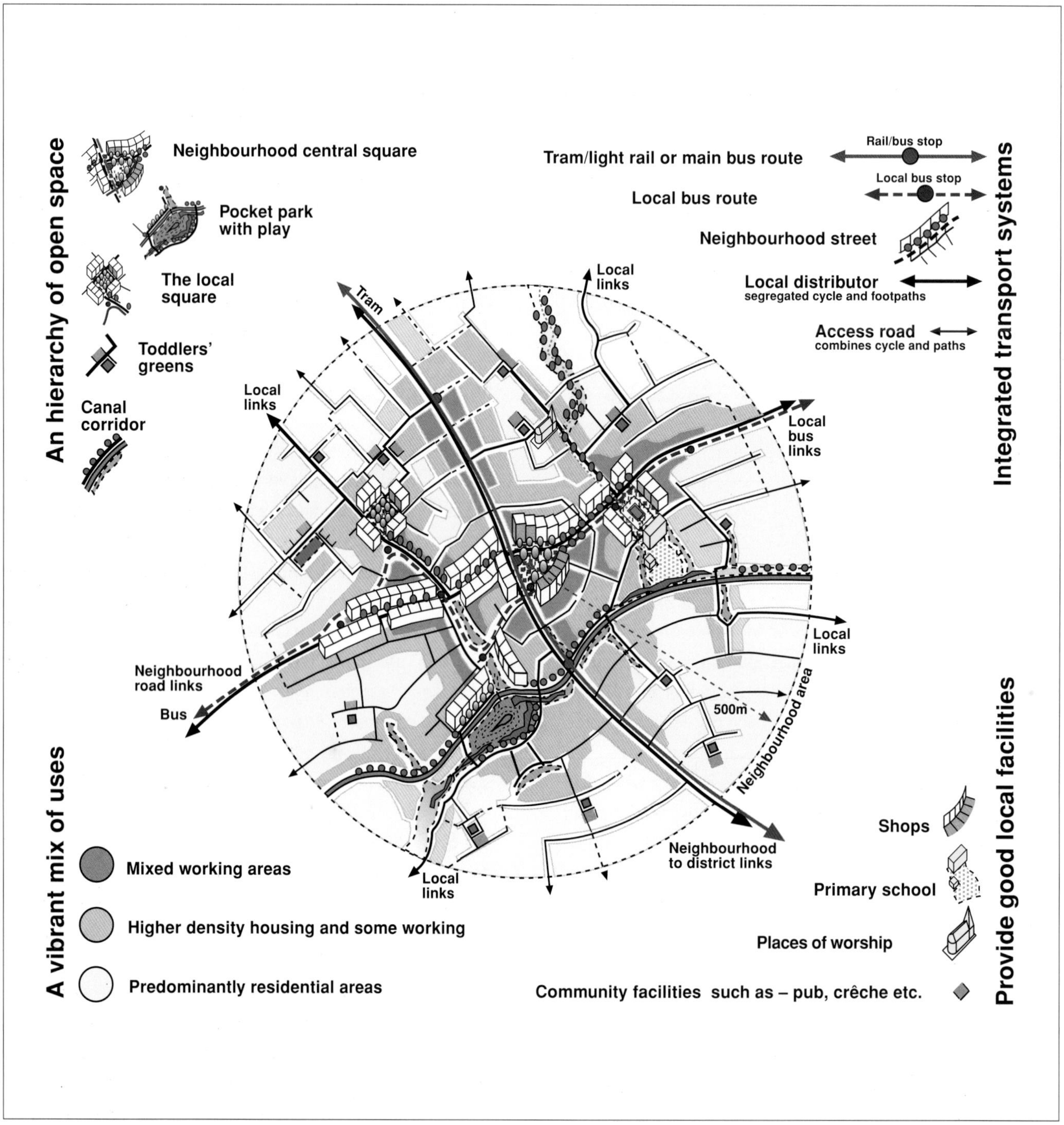

(Andrew Wright Associates)

If we compare this more flexible approach to the English situation, then it clearly raises serious issues about how we allocate and fund housing for those who cannot pay for market housing. Our system has encouraged the concentration of poverty, need and families with problems, in a residualised social housing sector, as the worst cases move to the top of the list and often end up being concentrated in one area. Instead, we need to support the design of neighbourhoods where different types of housing are fully integrated. This requires changes to our planning and funding systems. We return to this important issue in Chapters 8 and 13 of the report.

RAISING THE QUALITY OF NEW HOUSING

Long-life, loose-fit, low energy buildings

To ensure sustainable urban development, new housing must be designed to respond to the interlinked concepts of 'long-life', 'loose-fit' and 'low energy'. Together these ensure that buildings are built to last, by considering each structure as a long term investment, involving:

- the employment of durable materials and efficient systems of fabrication;
- designing for changing user demands and lifestyles by providing flexible and cost-effective layouts, finishes and materials;
- ensuring resource efficiency by reducing energy use through building massing and configuration, exploiting passive energy design and employing appropriate environmentally responsible construction techniques.

The Task Force's visits to recent residential developments in Spain, Germany and the Netherlands confirmed that in these countries the quality of thinking and the quality of implementation in housing design is significantly more advanced than in England. Houses and apartments – built by the private and public sector alike – are designed to much higher architectural and environmental standards. This does not mean more expensive materials or a refined 'aesthetic', but a better understanding of the 'fit' between housing design and user requirements.

In some instances this translates into residences with a lower level of specification or fit-out than we might expect in England, but increased adaptability and reduced capital costs. Fixed elements such as kitchens, bathrooms, wall and flooring materials may be excluded or left 'raw', allowing occupants to make their own functional and aesthetic choices, investing their own money in the design of the domestic environment.

Much of the contemporary Dutch housing visited by the Task Force provided more generous space standards in the size of rooms, allowed greater flexibility of layout to respond to changing lifestyles, ensured better access to natural daylight with larger and well-insulated windows, and offered its inhabitants an improved relationship to the exterior through balconies, terraces and communal spaces. Average floor space in new German homes can be as much as 50% greater than English equivalent house types with lower construction costs.[2]

The challenge of reducing construction costs and increasing quality in housing is central to achieving an urban renaissance. Proper research and development, together with the advantages of mass production, have brought innovation and value to the consumer in other industries, such as car manufacturing and the electronics industry. The English housing sector must respond with similar investment in research, development and experimentation in order to respond to the changing needs of the market and achieve higher goals in terms of sustainability and value-for-money. We need to keep in mind that the use of a building changes much faster than the life of a building.

2 'Building the 21st Century House'; URBED (1998)

The Slachthuisplein district in The Hague: market housing or social housing?

These practical lessons should be assimilated from overseas practice and built into the design, construction and procurement of new housing in England, focusing on the following areas.

- Generosity of space: increasing floor space and allowing for higher ceilings. The present planning system encourages the lowest level of floor-to-ceiling space by fixing a height and then allowing the developer to optimise the area in-between. The developer then seeks to cram in as many floors as possible. It would be preferable to allow more generosity in terms of overall height and instead, insist on higher minimum floor to ceiling heights for individual floors.

- Quality of construction: getting the basic design and quality of construction right. This requires a relaxation in specification standards on interior finishes and the provision of fitted kitchens, carpets, etc.

- Optimisation of off-site construction: gaining efficiencies by expanding the use of off-site construction of the basic housing shell, and adding design variety through the facade and the external finishes.

- Flexibility of building: establishing a housing sales policy based on the amount of floor space rather than just the number of bedrooms, and making more use of flexible partition walls so that internal space can be re-configured to meet the changing needs of a household – such as an extra bedroom for a new arrival or extra space to use as a work area.

The importance of these issues raises the question of whether there is a case for re-introducing some form of minimum space standards in respect of total floor space areas and ceiling heights for different types of housing. Our concern is that this may unduly constrain innovation in design. The main benefit would be to outlaw the worst of the 'box' units of some of the volume house-builders and social housing providers. We remit this issue to the Government to consider further.

Improving environmental performance

Whilst regulations have contributed substantially to improving the environmental performance of new buildings in recent years, much more can be done. In respect of energy alone, there are now excellent technical opportunities to design new buildings that require a minimum of external energy input, using solar gain from both passive and active solar systems via photovoltaic panels, (which can transform buildings from net energy users to net energy producers), fuel cells, Combined Heat and Power (CHP) systems etc. The type of buildings we develop impacts upon how much energy we use. For example, the average fabric heat loss of a dwelling in, say, a block of nine city apartments is 40% less than equivalent sized detached dwellings.[3] We also need to consider the overall environmental performance of whole development plots as well as the individual buildings, reflecting the full range of impacts arising from within the curtilage of the home, including water management and use of materials.

3 Source: Ove Arup & Partners (1999)

Figure 2.9: New developments in environmental design can help reduce the energy consumption of a typical dwelling and create more sustainable urban neighbourhoods

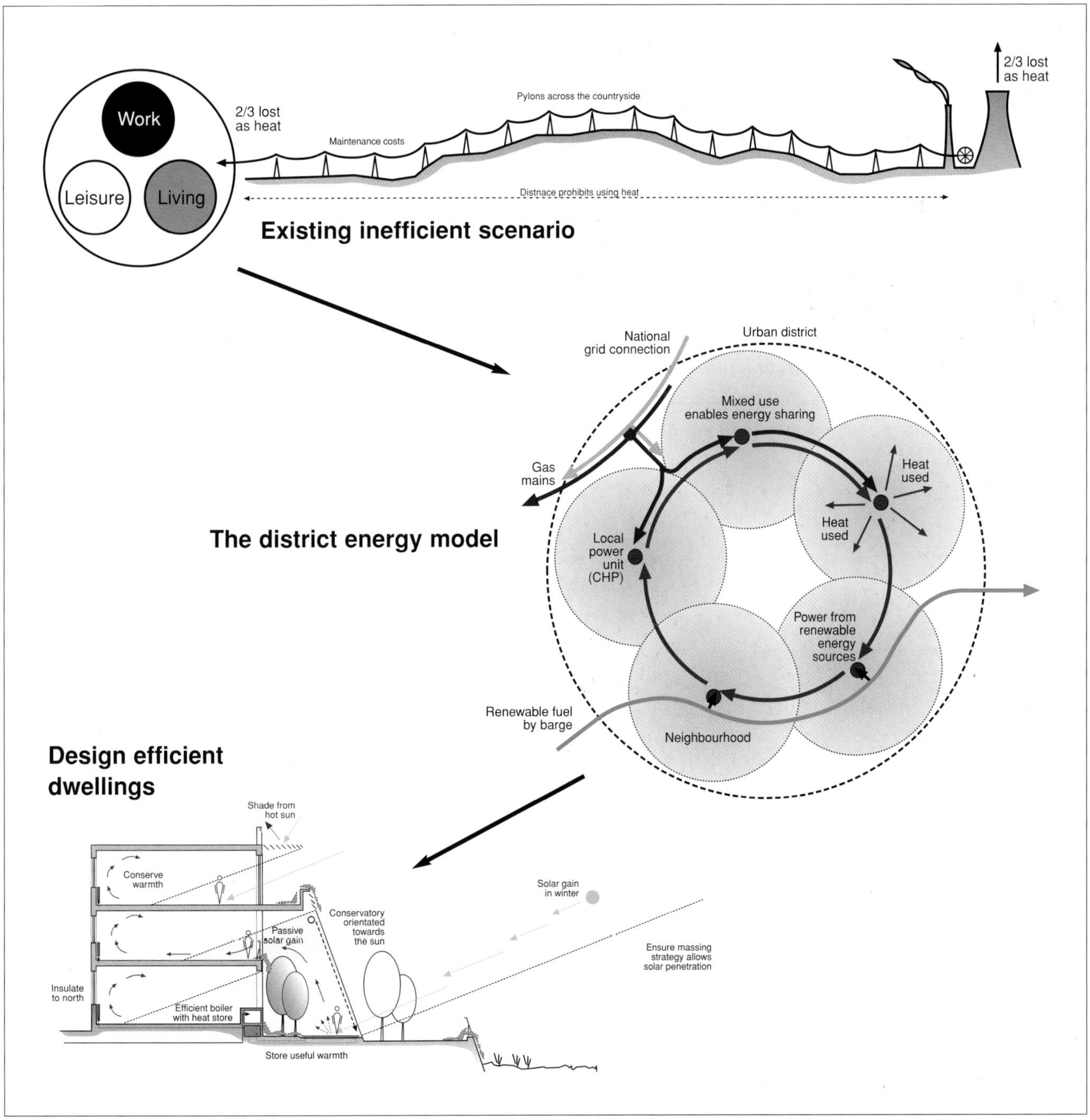

(Andrew Wright Associates)

In respect of energy and water management, there is an opportunity to link explicitly the environment performance of our homes to the costs of owning and running them. If we can establish this connection in the minds of the customer, so that such standards become the norm, then house-builders are much more likely to factor in any additional costs from the outset, rather than regarding higher performance standards as an additional luxury, reflected in a higher sales price. Site development briefs and public funding guidance could establish minimum environmental ratings, below which approval would not generally be given. Building on the work of the Building Research Establishment and others, our recommendation is:

- **Introduce a mandatory double performance rating for houses combining a single environmental rating and a single running cost rating, so that home-buyers know what level of building performance they are getting for their money. (4)**

DEFINING SUCCESS: KEY PRINCIPLES OF URBAN DESIGN

Towns and cities can offer a range of different types of urban living, to satisfy a very varied range of needs. They allow people different 'trade-offs': between, say, liveliness and calm; mix and uniformity; high and low density; private gardens or nearby parks. The people who can exercise choice do so. They move to the 'best' bits of town, to enjoy the possibilities that are offered. Our task is to widen that choice – so that many more people can have the opportunity to live in lively, successful, enjoyable towns, built to the standards and qualities of the best.

We have developed a framework of design principles for creating more liveable places. On their own, these cannot guarantee successful places. They cannot even ensure good design, but they can provide a set of ground rules for starting

Dutch design and construction skills (Maccreanor Lavington Architects)

to think about a site or area – whether an empty brownfield or greenfield site, or the refurbishment of an existing housing estate or urban area. As such, they can provide the basis for criteria for assessing plans and proposals.

1. Site and setting
The layout of a development site must recognise its social, and physical context, and seek to integrate with existing patterns of urban form and movement. Design proposals should recognise that each location is different; that each place relates differently to the town centres, facilities and transport routes in its hinterland.

2. Context, scale and character
Designs should respect local traditions and relationships, and draw on them to inspire and guide new forms of development. Re-using existing buildings and consolidating existing public spaces will contribute to achieving continuity and integration.

3. Public realm
Priority must be given to the design of the public realm. From the front door to the street, to the square, the park and on out to the countryside, designs should create a hierarchy of public spaces that relate to buildings and their entrances, to encourage a sense of safety and community.

4. Access and permeability
A user-friendly public realm should make walking and cycling easy, pleasant and convenient by keeping the size of urban blocks small, with frequent pedestrian cut-throughs to make a new development permeable and accessible to the existing neighbourhood. Car dependency should be minimised and integration with public transport maximised.

5. Optimising land use and density
The design potential of vacant urban sites and buildings should be optimised by intensifying development and uses in relation to local shops, services and public transport. Any development designed around higher densities, should take account of privacy, sound insulation and safety.

6. Mixing activities
Diversity of activity and uses should be encouraged at different levels: within buildings, streets, urban blocks and neighbourhoods. Careful planning, design and siting can be used to resolve potential conflicts.

7. Mixing tenures
To avoid single housing tenure, of whatever kind, designs should offer a wide choice of tenure options at urban block, street, and neighbourhood level, in a way which does not distinguish tenure by grouping or house type. New development should also be used to bring balance into existing mono-tenure areas.

8. Building to last
Buildings should be designed to be durable over many generations and through changing social and economic needs, providing adaptable and flexible environments that are not fixed in single-use, single-occupier roles.

9. Sustainable buildings
Buildings, landscape and public spaces should be designed and built to high standards, aesthetically and structurally, with durable materials, appropriate technology and orientation that minimise energy use and encourage recycling.

10. Environmental responsibility
Land should be regarded as a scarce finite resource. Development projects should be as compact as possible and should enhance the environment, not just limit damage, by respecting biodiversity, harnessing natural resources and reducing the call on non-renewable resources.

BARCELONA AND THE OLYMPIC VILLAGE

Barcelona is celebrated as a contemporary model of urban regeneration. The unique synergy between civic leadership, urban design and implementation has been rewarded by the prestigious 1999 RIBA Royal Gold Medal for Architecture.

The Catalonian capital re-invented itself throughout the 1980s and 1990s with a series of urban design initiatives that improved the quality of public space in the city and radically enhanced its infrastructure. Under Mayor Pasqual Maragall and architect Oriol Bohigas, the city created 150 new public squares at the heart of urban communities. The city succeeded in winning its bid for the 1992 Olympics and coupled this with a strategy of urban regeneration that has paid long term dividends to the citizens of Barcelona, rather than making a short term profit for the event organisers.

The Olympic Village, planned by MBM Architects, is a model of successful regeneration of a large brownfield site. Located a few miles from the old city centre on a tract of previously contaminated industrial land, the new neighbourhood is now inhabited by a mixed community of over 8,000 people. The project reunites the old city with its waterfront, a typical condition of industrial ports and maritime centres. More than 12 million people have visited the area since the Olympics, contributing to the revitalisation of the local economy and establishing a new city identity at a regional, national and international level. This creative strategy is guiding the next stage of urban redevelopment, several kilometres along the waterfront.

The new urban district is a simple extension of Barcelona's 19th century grid layout. Five-storey apartment buildings are arranged along traditional streets with large internal courtyards and communal gardens. A wide range of commercial and retail facilities are distributed at street level, with a concentration of hotels and restaurants around the Olympic Port, close to the underground station and public transport facilities. The Olympic Village was designed at a density of 200 dwellings per hectare which was considered the lowest acceptable threshold of population density that could sustain a varied economy of local shops and facilities.

Barcelona: aerial view of the waterfront before regeneration

Barcelona: aerial view of the Olympic village after regeneration

IMPROVING THE DESIGN PROCESS: THE SPATIAL MASTERPLAN

A major commitment is required to implement a new framework for quality urban design, to ensure that the ten core principles are translated at a national and local level. This requires a careful appraisal of the planning and development processes, identifying the tools that can be used to promote successful and sustainable urban environments.

The spatial masterplan is a synthesis of the design-led approach to urban development. As such, it is a fundamental ingredient in achieving an urban renaissance in English towns and cities. Most successful urban projects analysed in this report – Barcelona, Rotterdam and Greenwich, for example – have been based on implementing a spatial masterplan which has driven the development process and secured a high quality design product.

Unlike conventional two-dimensional zoning plans, (which tend simply to define areas of use, density standards and access arrangements), the 'spatial' masterplan establishes a three-dimensional framework of buildings and public spaces. It is a more sophisticated visual 'model' that:

- allows us to understand what the public spaces between the buildings will be like before they are built;
- shows how the streets, squares and open spaces of a neighbourhood are to be connected;
- defines the heights, massing and bulk of the buildings, (but not the architectural style or detailed design);
- controls the relationship between buildings and public spaces, (to maximise street frontage and reduce large areas of blank walls, for example);
- determines the distribution of uses, and whether these uses should be accessible at street level;
- controls the network of movement patterns for people moving on foot, cycle, car or public transport;
- identifies the location of street furniture, lighting and landscaping; and,
- allows us to understand how well a new urban neighbourhood is integrated with the surrounding urban context and natural environment.

The spatial masterplan therefore provides a vital framework for development. As such, it requires the involvement of a range of different design professionals – architects, landscape and urban designers, engineers, planners, project co-ordinators – as well as the key stakeholders. It therefore plays an important part in building consensus and support for a project, by involving development agencies, landowners, local government, developers and the local community in its preparation.

A spatial masterplan, when accompanied by design guidelines in the form of Supplementary Planning Guidance or a more informal code or brief, should provide sufficient detail to allow statutory bodies and project sponsors to evaluate their performance against design and development objectives, which are summarised in Figure 2.10.

The preparation of a spatial masterplan will normally be co-ordinated and sponsored by the local authority or one of the proposed delivery bodies set out in Chapter 5. In areas designated for regeneration, there may well be a partnership organisation, combining public, private and voluntary sector skills, which can co-ordinate the process. On some occasions, perhaps in the context of a development competition, the onus will be on the private sector developer to define the physical concept plan for the regeneration project. Many complex development sites may benefit from working with an independent project co-ordinator or Local Architecture Centre, to provide advice and expertise on managing the design and consultation process (see later).

Figure 2.10: Spatial masterplanning – checklist of design issues

Urban form and public space

- relationship between development and wider metropolitan or regional context
- urban structure and grain of streets and public routes
- identity and sense of place
- design, shape and scale of major public spaces
- variety of built form and urban block structure
- location of building entrances along streets and public spaces
- distribution of residential, commercial and community facilities
- development densities, plot sizes and ratios
- intensification of public realm
- landmarks and public buildings
- public art
- use of natural features including trees, planting and water
- design and materials of hard and soft landscaped areas
- pavement widths and street furniture
- lighting and safety
- 24-hour use

Movement

- integration with existing pedestrian, vehicular and public transport routes
- location of public transport facilities
- integration between different movement modes (foot, cycle, car, public transport)
- accessibility of facilities within five and ten-minute walking and cycling distances
- car parking standards and location of car parking spaces
- traffic calming measures
- disabled access

Building design

- building layout and orientation
- variety of massing, materials and architectural expression
- flexibility of internal layout
- work/live and lifetime homes
- disabled access
- materials and maintenance
- visual link between buildings and streets – openings and entrances
- use of external spaces – balconies, roof terraces, porches
- overlooking distances

Environmental design

- massing and thermal performance
- passive environmental design
- exposure to sunlight and natural daylight penetration
- energy efficiency
- renewable energy sources
- Combined Heat and Power (CHP) provision
- grey water recycling
- reedbed filtration
- thermal and acoustic insulation
- household waste management
- landscape, biodiversity and ecology

Community issues

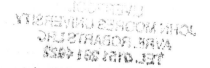

- play areas and community facilities
- proximity to existing or proposed school facilities
- adult education and family learning opportunities
- sports and childcare facilities
- training opportunities and job creation
- management and stewardship
- the wired community
- complementary community initiatives

In summary, to be effective the masterplanning process must be:

- visionary and deliverable: it should raise aspirations for a site and provide a vehicle for consensus building and implementation;
- fully integrated into the land use planning system, but allowing new uses and market opportunities to exploit the full development potential of a site;
- a flexible process, providing the basis for negotiation and dispute resolution;
- a participative process, providing all the stakeholders with a means of expressing their needs and priorities; and,
- equally applicable to rethinking the role, function and form of existing neighbourhoods as creating new neighbourhoods.

Our recommendation:

- **Make public funding and planning permissions for area regeneration schemes conditional upon the production of an integrated spatial masterplan, recognising that public finance may be required up front to pay for the masterplanning. (5)**

PROCURING EXCELLENCE IN URBAN DESIGN

It is through the procurement process that local authorities and their regeneration partners establish the level of expectation about the quality of design. Two critical components of this process are the preparation of development briefs and the use of competitions.

Development briefs

Many of the documents produced by public authorities and regeneration partnerships which purport to be development or design briefs are, in fact, little more than marketing brochures to attract private sector interest in a difficult urban location. Recent research carried out for DETR found that the current standard of all the different types of brief being produced in this country was 'very mixed'.[4]

The development brief should set out the vision for a development, and ground it firmly into the physical realities of the site and its economic, social, environmental and planning context. Apart from its aspirational qualities, the brief must clearly include key objective factors including site constraints and opportunities, soil conditions and infrastructure, existing transport and access, planning constraints and regulations, and set out the proposed uses, areas, mix of tenures, development densities and other relevant design requirements.

The brief plays a crucial role in setting the highest achievable standards of environmental design and construction by requiring energy efficiency and built-in sustainability. In the recent Millennium Communities design brief for Allerton Bywater, near Leeds, targets included 50% reduction in energy consumption, 50% household waste reduction, 30% reduction in construction costs, 25% reduction in construction time and 0% defects at handover, in comparison with normal practice – setting higher standards of environmental and construction efficiency than those required by Building Regulations.

Depending on the status and size of the development, it may be appropriate for the development brief to require an analysis of the impact of the development on the local economy. Similar attention should be paid to community consultation and stewardship, using the brief as a vehicle for expressing local views and aspirations, and setting out a clear programme of consultation and participation.

4 'Planning and Development Briefs: A Guide to Better Practice'; DETR (1998)

Figure 2.11: An integrated spatial masterplan requires an integrated design team

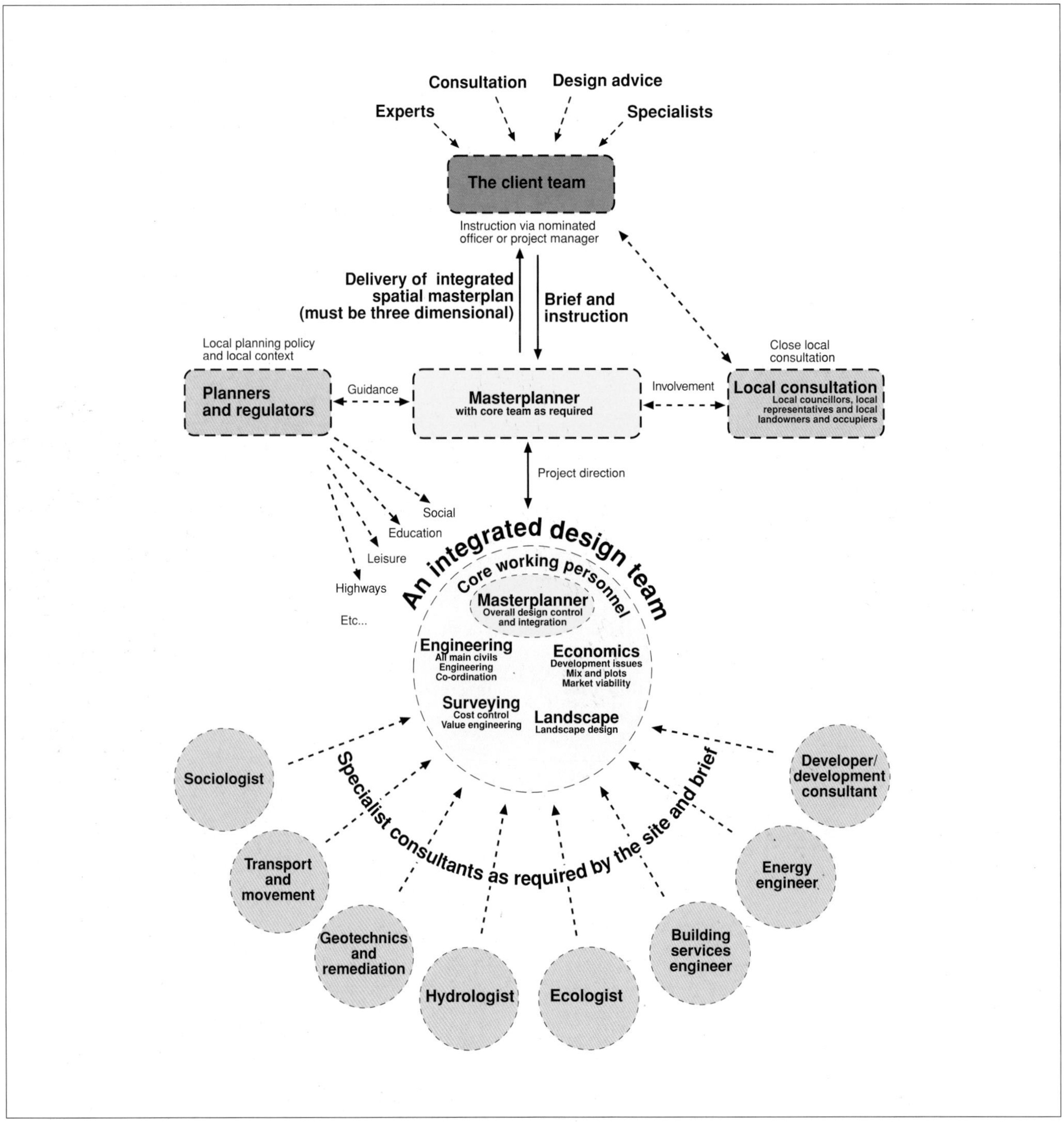

(Andrew Wright Associates)

Design competitions

Design competitions are an excellent way of procuring quality in urban development. They provide an open, transparent and democratic process which, if well managed, produces value-for-money and optimises the design and development potential of a site. Most of the successful projects visited by the Task Force were the result of competitions sponsored and organised by the public or private sector. They have resulted in well-built urban neighbourhoods, enjoyed by their inhabitants who are proud of the high design quality of their environment. Competitions add value to urban regeneration.

There is growing evidence in the UK, partly influenced by the National Lottery and EU procurement rules for public projects, that design competitions can yield high quality buildings and spaces. The new Scottish Parliament in Edinburgh and the Tate Gallery of Modern Art in London are two examples of the new generation of public buildings commissioned through an international competition. Yet, we have some way to go to transform the culture of the development industry, and particularly, the volume housing sector.

In visiting regeneration projects overseas, we were also struck by the willingness to use competitions to test innovative urban design approaches. In the Netherlands, this

Experimenting with car-free residential neighbourhoods in the DWN Terrain, Amsterdam

included car-free developments in Amsterdam and new approaches to suburban development outside the Hague. In Germany, the Federal Government were testing different maximum car parking standards and in the town of Nordhorn, we saw innovation in the use of sustainable land reclamation technologies as part of an integrated urban design process. Until recently, English authorities have seemed comparatively reluctant to use competitions to test different types of integrated solution to common urban problems.

The quality of the competition process will, inevitably, depend of the quality of the design brief, the calibre of the selection panel and the expertise of the advisers involved in assessment and evaluation. The selection panel should include representatives from the stakeholder organisations alongside independent architectural experts. To be effective, the briefing and competition procedure requires time and resources which are seldom considered at the outset of the development project. The cost of this critical stage may be up to half a percent of the total building costs, but provides real value-for-money in terms of delivering a high-quality product that builds support and consensus for the project. Competitions are a key element of a participatory and inclusive planning process.

There are a number of types of competition which be used to select urban design and masterplanning teams.

- Competitive interviews: where a shortlist of architects are interviewed by the selection panel and a single team is appointed to develop a masterplan.
- Two- or three-stage design competitions: where a number of design teams are commissioned to develop design schemes and a winner is chosen on the basis of submitted proposals.
- Open, anonymous design competitions: where a wide range of competitors submit a design proposal and a single winner is appointed to develop the scheme.

The direct involvement of several Task Force members in the Millennium Communities competitions has shown that a well organised competition can have a beneficial impact on the quality of the design product in this country as well. What we have learnt from the Millennium Communities competitions and other competition processes is that there are a number of features which need to be captured and disseminated as best practice.

- Competition briefs need to be explicit about their aims and objectives, and the decision criteria.
- Every effort should be made to promote competitions widely, and allow potential competitors sufficient time to make an appropriate response to an initial competition notice.
- There must be sufficient time and resources to develop an appropriate brief and for competitors to develop a full design response, (this could vary from 3–12 months).
- The composition of the assessment panel is a key factor in both stimulating a high level of entry from participants and guaranteeing the selection of a high quality solution.
- There must be a clear monitoring and review structure to ensure that the design and performance objectives are followed through during the construction and implementation process.

Recommendation:

- **All significant area regeneration projects should be the subject of a design competition. Funds should be allocated in any regeneration funding allocation to meet the public costs of such competitions. (6)**

GREENWICH MILLENNIUM VILLAGE: A CASE STUDY IN DESIGN PROCESS AND PROCUREMENT

The high-profile international competition for the development of the Millennium Village on London's Greenwich Peninsula is an interesting case study for the implementation of quality urban design in England. The initial brief called for innovative design responses which would act as a model of sustainable urban development across the nation. Thirteen development consortia submitted proposals for the creation of a new urban community. The quality of the first round of submissions was disappointing. Nearly all the schemes were uninspiring versions of low-density, single-use housing estates, dominated by the car, with little or no attempt to create a mixed-use focus for new residential communities.

In the second stage, four consortia were invited to develop their schemes further. A rigorous and demanding brief, coupled with a design-led Advisory Panel, ensured that all four schemes improved considerably during this phase of the competition. It is significant, though, that the two most interesting design responses came from non-UK architectural teams – the winning proposal for a Countryside Properties/Taylor Woodrow consortium by the Swedish architect Ralph Erskine with Hunt Thompson Associates, and the submission by MBM Architects of Barcelona.

The northern European approach of the Erskine scheme is designed around variety and quality of the public realm – with a range of streets, squares, open spaces and communal gardens forming the 'public armature' of the new urban community. The buildings are equally diverse in style, massing and construction providing the potential for individual expression and identity. The more intensely urban scheme by MBM adopted a regular urban grid of streets and alley-ways, reminiscent of Georgian London, which succeeded in integrating the different elements of the new neighbourhood with its surroundings. Both schemes, though different in style and character, displayed a profoundly 'urban' feel and grain that took account of how cities change and adapt over time, reflecting the need for a robust integrated spatial masterplan to guide urban developments of this scale.

The Greenwich Millennium Village (Countryside Properties plc)

DEVELOPING A NATIONAL URBAN DESIGN FRAMEWORK

The role of government

It will be the task of national government to draw together the existing policy threads on architecture and urban design, and to reinforce them to create the basis of a national urban design framework. The principal responsibility will lie with the Department of the Environment, Transport and the Regions, but there will also be crucial roles for the Department of Culture, Media and Sport, which is responsible for promoting excellence in architecture, and for the Department for Education and Employment, in contributing to the development of professional skills.

The Secretary of State for the Environment, Transport and the Regions is going to require the highest level of professional advice and support, in particular, on the coverage of urban design issues in planning and funding guidance, developing good practice guidance, advising on the design implications of other policy proposals, and generally helping to champion the cause.

This will require senior professional input from the following disciplines as a minimum – architecture, land use planning, transport planning, civil and building engineering, environmental science, ecological design, landscape architecture, housing management, construction, and private development and investment.

In this respect, there will be an important role for the new Commission for Architecture and the Built Environment, being established by the Department of Culture, Media and Sport. The evolving remit of the new body will encompass education and national design review functions, as well as the regional and community agenda. The Urban Task Force welcomes the formation of this new body and supports a close working relationship with DETR.

Translating the key themes of a national framework in terms of planning guidance, guidance to statutory agencies and public funding criteria, is crucial if we are going to address the quality agenda successfully. This cascade process could be assisted by the re-introduction of a national series of design bulletins to provide best practice guidelines to local planning authorities on the Government's design policies.

To the extent that there have been design policies in place over the last 20 years, these have rarely influenced the way that public funding programmes have been administered. The importance of high quality design merits barely a mention in statutory guidance to the new Regional Development Agencies, and there is little or no guidance on design criteria in respect of programmes such as the New Deal for Communities programme and the Single Regeneration Budget. Nor is it clear how design principles are to be incorporated within local authorities' housing or economic development strategies. At the same time, where design standards exist, such as those applied by the Housing Corporation or by the Home Office in respect of community safety, they show no strong consistency.

Government must also lead by example. The current series of Millennium Communities competitions will help to raise standards and test innovative design approaches. We can build on this initiative by attempting demonstration projects which combine experimentation in design and management, implementing many of the principles contained in this report, including a mix of uses and tenures, neighbourhood environmental management systems, innovative land remediation techniques and intensive 'aftercare'.

Recommendations:

- **Develop and implement a national urban design framework, disseminating key design principles through land use planning and public funding guidance, and introducing a new series of best practice guidelines. (7)**

- **Building on the Millennium Communities initiative, undertake a series of government-sponsored demonstration projects, adopting an integrated approach to design-led area regeneration of different types of urban neighbourhood. (8)**

Promoting public involvement

Securing high quality urban environments has as much to do with the public level of awareness of urban design as it is about the skills of the professionals involved in the day-to-day management and implementation of schemes. Increasingly, the design and land use planning system will work on the basis of pre-project preparation, based upon mediation and negotiation. This will apply to the preparation of development briefs, masterplans and supplementary design guidance. We will therefore need additional institutional capacity to manage the interface between politician, professional and public.

Our visits to Spain and the Netherlands highlighted the success of local architecture centres in this context. These provide venues for exhibitions, community planning events and day-to-day advice on development issues. The Dutch example includes a network of 30 centres, (one in each major town), fully supported by central government. In Spain, there is an architectural gallery in every provincial capital sponsored by the professional design institutions. In Bordeaux and Paris, there are several public architectural venues, funded by central and municipal government, that play an important role in the cultural lives of their cities. By comparison, the existing network of such centres in England is patchy. It is made up of a scattering of different local and regional bodies, all on a different footing and with varying priorities.

Local urban design or architecture centres will play an important role in achieving an urban renaissance in England. With a strong public agenda and independent status, architecture centres are the natural custodians of the debate on the future of the public realm and are uniquely placed to nurture a progressive, critical, cross-sector dialogue. They also play a crucial role in sustaining the active participatory processes needed to ensure urban regeneration schemes and projects are successful in the long term.

These centres should be properly resourced, be nationally co-ordinated by the Commission for Architecture and the Built Environment and linked to the proposed Regional Resource Centres for Urban Development described in Chapter 6. To secure this opportunity they need more than just funding. Tying in local government, the RDAs, the newly aligned regional cultural fora and, in the case of national case studies or projects, central government departments, is a prerequisite. Through the presentation of projects of local, regional and national significance and a range of urban issues for debate under the scrutiny of a public audience, they are very much part of the drive to raise both standards and expectations.

Any network of architecture centres needs to be supported by a national information database on best practice. The Resource for Urban Design Information (RUDI), established by Oxford Brookes University is an excellent model that should be consolidated and linked in to a wider information network.

Recommendation:

- **Establish Local Architecture Centres in each of our major cities. There should be a minimum network of 12 properly funded Centres, fulfilling a mix of common objectives and local specialisms, established by the end of 2001. (9)**

MAKING THE CONNECTIONS

To create liveable urban neighbourhoods which function as strong economic and social units, we have to improve transport connections in a way that promotes efficiency, is environmentally sensitive, and prioritises the needs of pedestrians, cyclists and public transport users.

Transport options have to be provided that people want to use. Few people will give up their cars completely, but many can be persuaded to reduce the use of their car if other options are sufficiently attractive.

There is a strong case. Urban traffic congestion is increasing and car traffic is predicted to grow by over one third in the next 20 years. Transport also constitutes a high percentage of household energy consumption, contributing significantly to carbon dioxide emissions. At the same time, as many as 13 million people live in households which do not own cars, and hence are effectively discriminated against by a transport system which prioritises the motor vehicle.[1]

Many overseas cities, such as Strasbourg, Curitiba and Freiburg, are a long way ahead of us in defining new urban transport solutions. At home, Edinburgh's Greenway system demonstrates how we can prioritise public transport, while the city of Oxford has successfully restricted increases in the use of the motor car. The remainder of this Chapter considers how other English towns and cities can catch up with the best, both at home and abroad.

It concludes that we should:

- reclaim the potential of the 'street' to meet many different community needs, as opposed simply to providing a conduit for motor vehicles;
- increase our investment in walking, cycling and public transport, and not just rely on the private sector to provide those extra resources;
- reduce the distances we travel by consolidating development within a compact urban form, close to existing and new travel interchanges.
- reduce the amount of land we give over to the motor car, particularly by reducing the amount of space within our towns that we use as surface level car parking.

1 Source: Richard D Knowles; University of Salford (1999)

CREATING SUSTAINABLE MOVEMENT PATTERNS

The planning system: setting the tone

In 1998, the Government published an Integrated Transport White Paper,[2] which set out a comprehensive strategy for improving our transport system in a way which will enhance the nation's economic health, reduce social disparity and create a healthier environment. Many of the proposals in the White Paper, when implemented, will lead to improvements in urban transport. There is, however, much more that can and should be done.

The starting point is the way in which we plan and design urban neighbourhoods. This determines the quality of our urban transport systems which in turn impacts upon both overall environmental quality and public health.

Designing a successful urban neighbourhood means thinking about journeys in a way which not only considers desired destinations and modes of transport, but as importantly, acknowledges the role of such journeys in responding to social, economic and environmental objectives. It requires the definition of movement frameworks which improve accessibility while reducing the need for car travel, take full account of the kind of movement demand a development will generate, and connect new areas to existing networks for travel by foot, cycle, public transport and car.

To ensure these objectives are met, the Government is providing the lead through national planning guidance. Transport considerations must also inform regional and local planning allocations and capacity assessments for new housing and business premises. In particular, requirements on development densities and car parking requirements should fully reflect the potential, and where relevant, the actual travel share of public transport.

Transport planning at regional and local level will be strengthened through the preparation of Regional Transport Strategies and Local Transport Plans. We consider the following principles to be important in the preparation of these documents:

- the need to integrate land use and transport planning as closely as possible at both levels;
- securing better integration and accessibility of public transport services;
- integrating different transport types and creating a clear hierarchy based upon the most sustainable options;
- establishing clear long term priorities for investment.

Recommendation:

- **Place Local Transport Plans on a statutory footing. They should include explicit targets for reducing car journeys, and increasing year on year the proportion of trips made on foot, bicycle and by public transport. (10)**

Edinburgh Greenway: Giving the buses priority (City of Edinburgh Council)

2 'A New Deal for Transport: Better for Everyone'; DETR (1998)

THE STRASS PLAN: EASING TRANSPORT TENSIONS IN STRASBOURG

In 1992 the city of Strasbourg, in eastern France, decided to improve the environmental efficiency of its transport system. Recognising the need to make better use of its rich heritage and to improve quality of life for citizens and tourists alike, the city sought to free up the centre of the city from congested traffic and promote much greater use of public transport, walking and cycling. The result was the Strass Plan.

Many central streets and squares were re-arranged. Place Kléber, once dominated by traffic, is now at the heart of a 2.8 hectare pedestrianised area connecting the historic Cathedral and Petite France districts across the city. New street furniture and open spaces have been added. The number of pedestrians using the area has increased markedly.

The bicycle network in Strasbourg is now the largest in France. 106 kilometres of cycle lanes have been created in the city itself, along with comprehensive provision of rental points, lockable stands and guarded parking areas. 15% of local people now use bicycles daily. The aim is to increase this to 25%.

A tram system has been introduced to provide smooth access from the suburbs and neighbouring towns straight into the city centre. The trams transport 60,000 people a day into and around the city, way above original forecasts.

The entire bus network was re-planned to link in with the tram network, making a total increase in public transport provision of 30%. Experimental use is also being made of a fleet of non-polluting electric vehicles for rent at public transport interchanges.

The plan goes beyond the city boundaries. High speed east-west rail links are planned to improve non-motorway access to London, Paris and Brussels, and through Germany, Austria and Hungary, as Strasbourg looks forward to becoming a bridgehead to Eastern Europe.

Into the future: the tram system at Strasbourg (TRANSDEV)

Getting the connections right

In Chapter 2 we set out the importance of creating and sustaining a 'permeable grid' in our towns and cities. This describes a layout of buildings and spaces which allows easy and efficient movement of both goods and people between different places.

Connecting a development to the rest of the town or city is a key priority in designing successful urban form. This is as relevant to new settlements and settlement extensions as it is to the regeneration of existing areas.

The starting point for any new urban development is to establish how routes from the development will knit in with the existing infrastructure. Historic routes need to be explored and understood in the context of brownfield sites in particular, as redevelopment in these locations represents a chance to re-connect the city. The diagrams below show how the regeneration of Hulme, Manchester enabled the original urban street pattern to be re-established.

We also need to get the connections right between transport interchanges, particularly railway stations and the rest of the town. Cities such as Chester demonstrate the benefits of creating ease of interchange between trains and buses. Secure cycle storage at stations such as Chester, Oxford, York and London Waterloo add further flexibility, but still fall short of levels of storage provision in, say, most Dutch cities.

To ensure that a neighbourhood is well integrated with its urban context, it must be well connected to its immediate neighbours and provide a clear structure of accessible routes within the neighbourhood itself, which lead from one destination point to another.

Whilst increased mobility is a sign of vitality and contributes to a healthy level of street-life, vehicular traffic should not dominate the experience of the pedestrianised street. For this reason vehicular routes should be carefully planned to coincide with, but not overwhelm the network of public streets and places. Some streets can and should be limited to public transport; others just to cyclists and pedestrians.

Figure 3.1: Hulme through the ages, from Victorian terraces, to 1960s deck access, to mixed low and mid-rise street pattern

Source: Mills Beaumont Leavey Channon, Manchester

In all cases public routes within a neighbourhood should be designed to provide the appropriate environment for pedestrians first, and then vehicles of different types.

The antithesis of this form of integrated development is the layout of some of our most recent urban and suburban residential developments. Tree-like street networks, based on the use of many cul-de-sacs, and designed to limit through movement, have negative impacts for cars and people. For cars, they concentrate congestion at the 'root of the tree', usually where the main estate access road meets the main distributor road. For buses they often form tortuous and slow routes as they literally have to go round the houses. For pedestrians they create indirect journeys which send people back to their cars even for the shortest distances. And in design terms, they create fragmented layouts which waste valuable land and open space.

Planning movement at the neighbourhood level should therefore be based on an intelligent analysis of the area's needs and potential, not the blanket application of guidance which is treated as prescriptive standards. One example of this is the Government's own Design Bulletin 32, 'Residential Roads and Footpaths Layout Considerations'. This document has become a set of 'rules' required by local authorities to fulfil technical requirements for new road layouts. It has often led to poor design solutions by creating road junctions on a scale totally divorced from actual safety requirements, and wasting land in the process. Documents such as this should be replaced by design guidance which provides good practice guidelines, not prescription.

At the same time, we must ensure that over-restrictive use of 'safety audits' do not defeat the agreed objectives of good design and integrated movement planning. Safety is extremely important, but too often the judgement by a single highway engineer goes uncontested. Innovative design solutions are not considered, and the answer can be wasted space, more tarmac and no additional safety.

Streets as places

For every street we need to be asking:

- what job should it be performing;
- who uses it and why;
- what would people like it to be used for;
- how well is it performing its function;
- how can greater priority be given to non-traffic roles;
- could we re-engineer the street to play a different role?

Figure 3.2: Two sides to every street: permeable and non-permeable urban forms

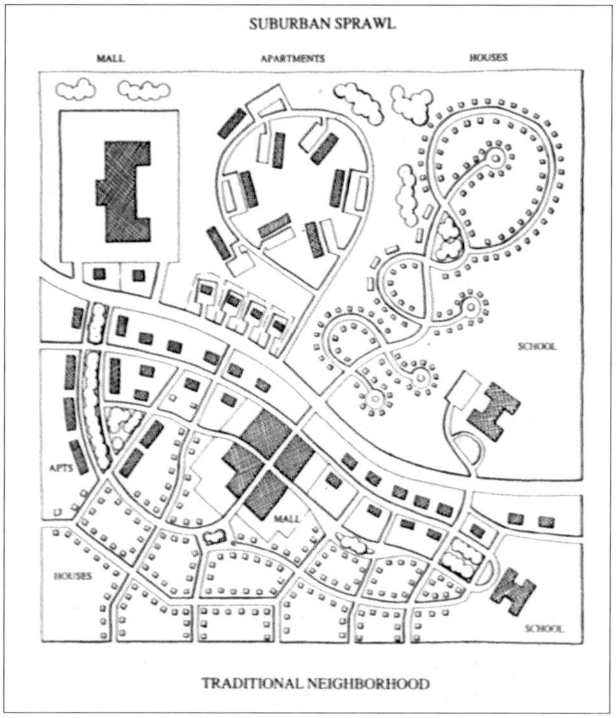

Source: Duany Plater Zyberk, Miami

Figure 3.3: Planning the integrated transport system

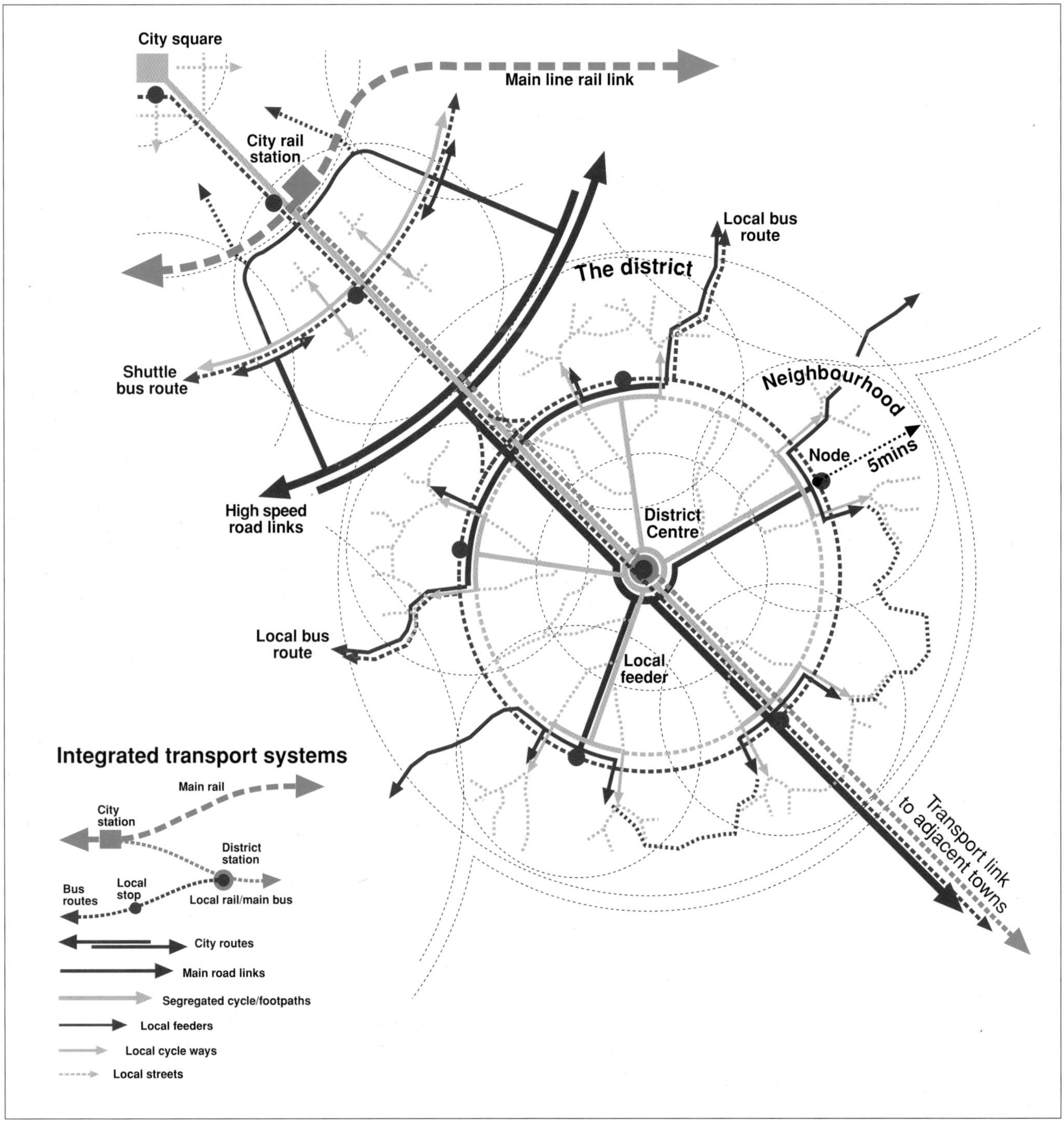

(Andrew Wright Associates)

At the top of the road hierarchy, the role and function of major roads must be recognised as changing when they enter urban settlements. While they remain streets based upon ease of movement for traffic, these roads should become much more clearly managed with greater priority given to public transport through dedicated lanes, and speeds should drop to enable appropriate development alongside the highway. Within a short space of having entered the urban settlement, the road should form part of the overall fabric of the town or city.

In view of this, and because of the mistakes of the past, we must prioritise expenditure on ameliorating the worst effects of those major roads which have dissected towns or neighbourhoods. This includes a number of the major ring road schemes which have thrown a concrete collar around the centres of our towns and cities. Wherever possible, we need to re-integrate these highways with the rest of the urban transport structure. Perhaps most importantly, we need to give pedestrians ease of access across these major roads. One example is the inner ring road in Dortmund.

Outside the main railway station, traffic is held back from a 20 metre wide pedestrian crossing. The crossing goes 'straight through', on one phase of lights, without the need for any 'cattle pens' or railings. As a result, people flow through from town centre to the railway station on the most convenient alignment. Although this is one of the busiest roads in the city, there is no question about who has priority – it is the pedestrian.

For smaller local streets to work as social places, we need to re-think the way we design both the pedestrian spaces and the carriageway so that the impact of vehicular traffic is minimised. This means slowing traffic down while at the same time improving the design of the street as a place, rather than a transport corridor. Dramatic improvements can be made by, for example, simplifying signing, street furniture and road markings so that their visual impact is minimised. Many useful recommendations have already been set out in this context in the DETR's companion guide to Design Bulletin 32 – 'Places, Streets and Movement'. Drivers need to be made aware that they are entering a pedestrian sensitive environment. Speed limits will often need to be reduced. To respond to this, the Government will need to complete its national review of speed policy and speed limits quickly. Limits of 20mph and lower could become the norm in most urban residential areas and high streets. Where traffic calming is also introduced to an existing street it needs to be designed with pedestrians and cyclists in mind.

Crossing the inner ring road in Dortmund (Tim Pharoah)

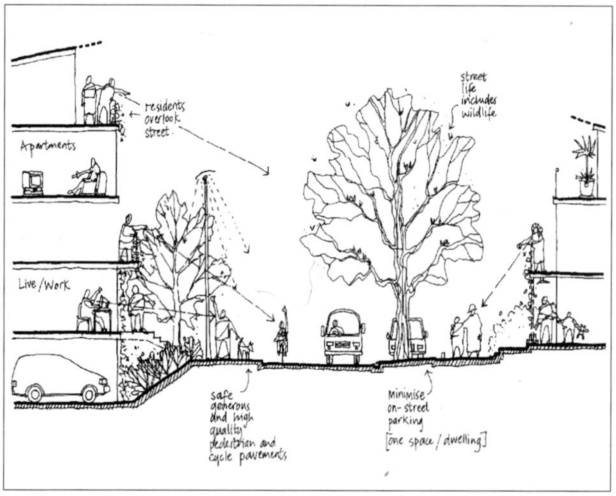

Streets can create a suitable environment for people and vehicles

Figure 3.4: A tale of community interaction in San Francisco: the lighter the traffic, the more chance of knowing your neighbours

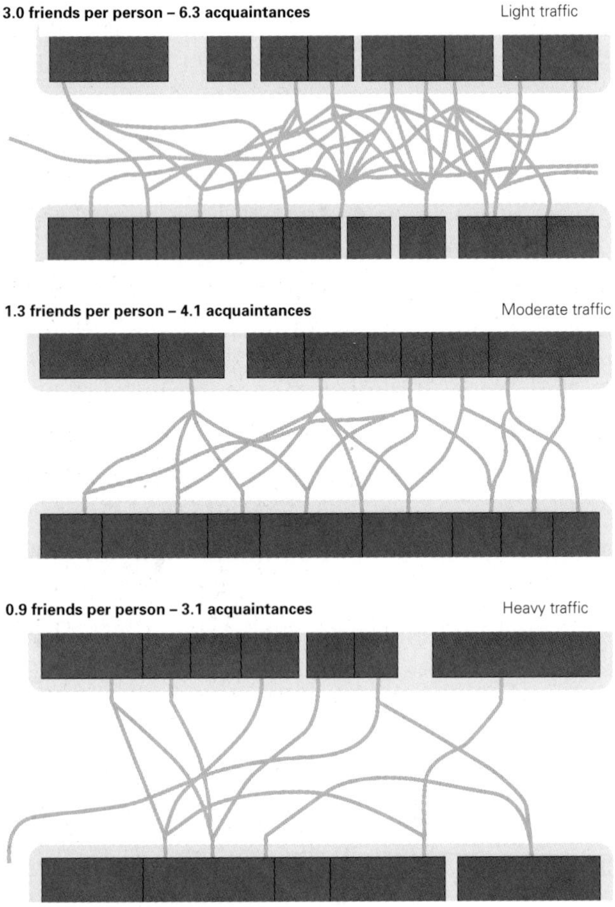

Three streets in San Francisco (Lines show friends and acquaintances)

Source: Appleyard and Lintell (1972)

To this end, we would like to see the formal introduction of Home Zones in this country. Based upon the best German and Dutch examples, Home Zones are groups of streets which create living spaces, where pedestrians have absolute priority and cars travel at little more than walking pace. They are not private enclaves, in that they still allow people to pass through a neighbourhood from one place to another, but they do change the way in which such journeys can be made. On entering a Home Zone, drivers pass prominent road signs and other entry features that make them aware of the change in legal status. Once past the signs, the drivers know that, just like a zebra crossing, they will be responsible for the injuries they cause. The streets themselves have features which force drivers to drive slowly and safely – speed tables, trees and bushes, extended pavement areas etc. The crucial point about Home Zones is that the decision to give an area Home Zone status has local support.[3]

Our recommendation is:

- **Introduce Home Zones in partnership with local communities, based on a robust legal framework, using tested street designs, reduced speed limits and traffic-calming measures. (11)**

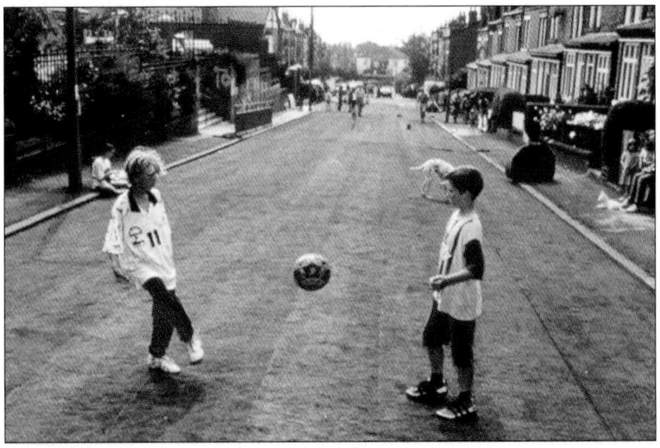

Pioneering the way for Home Zones in Leeds?

3 'Home zones: reclaiming residential streets'; Children's Play Council

CREATING A NEW SET OF TRAVEL CHOICES

Over the last fifty years the planning of development has been dictated primarily by the demands of the car user. This, not surprisingly, has had the effect of encouraging car use, even for journeys which would be much better made by walking or cycling. This change reflects, in part, a major cultural shift in England. For example, to take just two places the Task Force visited, Hull and Rotterdam face each other across the North Sea, have a similar climate and topography, but have a dramatically different attitude to cycling. To reverse this trend means designing with all forms of movement in mind.

Prioritising walking and cycling

The Government's Transport White Paper gives priority to walking and cycling as 'forms of transport' in their own right and expects to see this reflected in local plan preparation. Local authorities are recommended to adopt a similar stance and prioritise walking and cycling projects, and other transport projects in which walking and cycling form a significant part.

Walking

Some 80% of all journeys under one mile are undertaken on foot and 28% of all journeys in total.[4] Almost all public transport trips involve at least one walking stage. The obvious way to encourage walking is to win back space for people on foot, and to encourage street facilities and functions which make it attractive to walk, with well-designed seating areas, public art, planting and paving, and less traffic. In many parts of urban England, walking is a dreadful experience of trying to negotiate obstacles, moving and non-moving, which prevent you from getting where you want to go. We have to decide on the main purposes of our urban streets. Is Brixton High Street primarily a local district centre and meeting place, or is it principally the main road from London to Brighton? Which takes priority?

HALIFAX: ON THE MOVE

Nestling in the Pennine hills of Yorkshire's West Riding, the town of Halifax has adopted a number of innovations to improve the appearance and quality of visitor experience in its historic core.

Crossley Street, one of the main streets in the centre of the town, has been transformed by an environmental scheme. Flat-topped road humps have been installed to slow traffic and aid pedestrians. The footways have been extended to narrow the carriageway at each end of the street. In the central area, a restricted parking zone has been introduced which obviates the need for yellow lines.

Great importance has been attached to the appearance of the finished scheme and its setting in the heart of a conservation area, and to the needs of people with reduced mobility. Street furniture has been kept to a minimum and specially designed unlit low level road signs were used. Attention to detail and quality of finish includes the use of specially manufactured brass studs, which were set in the stone paving to replace conventional tactile paving at crossing points.

The changes have been a success. Vehicle flows and speeds, and parking activity, have fallen, while pedestrian use and resident and visitor satisfaction have increased. The results of a recent survey bear this out. 51% of those interviewed felt that the changes had made it easier and safer to cross the road, 73% felt that the scheme had improved ease of walking on the footway, while 80% felt that the appearance of Crossley Street had been improved.

Pedestrian routes need to respond to 'desire lines' and connect the places where people want to go in a direct and convenient way. Development plans should identify clear areas and routes where pedestrians will be given priority and walking generally encouraged.

4 National Travel Survey, in 'Walking in Great Britain'; TSO (1998)

We actually know very little about the local travel patterns and the motivations of the urban pedestrian. We need more effort made at national and local level to understand local pedestrian patterns within particular localities, attitudes to the walking environment and pedestrians' own priorities for improvements. Each local authority should undertake ongoing analysis of key origins and destinations for local walking journeys – hospitals, stations, libraries, high streets etc. – and developing policies and plans both for overcoming obstacles on the routes between them, and for making them more secure and user-friendly.

Cycling

Today, just 1% of all journeys in England are by bike. Fifty years ago, it was 25%. The demands of cyclists are relatively easy to accommodate with the right street design and traffic management. On low speed streets, (below 30 kph/20 mph), cyclists can mix with vehicles. On busier streets with higher traffic speeds there should be clearly defined cycle lanes with special provision for cyclists at junctions. It is anomalous that the busiest streets at rush hour are extremely slow moving but often still too dangerous for cyclists. If, and only if, pavements can be made wide enough by reducing the width of roads, we can follow the continental practice of creating dedicated lanes for cyclists alongside pedestrians.

The development of comprehensive cycle networks must continue to be a priority – both within and across local authority boundaries. The problem at the moment is that where such networks do exist, they are often far too notional and do little to encourage cycling amongst non-cyclists. They are poorly enforced, and often cluttered by on-street parking. And at the points at which priority is most needed, such as roundabouts and busy intersections, the provision disappears. A disconnected network is next to useless.

Instead, we need to strengthen networks by:

- wherever possible, enabling a clear physical separation on major roads between cycle lanes and carriageways;
- where separation is not possible, ensuring adequate widths of lanes to increase feelings of safety;
- increasing enforcement and penalties for mis-use of cycle lanes.

Safe, secure integrated networks are therefore a necessity but they must be accompanied by a strong promotional campaign which advertises the route.

Following the example of stations such as London Waterloo, standards should be established for the provision of cycle storage facilities at all significant public and commercial facilities, including railway stations. This should be backed up by a clear expectation on developers, through the planning process, to design in storage provision.

In the longer term, we should perhaps look at how insurance rules influence behaviour patterns and alter the transport hierarchy. One option would be to change insurance legislation so that damage and injuries suffered by cyclists in collision with car users should be automatically liable to the car user's insurance company, (a practice which helps underline transport priorities in the Netherlands).

Making arrangements for cycle storage: Central Station, York (Jem Wilcox)

Our recommendation:

- **Make public funding and planning permissions for urban development and highway projects conditional on priority being given to the needs of pedestrians and cyclists. (12)**

Improving public transport

Creating a virtuous circle

Our urban public transport systems fail to provide people with the choice and the incentive to get out of their cars. A recent Audit Commission survey showed that around a third of car drivers considered that buses and trains did not cover the right routes for them and almost a quarter considered services to be too unreliable to make the switch.[5]

To address the deficiencies of the current system requires an integrated response which responds to concerns over reliability, linkage, quality of vehicle, and capacity. Public transport operators need to respond to the new opportunities associated with the revival of urban neighbourhoods to deliver faster and more flexible services which increasingly offer a reasonable competitor to everyday car use. New development needs to build in access standards for public transport from the outset, and this could be backed up by a dedicated national guidance note on how this can be achieved.

At the same time we need to make sure that transport hubs benefit from the maximum catchment population possible to sustain existing services. Today, many sites which were previously developed but now lie vacant are close to actual – or potential – transport nodes. In redeveloping such sites we can effectively strengthen the public transport network by providing more public transport patronage. This in turn permits higher service levels to be provided commercially, which can encourage lower car ownership and an overall reduction in car use by those who do own cars, facilitating more intensive developments with reduced car parking provision and so on.

5 'All aboard'; Audit Commission (1999)

To promote this we must ensure that:

- we prioritise development opportunities on the basis of their proximity to the existing and potential public transport networks;
- we make it as simple as possible for people to access public transport services with minimum effort and pre-planning.

We also face a necessary but uphill task in securing better access to public transport for many suburban estates which have been entirely developed around the needs of the car. Low density layouts and the lack of clear neighbourhood centres deter people from using public transport as well as discouraging providers from supplying the services.

Improving service information is crucial. In all our major towns and cities, there should not only be a dedicated telephone information service on all public transport routes, there should also be a face to face information point and computerised 'real time' travel guides at the railway station and in the town centre. We can also build on the experience of the Greenwich Millennium Community in piloting the availability of 'real time' community travel information, including local bus and train times, on home digital systems and over the Internet.

Our recommendation:

- **Set targets for public transport within Local Transport Plans that specify maximum walking distances to bus stops; targets on punctuality, use, reliability and frequency of services; and standards for availability of cycle storage facilities at stations and interchanges. (13)**

the fares. Poorer people often can only afford to pay as they go, so that they cannot take advantage of cheaper multi-journey fare options. Another priority must therefore be to re-integrate these communities back into our urban transport systems.

To achieve this, we need to combine a number of options:

- give priority in defining cycle routes to link estates to centres;
- reduce bus fares from peripheral urban areas to the centre, usually by creating a flatter fare structure;
- make use of mini-bus services that can run continuously but are cheap;
- be more customer oriented; for example, running cheap buses from the estate to the supermarket at particular times of the day.

Recommendation:

- **Ensure every low income housing estate is properly connected to the town and district centre by frequent, accessible and affordable public transport. (15)**

Investing sufficient resources

The outcomes of the Comprehensive Spending Review, announced in 1998, brought good news for those seeking greater public investment in transport, which is scheduled to rise by £988 million over the next three years to £3.67 billion.

The Government has also made clear that there will be a re-prioritisation of resources away from major highways towards local transport provision, with the accent on the more sustainable forms of provision. Although it is difficult to monitor the split of expenditure accurately, figures provided by DETR suggest that the annual proportion of transport expenditure dedicated to non-private transport is just over 55% at the current time. Local authorities will also have a small single pot of capital resources to spend in accordance with their local transport plan. This devolution of power over decision-making fits with promoting the primary strategic role of local authorities, and we would like to see an increasing proportion of transport expenditure devolved to regional and local levels.

The development of comprehensive area regeneration strategies will inevitably require significant investment in transport infrastructure. Some of that resource will come through the regeneration budgets but this needs to be backed up by targeting of mainstream programmes. The main priority of that targeted funding must be to shift the balance of transport users in favour of public transport.

The regeneration agencies also need to be given sufficient freedom to invest in transport measures, rather than having to rely on the availability of other funding sources. This is not about providing access roads to new industrial units, which has tended to be the limit of the agencies' involvement in the past. Instead, they should be able to use a mix of capital and revenue finance to support the transport needs of new mixed use developments. This may be particularly relevant in the early stages of a development where the population catchment is insufficient to justify public transport provision without additional subsidy.

Stratford Bus Station: investing in public transport as part of a wider regeneration strategy

(Dennis Gilbert/View)

Our recommendations are:

- **Commit a minimum 65% of transport public expenditure to programmes and projects which prioritise walking, cycling and public transport, over the next ten years, increased from the current Government estimate of 55% this year. (16)**

- **Give priority to the public transport needs of regeneration areas within Local Transport Plans and public funding decisions. (17)**

- **Allow Regional Development Agencies and other regeneration funding bodies to provide funding for transport measures that support their area regeneration objectives. (18)**

Reducing car use

The Government's current transport agenda fails to promote reduced car ownership. Indeed, a recent report suggested that the current tax system actually discriminates against people giving up their cars.[8] At the same time, we are making little impact on levels of car use.

85% of all transport journeys start or finish at home.[9] About 40% of those journeys are by people travelling to and from work. The average commuting time in our country is now 40% higher than 20 years ago. Many of those commuters spend too long in their cars stuck in traffic jams.

Persuading people to come back and live work at the heart of our towns and cities would help ease the commuter problem. That is the long term goal. In the shorter term, measures already promised in the Integrated Transport White Paper, such as road charging, dedicated multi-occupancy vehicle lanes and work-place parking charges must be introduced as quickly as possible.

THE SCHOOL RUN

The trend in car use for the school journey is sharply upwards with car travel nearly doubling over the last ten years. Well over a third of primary pupils now travel to school by car and so do over a fifth of secondary pupils. One in five cars on the road at the morning peak of 8.50am is taking children to school. Other European countries such as Germany have experienced only a small fraction of the increase in car use for school runs in the UK. The following table shows how the number of children walking to school has declined dramatically since 1971.

Figure 3.5: The decline in the number of primary school children walking to school

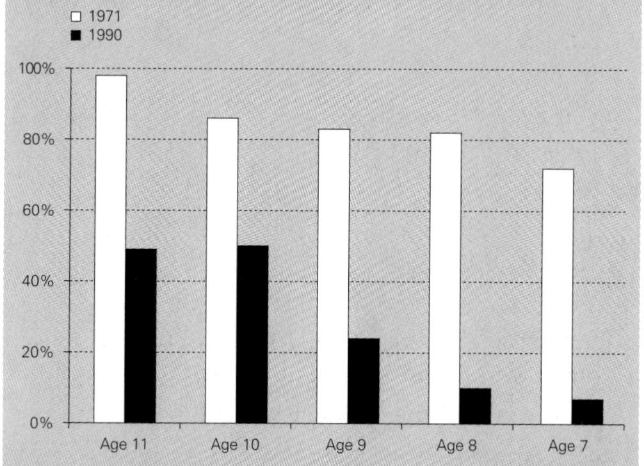

Source: Hillman (1993)

There is a need to check the huge growth in the number of children who are driven to school by providing realistic alternatives. We know that for some people, the twin imperatives of time and safety will mean that the car must continue to be used, but there are many parents and children who could reap health and social benefits from leaving the car at home.

We particularly want to see initiatives that involve the school itself – governors, teachers, parents and children – planning together how to provide more sustainable travel options.

8 'House of Commons Environmental Audit Committee Report' (1999)
9 National Travel Survey 1994

Figure 3.6: Average journey length in Great Britain

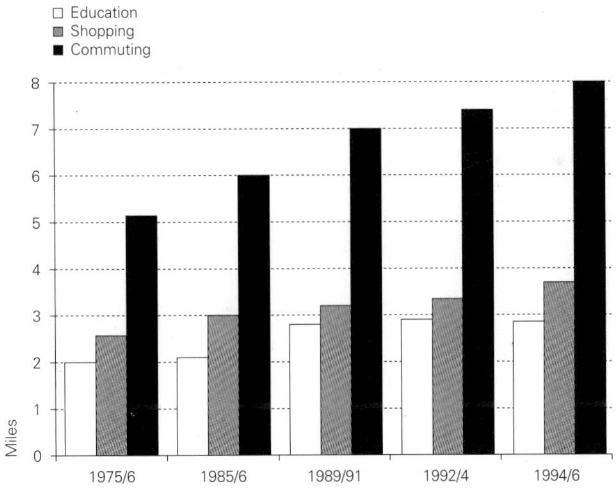

Source: DETR (1998)

We also have to recognise changing trends in commuter journeys. One of those trends is a growth in non-central work trips. In other words, people are travelling between neighbourhoods within the same town or city, often between two suburban areas. There are few circular or orbital public transport options. The city of Paris has responded to a similar need with the development of the Orbitale route, using light public transport on reserved tracks, inside the inner and outer suburbs of Paris, making public transport journeys easier from suburb to suburb. We need to be thinking of similarly innovative solutions. The lessons we can perhaps learn from the Orbitale system are that:

- circular systems must link well to radial routes, building a web of interchanges that attract a mix of walk-in catchments and people making connections;

- they must be targeted on areas where they can make a real difference to travel choice; fast well-integrated orbital bus and tram routes at different distances from the city centre;

- these inter-neighbourhood routes can generate greater social inclusion, in terms of their potential to connect deprived areas with job creating areas; e.g. South Acton to Park Royal in West London; Speke to Norris Green in Liverpool; North and East Manchester to Manchester Ringway airport.

On a wider scale, new types of urban patterns are developing. One example is the 'network city' where a number of towns and cities within a region increasingly operate as a network in which people, live, work and recreate using various spaces that do not conform with normal commuter patterns along travel-to-work corridors into the major city centre. Examples abroad include the Frankfurt region, the Randstad in the Netherlands and Emilia Romagna in Northern Italy. Increasingly, an English region such as the East Midlands is developing similar characteristics, with profound effects for transport planning.

It is therefore important that Regional and Local Transport Plans specifically address unmet and poorly met travel needs, especially orbital journeys and sub-regional travel patterns, and produce proposals to address them.

Figure 3.7: The process of reducing car use in towns and cities depends on a series of interlinked factors

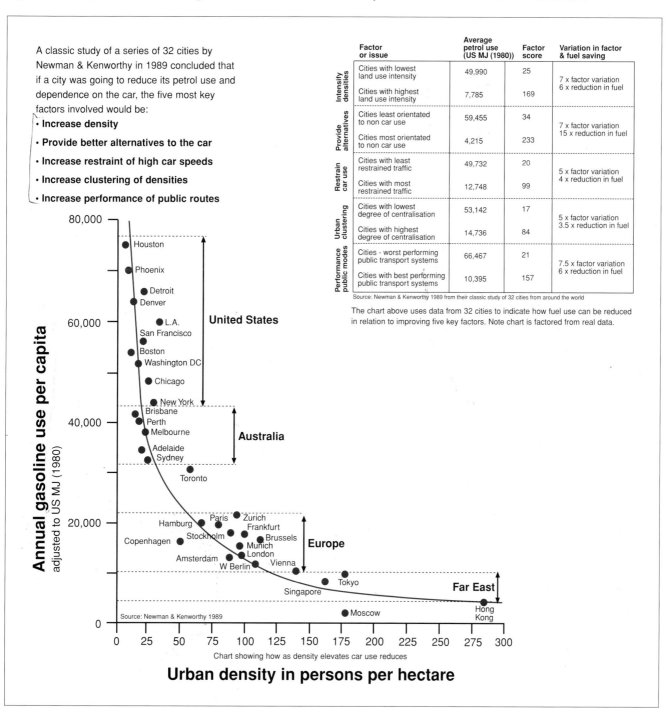

A classic study of a series of 32 cities by Newman & Kenworthy in 1989 concluded that if a city was going to reduce its petrol use and dependence on the car, the five most key factors involved would be:

- **Increase density**
- **Provide better alternatives to the car**
- **Increase restraint of high car speeds**
- **Increase clustering of densities**
- **Increase performance of public routes**

	Factor or issue	Average petrol use (US MJ (1980))	Factor score	Variation in factor & fuel saving
Intensify densities	Cities with lowest land use intensity	49,990	25	7 x factor variation 6 x reduction in fuel
	Cities with highest land use intensity	7,785	169	
Provide alternatives	Cities least orientated to non car use	59,455	34	7 x factor variation 15 x reduction in fuel
	Cities most orientated to non car use	4,215	233	
Restrain car use	Cities with least restrained traffic	49,732	20	5 x factor variation 4 x reduction in fuel
	Cities with most restrained traffic	12,748	99	
Urban clustering	Cities with lowest degree of centralisation	53,142	17	5 x factor variation 3.5 x reduction in fuel
	Cities with highest degree of centralisation	14,736	84	
Performance public modes	Cities - worst performing public transport systems	66,467	21	7.5 x factor variation 6 x reduction in fuel
	Cities with best performing public transport systems	10,395	157	

Source: Newman & Kenworthy 1989 from their classic study of 32 cities from around the world

The chart above uses data from 32 cities to indicate how fuel use can be reduced in relation to improving five key factors. Note chart is factored from real data.

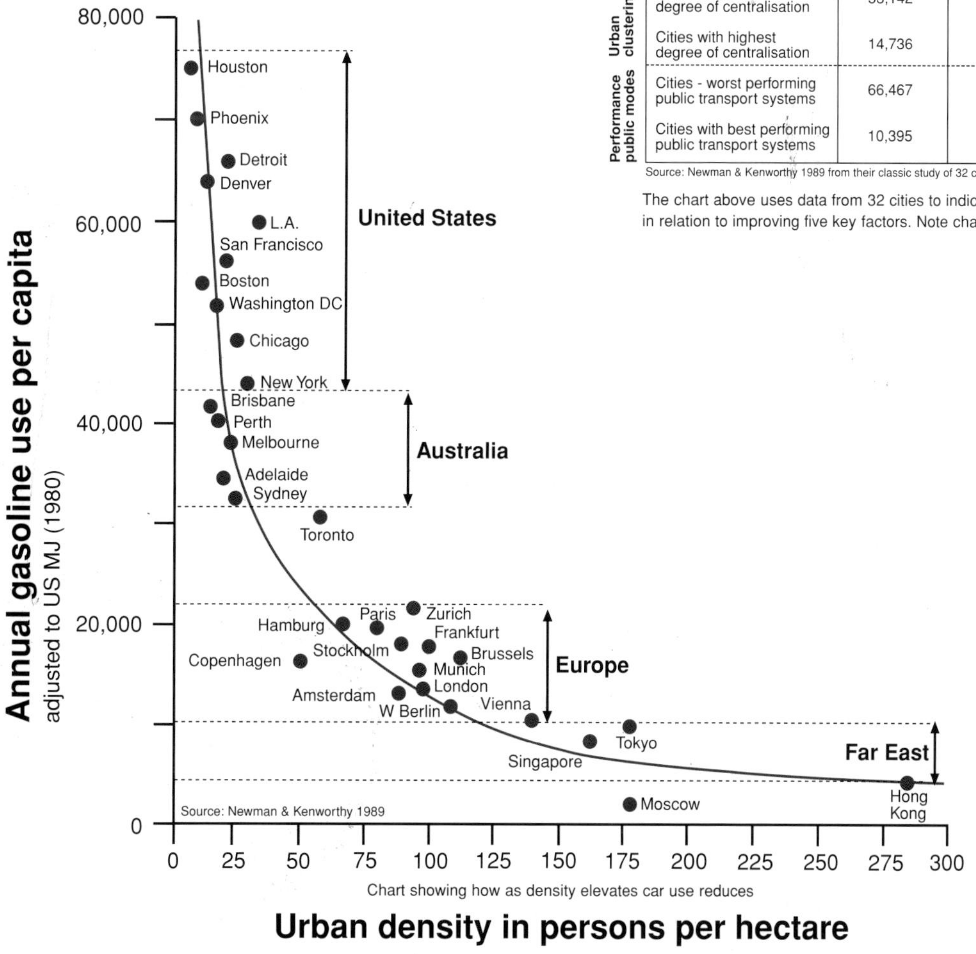

(Andrew Wright Associates)

FREIBURG, GERMANY: INTEGRATING TRANSPORT THROUGH DESIGN AND MANAGEMENT

The German city of Freiburg has shown how it is possible to virtually stop the growth of car use, even when car ownership is growing. Freiburg's car ownership rose from 113 per 1,000 people in 1960 to 422 per 1,000 in 1990. But despite the growth in the availability of cars, car use has remained virtually constant since 1976, while public transport passengers have increased 53% and bicycle trips have risen 96%.

The success in Freiburg in 'taming the automobile' is due to three main transportation and physical planning strategies:

- sharply restricting automobile use in the city by pedestrianising the city centre, instituting area-wide calming schemes (including a city-wide speed limit of 30km per hour in residential areas) and making car parking more difficult and expensive;
- providing affordable, convenient and safe alternatives to auto use, by extending and upgrading its light rail system and using buses as feeders to the rail system;
- strictly regulating development to ensure a compact land use pattern that is conducive to public transport, bicycling and walking.

Kaiser Josef Station, Freiburg, Germany (Dr Klaus Weigandt)

PARKING

Secure car parking is one of the most important factors in an individual's choice of home. Given the choice, people will select both homes and neighbourhoods that afford safe storage for vehicles. Parking is also critical for many businesses, and surveys consistently point to the perceived importance of both customer and supplier parking for commercial enterprise – especially retail.

We cannot, however, go on as we are. Providing parking space for vehicles is using up vast tracts of our urban land. Much of this could be put to far better use, to accommodate housing development or create new squares and parks, reversing the car's erosion of urban open space. If we have now abandoned 'predict and provide' in respect of housing provision, and traffic forecasts have effectively forced the abandonment of 'predict and provide' in respect of roads, then it is time we also abandoned 'predict and provide' in respect of parking requirements and set some maximum standards.

Planning residential parking provision

There are two main elements to reducing car parking – private residential and private non-residential provision. There is now a growing number of test case developments, which have successfully negotiated a wholesale shift in patterns of car ownership and hence residential car parking in this country. Car-free or virtually car-free developments show that the relationship between people and cars can be changed. There are about 200 successful car-free housing schemes operating in different parts of Europe. While such innovations have yet to gain anything more than marginal public acceptance, we need to learn from these examples and promote new developments that reduce dependency on the car as a primary means of transportation.

While the opportunities for a more radical approach to car ownership and car parking do exist – for example in the context of special needs housing or housing close to public transport – the vast majority of new developments are still very traditional in dealing with these issues. Planning authorities should not automatically insist on off-street car parking. There are plenty of older parts of our towns and cities that have no off-street car parking. Good on-street management control, prioritisation for residents and reduced car dependency contribute to making these environments attractive to a wide group of urban dwellers.

Recommendation:

- **Set a maximum standard of one car parking space per dwelling for all new urban residential development. (19)**

Planning non-residential parking provision

Private non-residential parking is an even bigger problem because it fuels traffic growth. The planning system has allowed private developers to get away with demand-based provision, often on the basis of exaggerated demand. We must therefore change the way in which the planning system influences the design of commercial facilities, so as to maximise access for pedestrians, cyclists and public transport, to integrate with other uses. Planning guidance should establish a range of maximum private non-residential parking standards, the range to reflect different sizes and locations of development.

Metro Centre, Gateshead (Martin Bond Environmental Images)

In mixed residential and commercial developments we also need to look at the possibility of shared parking spaces which alternate between business and resident designation. We can also learn from countries such as France, Holland and Spain which may make far greater use of underground parking, both for residential and commercial provision.

There are examples where we need to increase car parking. One such case is to prevent out-of-town traffic entering the town or city centre by extending park-and-ride schemes. Oxford, for example, has done this very successfully. In doing so, we have to make the joint cost of parking and catching public transport for the remainder of the journey into town, substantially cheaper than parking in the city centre. Otherwise, park-and-ride will not work. There also has to be sufficient car parking provision at suburban railway stations for the same reasons.

Car parking charges

As well as using the planning system to reduce private non-residential parking provision, we can also consider the use of financial instruments. In its White Paper, the Government chose not to introduce any form of taxation on commercial car parking at present, other than workplace charging, and even this limited charging mechanism is to be subject to local authority discretionary powers.

It would be equitable to extend the workspace parking charge to all forms of private non-residential car parking. It would still be relatively easy to extend the proposals for business parking to include customer (e.g. retail and leisure) parking when the legislation comes forward. In doing so, we should ensure that local authorities do not compete against each other by reducing rates and, crucially, that out-of-town or edge-of-town superstores do not use superior profit margins or higher food costs to subsidise the cost of the tax to the customer by paying it for them. These concerns would suggest that, although the charge would need to be collected from the business through a mechanism such as an additional charge to the Unified Business Rate, it should be mandatory on those businesses to pass on the charge in full to their customers at the point of use of the car park.

Any charge should be modest to start with, and increases specified over a number of years, allowing owners/end users to make adjustment plans, by reducing their car parking provision and improving access for other forms of transport. In addition, like other special charging mechanisms, such as the landfill tax, there may need to be a small number of exemptions, including:

- a minimum threshold so that smaller stores in both urban and rural areas with just a small amount of off-street car parking are not penalised; this could be based upon floor area, maximum occupancy levels or rateable value;
- a discretionary power to provide an exemption for regeneration areas (see Chapter 5) where there is a need for short term help to stabilise the position of existing retail businesses and attract new ones.

Revenue raised through the tax should be hypothecated at either the national or regional level to provide additional transport finance for urban regeneration schemes.

The Task Force's recommendation is:

- **Extend plans to tax workplace charging to all forms of private non-residential car parking provision. (20)**

IN SUMMARY

The Integrated Transport White Paper committed the Government to "...minimise transport's demand for land." The design principles and policy recommendations which are set out in this Chapter will help to minimise the urban land-take of transport. But they could also complement many other objectives. Getting the movement patterns in our towns, cities and urban neighbourhoods right is critical to achieving a viable mix and density which will in turn further enhance urban capacity.

Our principal conclusion is that we can only increase the 'carrying capacity' of urban areas – through density or mix – if we reduce the need for car travel. If we do not achieve this, then the spaces between the buildings get blocked up by cars, either parked or moving. Therefore, while an urban movement framework should make provision for all forms of movement, it should positively discriminate in favour of walking, cycling and public transport.

To achieve this prioritisation we have to accept that, for the foreseeable future, many people will still choose to use their cars whatever the other options. Our objective should be that they have to pay a more realistic charge for the social and environmental costs which they are currently passing on to others.

We will have to improve public transport provision out of all recognition. We will have to reduce car parking provision and we will have to design our streets in a way which promote access and movement on foot and by bike.

Urban transport will require more resources to achieve these important changes.

SUMMARY OF RECOMMENDATIONS	Responsibility	Timing
Key recommendations		
Introduce Home Zones, in partnership with local communities, based on a robust legal framework, using tested street designs, reduced speed limits and traffic-calming measures.	DETR	By 2002
Place Local Transport Plans on a statutory footing. They should include explicit targets for reducing car journeys, and increasing year on year the proportion of trips made on foot, bicycle and by public transport.	DETR, local government	By 2001
Commit a minimum 65% of transport public expenditure to programmes and projects which prioritise walking, cycling and public transport, over the next ten years, increased from the current Government estimate of 55% this year.	DETR, HM Treasury	Ongoing
Other recommendations		
Make public funding and planning permissions for urban development and highway projects conditional on priority being given to the needs of pedestrians and cyclists.	DETR, RDAs and other funding providers	Immediate and ongoing
Set targets for public transport within Local Transport Plans that specify maximum walking distances to bus stops; targets on punctuality, use, reliability and frequency of services; and standards for availability of cycle storage facilities at stations and interchanges.	DETR, local authorities	By 2000
Give priority to the public transport needs of regeneration areas within Local Transport Plans and public funding decisions.	Local authorities and funding providers	Ongoing
Allow Regional Development Agencies and other regeneration funding bodies to provide funding for transport measures that support their area regeneration objectives.	DETR	By April 2000

	Responsibility	Timing
Extend a well-regulated franchise system for bus services to all English towns and cities if services have not improved substantially within five years.	DETR	Decision by 2004
Ensure every low income housing estate is properly connected to the town and district centre by frequent, accessible and affordable public transport.	DETR, local government	By 2000
Set a maximum standard of one car parking space per dwelling for all new urban residential development.	DETR	By end of 1999 through PPG3 and PPG13
Extend plans to tax workplace charging to all forms of private non-residential car parking provision.	DETR, HM Treasury	By 2001

PART TWO

MAKING TOWNS AND CITIES WORK

MANAGING THE URBAN ENVIRONMENT

Many people reject our towns and cities, and choose to live elsewhere, because they are badly managed and maintained. More than 90% of our urban fabric will still be with us in 30 years time. The state in which we hand these assets over to the next generation depends entirely on how we look after them over that period. If we want to make the most of our existing urban assets, sustain the results of new investment and promote public confidence in our towns and cities, we must manage our urban environment carefully.

This means keeping our streets clean and safe, mending pavements, dealing with graffiti and vandalism, and maintaining attractive parks and open space. It is about the way we manage environmental services and the amount of money that is available for the task at hand. It is excellence in delivery combined with sufficient investment which will help to maintain urban neighbourhoods as attractive places.

In some places we have to reverse years of neglect. In others, it will require a more careful consideration of how to preserve the quality of historic or newly regenerated environments. Everywhere, we must secure real trusteeship.

This Chapter considers what has gone wrong with the management of our urban environment and, in proposing new solutions, concludes that:

- we have to manage the whole of the urban environment more strategically which means giving more powers and resources to local authorities to do the job;
- we have lost much of the crucial interface between town hall managers and citizens. We need a network of dedicated environmental managers, wardens, caretakers and community-based management organisations to ensure that the services which are provided are those which people themselves need and prioritise;
- there are parts of our towns and cities, such as town centres and council estates, that have special management requirements, and we need to reflect those needs in management structures and resource allocation decisions.

THE STATE OF OUR URBAN ENVIRONMENT

There are many different types of services involved in managing urban areas. They include:

- local environmental services: e.g. street cleaning, refuse collection, grounds maintenance, parks management, regulation and enforcement of traders, street lighting;
- security services: e.g. policing, enforcement, guarding;
- housing management and maintenance: e.g. tenancy relationships, repairs;
- other property: e.g. estates management, repairs of all publicly and privately owned property;
- local transport and utilities: e.g. buses, trains, gas, electricity, water;
- local amenities: e.g. waterways, shopping malls;
- local personal services: e.g. health, social care, advice and information giving;
- education and leisure: e.g. schools, colleges, adult education, youth clubs, leisure centres.

The Prime Minister's Social Exclusion Unit (SEU) is looking at some of these types of service provision, concentrating on the needs of the most deprived neighbourhoods.

The available data suggests that urban areas, and in particular, deprived neighbourhoods, are under-performing against most of the service headings:

- in education: inner city residents have been found to be more than 50% more likely to leave school without graded results than residents in all other areas;[1]
- in health: the mortality rate for the 44 most deprived boroughs (all urban) is 30% higher than the national average;[2]
- in community safety: 10% of residents in inner city areas are burgled once or more in a year, twice the rate of anywhere else, and 25% of ethnic minority residents in low income multi-ethnic areas say racially motivated attacks are a very or fairly big problem for them;[3]
- in housing: 20% of all dwellings in England face urgent repair costs of more than £1,000 and the level of housing investment as a percentage of GDP is below most other EU countries, and less than half that of Germany.[4]

In this Chapter, in accordance with our remit, we are focusing mainly on local environmental services, but there is a need to address all aspects of service management if we are to convince people to move back into urban areas.

The urban realm is showing the strain after years of under-investment. In a recent survey:

- 26% of households in England thought that their neighbourhood had got worse in the last two years, compared to just 10% who thought it had got better;[5]
- 34% of people living on council estates felt things had got worse.

People were similarly pessimistic about how their neighbourhood would change in the future.

1 'Urban Trends 2'; Policy Studies Institute (1994)

2 'Bringing Britain together: a national strategy for neighbourhood renewal'; Social Exclusion Unit (1998)

3 Sources: Home Office (1996, 1994)

4 'Future housing needs and urban development'; OECD (1998)

5 'Patterns of Neighbourhood Dissatisfaction in England', Joseph Rowntree Foundation (1998)

Figure 4.1: Rank order of problems identified by householders in their area

Problem	**% of households who perceive this as a problem**
Crime	68%
Vandalism and hooliganism	55%
Litter and rubbish	41%
Dogs and dog fouling	34%
Graffiti	29%
Noise	24%
Neighbours	14%

Source: Survey of English Housing 1997/98

Figure 4.2: Relative extent of problems perceived by householders living in urban areas

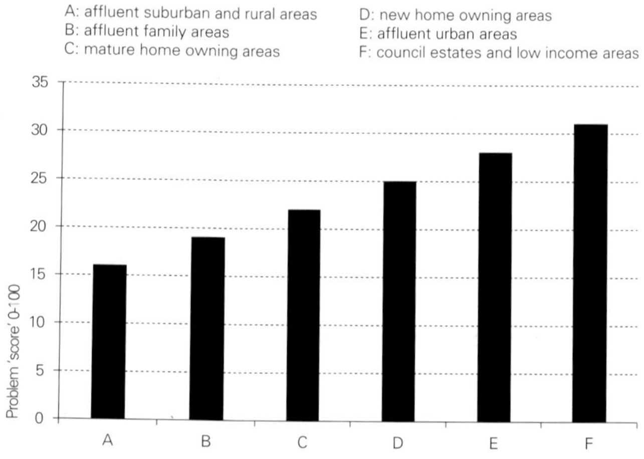

Source: Survey of English Housing 1994/95, using ACORN area classification

In addition:

- 18% of people living in affluent urban areas and 28% of households living in council estates and low income areas described the appearance of their area as 'fairly bad' or 'very bad'. This compares to just 4% of people living in affluent rural and suburban areas;
- overall, people living in deprived areas were twice as likely to be dissatisfied with their area as other households;[6]
- over 25% of council tenants expressed dissatisfaction with the maintenance of communal areas in purpose built blocks compared to 17% of households in housing association accommodation and 8% of people who owned their flat outright.[7]

These levels of dissatisfaction and pessimism about the state of our towns and cities reflect a widely held view that our towns and cities are run-down and unkempt. An assessment of the most recent performance data for local authority services goes some way to explaining why we have such a negative perception.[8]

Considering just the problems of litter and fly-tipping:

- only 34% of councils offer a back door household waste collection service;
- only 53% of metropolitan authorities offer an appointments service for the collection of bulky waste compared to 72% of councils across the whole of England;
- four times as many waste bins are missed during collection rounds in metropolitan areas compared to shire districts, with certain authorities such as Liverpool, Croydon and Wakefield, missing more than ten times the national average;
- monitoring the cleanliness of our city streets reveals that only just over 50% achieve an acceptable standard and less than 30% achieve a high standard.

A survey by the Tidy Britain Group in 1998[9] found that 47% of councils considered fly-tipping to be a 'significant problem' in their area, with domestic waste being the main problem. In the same survey, 60% of authorities were able to identify more than 40 different problem sites which regularly attracted fly-tipping activity.

6 'Survey of English Housing 1997/98'; ONS
7 Data from Survey of English Housing: Survey period – April 95–September 95; ONS
8 'Council Services Compendium for England 1997/98'; Audit Commission (1999)
9 Reported in Waste Manager vol. 27, no. 13 (1998)

The success of regulatory and enforcement policies will often be enhanced if local authorities integrate the different functions more closely. This might include bringing all the relevant professional staff together in a single team and establishing street level enforcement teams which can deal with a range of maintenance problems, rather than just having to deal with a single specialist function. The London Borough of Newham have just launched a 'Spotcheck' initiative which is designed to raise awareness and educate individuals and businesses about how their behaviour affects the quality of the surrounding environment, at the same time as taking enforcement action on a wide range of street scene issues, including illegal dumping, parking, abandoned vehicles etc.

Recommendation:

- **Make public bodies responsible for managing sites blighted by proposed major infrastructure schemes, even where they do not yet own the land. Local authorities should be empowered to take enforcement action if a responsible body reneges on its duties. (26)**

Crime prevention and community safety

There also needs to be a continuing consideration of how urban management relates to crime prevention and community safety. In a recent survey, 'crime and vandalism' were cited alongside more opportunities for young people, as the aspects of their area that most people wanted to see improved.[13] Residential and commercial burglary, thefts of, and from cars, racial crime, criminal damage, disorder, drug trafficking and misuse, nuisance and anti-social behaviours, are often perceived as negative parts of urban life. Patterns in many neighbourhoods and estates show a handful of persistent young offenders committing a majority of crimes. In many communities there has developed a sense of futility that nothing can be done and frustration with the ineffectiveness of the criminal justice system to deal with persistent offenders.

People's perception of crime is often out of line with the actual position. Research has shown that the public's lack of confidence in the police results in many crimes being unreported. The Macpherson Report[14] has documented how lack of confidence in police among black and ethnic minority communities is a particular problem, requiring a wide range of actions across public authorities.

Figure 4.4: Complaints about vandalism to houses and gardens, as percentage of housing stock (1994)

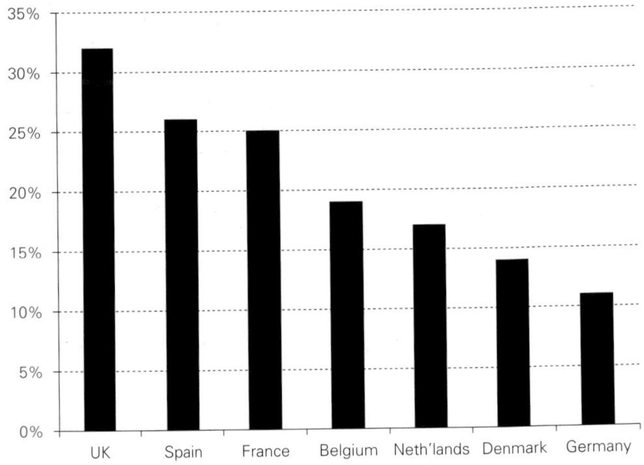

Source: OECD (1998)

The Crime and Disorder Act, adopted in July 1998, goes a long way towards addressing these public concerns. Its message is that communities should not have to tolerate living in fear of crime, and it introduces a range of tough measures to deal more speedily with offenders and crime prevention. It also recognises that crime will only be addressed through dealing with its causes – social exclusion, unemployment and deprivation.

The Act places a new statutory responsibility upon local authorities, along with the police, to form a partnership with other agencies to develop three year strategies for reducing crime in their areas. The first set of strategies has recently been published. It is important that these strategies include:

13 'Survey of English Housing 1995/96'; ONS (1997)

14 Home Office (1999)

Crime and vandalism were cited as the most important aspects of their area that people wanted to see improved (Richard Greenhill)

- policies and guidance for designing out crime. As we established back in Chapter 2, this points to the creation of lively areas with public spaces that are well overlooked. Interconnected streets and a fine grained mix of uses and buildings with plenty of windows and doors that face onto streets can contribute to overall levels of safety and security;

- joint action by all agencies to reduce crimes of public concern through concerted action by local authority environmental services, housing management, schools, social services, police, probation and health;

- engaging residents and businesses in the fight against crime, through neighbourhood watch and local partnerships on estates and in neighbourhoods, schools and public spaces;

- practical ways for applying new statutory orders for tackling racially motivated crime, anti-social behaviour, truancy, sex offenders and child curfews;

- bringing together the local services of the police, housing management, security, enforcement and environment management to focus on crime and vandalism 'hotspots';

- improving public confidence in the police, in particular, by implementing the recommendations of the Macpherson report by improving the recording of racist crime and supporting its victims.

Our recommendations:

- **Strengthen enforcement powers and sanctions against individuals or organisations that breach regulations related to planning conditions, noise pollution, littering, fly-tipping and other forms of anti-social behaviour. (27)**

- **Use fines from criminal damage and community reparation to repair and maintain the local environment, according to local people's stated priorities. (28)**

The need to know whether management is making a difference

Effective managers have to know whether inputs are having the intended effect. There are three main elements to this:

- being able to compare performance with similar urban areas, against a common set of indicators;
- developing much more detailed knowledge about how an urban area is changing over time;
- establish what constitutes best practice, and empowering the highest performing authorities to achieve even higher standards through the application of greater flexibilities and powers.

The Audit Commission's performance indicators for 1999/2000 will measure the following aspects of managing the urban environment:[15]

A2	Access to and use of local authority buildings
D	Refuse collection
I	Providing recreational facilities
J1-3	Keeping land and highways clear of litter and refuse
J4	Providing public conveniences
J5	Environmental health and consumer protection
P	Maintaining highways and streetlights

This is an incomplete list and it is fragmented between several different performance headings. Thus, a section entitled, 'Looking after the Local Environment', is actually very narrow in scope. We need to move towards a more comprehensive set of indicators, grouped together, which are based more firmly on outputs and outcomes, rather than service inputs, and which cover the whole of the urban environment. One means of achieving this may be to incorporate some of the Government's Sustainable Development Indicators.

At the local level, one of the main priorities for local authorities is to establish a clear baseline position of the state of the environment in different neighbourhoods and districts, based upon a mix of objective indicators and public perceptions. The choice of the indicators themselves will need to be developed in consultation with local people. The monitoring and evaluation of management performance will then have several purposes – to feed in to the definition of service plans, to inform procurement decisions and to provide the basis of feedback to the community. It will mean that borough-wide performance information has to be disaggregated by service and by neighbourhood.

Recommendation:

- **Review the performance indicators used by the Audit Commission as they measure standards of management of the urban environment, to produce a more comprehensive and better integrated set of measures. (29)**

15 'Performance Indicators for the financial year 1999/2000'; Audit Commission (1998)

IN SUMMARY

Quality of management is a crucial factor in the success of all urban neighbourhoods. It is the question of which services are delivered, by whom and to whom, and to what standards, which will determine the overall quality of the urban environment.

Local services are best delivered through a combined framework of strong strategic municipal government and responsive service management. In this Chapter, we have set out how such a framework can be structured, combining local leadership, clear and transparent management, devolved management in certain circumstances, responsive service delivery, upstream solutions and a commitment to evaluate progress.

In the next Chapter, we consider the situations when good urban management and maintenance are not enough, and more radical intervention is required. Regeneration is never, however, a substitute for urban management. Regeneration should mark a step change from one phase of urban management to another. A neighbourhood should move from a regime of preventative management, through regeneration to dedicated after-care and continuing improvement.

SUMMARY OF RECOMMENDATIONS	Responsibility	Timing
Key recommendation		
Assign a strategic role to local authorities in ensuring management of the whole urban environment, with powers to ensure that other property owners, including public utilities and agencies, maintain their land and premises to an acceptable standard.	National government, local government	By 2002
Summary of other recommendations		
Provide an above-inflation increase in central resources allocated to local authorities for managing and maintaining the urban environment in each of the next seven years.	HM Treasury, DETR	Annual
Establish single points of contact within local authorities, which have decision-making authority for the whole range of environmental services devolved to designated estates, neighbourhoods or town centres. In some cases, particularly social housing estates, this should include the appointment of super-caretakers or wardens.	Local authorities, housing associations.	Ongoing
Place Town Improvement Zones on a statutory footing, enabling local authorities to work with local businesses to establish jointly-funded management arrangements for town centres and other commercial districts.	DETR	By 2002
Pilot different models of neighbourhood management which give local people a stake in the decision-making process, relaxing regulations and guidelines to make it easier to establish devolved arrangements.	DETR	Ongoing
Make public bodies responsible for managing sites blighted by proposed major infrastructure schemes, even where they do not yet own the land. Local authorities should be empowered to take enforcement action if a responsible body reneges on its duties.	National government, local government	By 2001

HULME: RISING TO THE CHALLENGE

The slum clearance programme and subsequent building of one of Britain's largest system-built housing estates had disastrous results for Hulme. Initial high hopes for the 1970s redevelopment, designed to house 12,000 people – a fraction of those who lived in the area in the 1930s – were quickly dashed when evidence emerged of major problems, from heating inadequacies to pest infestation, high crime levels and symptoms of depression, isolation and ill-health which had been associated with the earlier slum conditions.

The early 1980s saw the start of a debate between community representatives, the City Council and central government about Hulme's problems and possible solutions. However it was not until April 1992, when Hulme City Challenge was launched with £37.5 million of government money, that there was a catalyst to fund a comprehensive programme to tackle the economic, social and physical problems of the area.

The City Challenge designation has helped Hulme to turn itself around. Three thousand deck access flats and maisonettes have been demolished and 4,000 new or refurbished homes are taking their place. Already, over 1,000 housing association homes, designed with close tenant involvement, and almost 1,000 private sector homes, are now occupied, including a 'foyer' scheme.

Commitments have also been secured for further private sector homes – flats, houses for sale and student accommodation.

The new Hulme is also providing new shops, offices, community and educational facilities, streets, squares and civic spaces alongside the new housing. Alongside these developments, a substantial programme of economic and social change has had a beneficial effect on the community's prospects. It is this integrated approach which has been crucial to the prospects for long term sustainable regeneration.

The Government has pledged to put in place a long term approach to economic development and regeneration policy, focusing its efforts on deprived areas. The first fruits of that policy are:

- the creation of Regional Development Agencies to promote the long term economic development of each of the English regions through the application of integrated funding solutions;
- strengthening the strategic role of local government in regeneration activities and working in partnership with the private and voluntary sector;
- continuing the Single Regeneration Budget but targeting it much more strictly on turning round areas of deprivation through an integrated package of regeneration measures;
- providing a new governmental structure for London, including a Mayor and a strategic authority to tackle city-wide regeneration issues such as transport, infrastructure and economic development;
- the introduction of the New Commitment to Regeneration initiative in partnership with the Local Government Association to enable a more co-ordinated strategic approach in applying available public resources to regeneration priorities;
- a growing commitment to involve neighbourhoods much more closely in the management and improvement of their areas, as evidenced by the New Deal for Communities programme for deprived areas;
- the introduction of education, employment and health action zones, followed by a cross-Government programme to co-ordinate the different Area Based Initiatives being run by different national departments.

Figure 5.1: How to make a patchwork quilt: summary of relevant government urban regeneration initiatives, 1981–1998

Initiative or Organisation	Operational period	Description
English Estates	1936–1993	With its roots in pre-war northern industrial development, English Estates constructed industrial and commercial premises in places where the private sector developers would not venture, often for the very good reason that nobody wanted to take their business there. Eventually subsumed by English Partnerships.
Derelict Land Grant	1949–1995	A long standing funding scheme that actually has its roots in post-war legislation. Provided 100% grant funding for local authority engineers to reclaim derelict land for new uses, mostly public open space.
Commission for New Towns (CNT)	1961–	The residual body for the individual New Town Corporations, concentrating on disposing its own sites and later, the UDCs. Eventually merged with English Partnerships.
Urban Programme	1969–1992	The first major government programme to be targeted on inner cities, its aim was to rebuild confidence and encourage investment, latterly in 57 Priority Areas.
Urban Development Corporations (UDCs)	1981–1998	Twelve English quangos set up to regenerate designated areas of our major towns and cities.
Enterprise Zones (EZs)	1981–1996	Fast-track planning and financial incentives for developers and occupiers willing to take the risk on unpopular commercial locations.
Urban Development Grant	1982–1988	Provided financial support for a wide range of urban development projects involving the private sector which would otherwise not have taken place.
Estate Action	1985–1994	Aimed to help local authorities transform unpopular housing estates into places where people wanted to live.

Initiative or Organisation	Operational period	Description
City Grant	1988–1994	Offered direct gap funding to the private sector for development schemes in priority urban areas which otherwise would not have been commercially viable.
Housing Action Trusts	1992–	Comprehensive quango-led transfer and redevelopment of social housing stock for a number of large social housing estates.
City Challenge	1992–1998	The first real attempt at a competitive bidding programme for regeneration funding. Resulted in 31 five year programmes, managed by partnerships who all received the same amount of money.
English Partnerships	1993–	National quango which subsumed City Grant, Derelict Land Grant and English Estates; grew quickly to a budget of over £400m but then lost its regional offices and their budgets to the RDAs. Now regrouping as a national body following a merger with the Commission for New Towns, but with an uncertain set of functions.
Single Regeneration Budget (SRB) Challenge Fund	1994–	A rolling programme of bidding rounds for local partnerships to secure resources for up to seven years for a mix of economic, social and physical regeneration schemes. Now in Round 5, it has become targeted on the most deprived local authority areas.
Estates Renewal Challenge Fund	1996–	Local authorities compete for Government resources to regenerate deprived estates, based on the transfer of the stock to a housing association or housing company, to allow a mix of public and private sector funding for renewal.

In putting forward recommendations on the delivery of urban regeneration, we wish to work with the grain of government policy. What we are seeking to do in this Chapter is test current policy apparatus against the key conclusions of the earlier evaluation reports and suggest where further changes are needed.

DEVELOPING A COHERENT URBAN REGENERATION POLICY

Integrating national and regional policy objectives

The single biggest priority for the Government in developing and implementing its regeneration policy over the next few years is to break down central government departmentalism. The Joseph Rowntree Foundation report on challenge funding and area regeneration found that government departmentalism is an important cause of fragmentation in regeneration policy at local level, '...making it particularly difficult to tackle complex interrelated issues on the ground'. The report further stated that while programmes like the Single Regeneration Budget have been useful in providing integrated responses to complex local needs, 'not all government departments and agencies have yet taken on board the issues and the lessons learned.'[5]

The Task Force's own findings support these conclusions. Too often, government departments are creating new initiatives without due consideration of how these initiatives will integrate with existing programmes and structures. While the principal regeneration programmes have now been brought together under the administration of Regional Development Agencies, a substantial number of other programmes run independently, often causing significant inefficiencies and confusion at the local level. The proliferation of Action Zones – employment, health and education – is a case in point. Local authorities and their partners bend their regeneration strategies to accommodate the new sources of funding, often distorting locally set priorities. As a general principle, we should be aiming for much more flexible funding programmes which can be adapted to meet the needs of an area. To achieve this, there is a need to:

- ensure that government initiatives and programmes are sufficiently flexible to enable local partnerships to interpret them in respect of their own administrative and service boundaries;
- integrate and rationalise existing area based initiatives wherever possible, including where these are managed by different government departments;
- deliver programmes through the regional structures; this means that certain government departments will need to strengthen their regional presence in the Government Regional Offices and the Regional Development Agencies;
- make greater use of block budgets for local government and their partners, extending the principle of a single mainstream capital funding pot to other special programmes (see Chapter 13).

Working alongside the Regional Chambers and the Government Regional Offices, the Regional Development Agencies have an important role to play in translating national policy objectives of individual government departments into a coherent and integrated economic development strategy for their region. This will, in turn, help determine their own funding priorities, and those of the Government Regional Offices and Housing Corporation. If the RDAs are to take a lead in determining the strategic regeneration of our urban areas at a regional level, then, through statutory guidance and resource allocation decisions, it must be made incumbent upon the RDAs to contribute fully towards the desired urban renaissance.

It is imperative that the Regional Development Agencies maintain and, if possible, increase the amount of public

5 'Challenge funding, contracts and area regeneration: A decade of innovation in policy management and co-ordination.'; Stephen Hall and John Mawson (1999)

investment being made into local urban regeneration strategies, including housing-led regeneration schemes. Over the last decade, a significant proportion of the Government's regeneration budget has been invested in the provision of housing, usually in funding the costs of cleaning up and servicing land, so that a scheme can be made economically viable. Such investment has been a feature of City Grant, the Urban Development Corporations, City Challenge, the Single Regeneration Budget and English Partnerships' Investment Fund. The RDAs' continued involvement in housing-led regeneration projects, particularly in resourcing site preparation, is vital if we are serious in our commitment to prioritise urban brownfield sites in locating new housing. The Regional Development Agencies should be given sufficient resources and set clear criteria for facilitating new housing on brownfield sites, to ensure that adequate funding is provided for land reclamation, infrastructure and servicing.

Enhancing the strategic role of local government

The strategic regeneration role of local government can now be derived directly from two changes:

- a new statutory duty to promote the economic and social welfare of their areas of administration;
- the Government's formal recognition of that role through its ratification of the European Concordat of Local Self-Government.

We welcome both these actions and hope that in time, this position will be strengthened further through the provision of a power of general competence, reflecting local authorities' democratic authority to find the best means of meeting the needs of their population.

The success of an urban renaissance is reliant upon the revitalisation of municipal authorities to provide strong, strategic leadership on behalf of their local populations. Last year's Local Government White Paper[6] endorsed the New Commitment to Regeneration programme. Pathfinder local partnerships, led by their local authorities, are drawing up comprehensive regeneration strategies for their areas. They are considering their spending needs over time to deliver those strategies, and looking to target all public expenditure flowing into the area towards achieving the agreed strategic objectives. The New Commitment programme can provide a mechanism for devolving more decision-making power down to the local level.

In strengthening the New Commitment programme, the Government also needs to be considering how this initiative, which is based around individual local authorities, fits with the need for city-wide strategic planning. This is a particular issue in respect of the six metropolitan conurbations. One option would be to encourage the local authorities in these areas to work with city partners to develop a formal city-wide vision within which the individual New Commitment strategies would be defined and operate.

Recommendation:

- **Strengthen the New Commitment to Regeneration programme by combining government departments' spending powers to deliver longer term funding commitments for local authorities and their partners. Central government should be a signatory to local strategies where they accord with national and regional policy objectives. (30)**

6 'In Touch with the People'; DETR (1998)

CONCENTRATING OUR REGENERATION EFFORTS

The case for a targeted approach

There is a balance to be achieved between universal provision of public resources to reflect the needs of the general population and the intensive targeting of such resources on particular urban areas in an attempt to achieve lasting change. Since coming to power the current Government has favoured the introduction of spatially targeted policy initiatives. The zones or special areas which have been created, have spanned most local policy areas. The Government's new imperative is to consider how these zones should interact and how the targeted initiatives can best be integrated.

One of the most recent studies which considered the requirements and impact of targeted area regeneration was the interim evaluation of the City Challenge programme, carried out by the European Institute for Urban Affairs in 1996.[7] From the outcomes of this report and some of the other programme evaluations carried out over the last few years, we have identified three main characteristics of successful area regeneration:

The need for a strategic approach

Without a strong strategic base, supported by higher tiers of government, and backed by a firm commitment of resources, it is impossible to target particular programmes or initiatives with confidence. The process becomes essentially reactive. An initiative is announced and local partnerships have a limited amount of time to pick an area that fits the programme and throw their hat into the ring. If the partnership is successful, the resources are gratefully received, but the task then begins of rationalising and reconciling the new initiative alongside everything else that exists.

SCHILDERSWIJK, THE HAGUE: MANAGING A NEIGHBOURHOOD IN TRANSITION

Schilderswijk is the poorest district of The Hague. Comprising 7% of the entire population of the city, the district has an unemployment rate of 41% of the labour force, 80% of residents of foreign descent, with an average annual income of 11,900 Dutch guilders, compared to an average of 19,550 guilders for the whole of the city. Most of the 3,300 hard drug users in the Hague live in this district, 78% of whom use opiates.

This social data paints a picture of decay and dereliction. Nothing could be further from the truth. In a programme stretching back to the late 1970s, the area has been comprehensively regenerated.

One of the current priorities is the quality of the public realm. Twenty-eight sites are getting a facelift – varying from refurbishing streets and squares, closing off semi-enclosed gardens, to putting windows in blank walls to provide natural surveillance. Each project is carried out in partnership with the local community and backed up by integrated enforcement teams.

The quality of the architecture is high throughout Schilderswijk. The 1.1 km high street has been completely re-developed over a period of seven years, bringing a coherence to the urban texture by applying a single set of design principles brought together in an Architectural Plan. Not all housing in the district has been replaced. A number of traditional mews streets have been retained as well a number of rows of refurbished three storey terrace houses.

After 20 years of urban regeneration Schilderswijk still has intense social problems, but the people live in an attractive environment, full of architectural variety, with excellent shops and facilities. The efforts of the Hague demonstrate that physical renewal is an essential part of the urban solution but it will never be all of the solution.

7 'City Challenge Interim National Evaluation'; European Institute for Urban Affairs; DETR (1998)

Schilderswijk, The Hague: retention of original mews complements new build projects

That is why the New Commitment to Regeneration programme is so important. Local authorities and their partners need the freedom to plan, over a long time period, how they are going to tackle priorities within their area, make linkages between different regeneration opportunities, give priority to the quality of urban design, manage decline in areas which are not going to be able to receive substantial resources in the short term and, generally, govern.

Integrating economic, social and physical measures

Previous area-based initiatives such as the Urban Development Corporations and the Enterprise Zones were predicated on a belief that the benefits of physical regeneration would flow to local people. Only with strong economic and social programmes as part of the package, will this happen. Where resources can be properly integrated, as in the case of City Challenge and the SRB Challenge Fund, then area regeneration projects are often able to cross normal service boundaries, encouraging service providers to consider how their services work in tandem, and consider what added value can be gained from a partnership approach to management and delivery.

Concentrating limited resources

Some of our urban areas have been in economic and social decline for 20–25 years. The only way to turn this around is sustained investment in physical, economic and social renewal. And yet, the amount of money available for tackling urban problems will always be limited. Area-based strategies provide the focus for combining resources from different Government, European and Lottery sources. Similarly, there is only a limited number of skilled regeneration practitioners.

Focusing our efforts on particular localities gives us the best chance of success, not least because the availability of long term public funding, supported by a flexible approach to how it is applied, gives the project partners the best opportunity to attract the private sector to work with them.

The City Challenge evaluation report summarised these and other advantages by stating that area regeneration can:

- enable a more strategic, integrated approach to regeneration;
- allow developments which require substantial pump-priming to take place;
- speed up developments which would otherwise be slower and more piecemeal;
- trigger further investment and related activity;
- add value by linking separate programmes, agencies and types of expertise.

We also, however, need to be aware of the following potential pitfalls:

- the danger of creating cliff-edges between areas benefiting from regeneration and neighbouring areas not in receipt of special funding, but in receipt of displaced social and economic problems;
- avoiding artificial regeneration time-scales; (City Challenge was five years), which may bear no relation to the time required to turn an area's fortunes around;
- avoiding a fragmented approach to the regeneration process, which fails to tie development activity to the economic and social needs of the local population.

We need a mixed funding model, which combines maximum flexibility for local authorities over the application of mainstream resources to the whole of the local population, with special regeneration programme resources which can be applied intensively to tackle the most urgent regeneration priorities. These choices need to be made in accordance with a long term local regeneration strategy.

The case for designating Urban Priority Areas

Some of the Task Force's proposals would benefit from targeting regeneration on particular urban areas. These measures include:

- preparation of spatial masterplans based on a clear development brief (Chapter 2);
- area implementation planning and higher performance requirements on local planning authorities (Chapter 8);
- extra compulsory purchase powers (Chapter 9);
- a package of fiscal incentives for owners, developers, investors and occupiers (Chapter 12);
- access to targeted public-private investment funds (Chapter 13);
- priority status for certain public funding programmes, including potential for block funding allocations (Chapter 13);
- the ability of local authorities to retain and recycle a proportion of local taxation for management and maintenance purposes (Chapter 13).

The impact of a number of these measures in combination will be greater than the sum of their parts. In addition, by applying funding and fiscal measures to carefully targeted areas, we can control the cost and optimise the impact of the measures in a way which is simply not possible if they are made more widely available. The planning and CPO measures reflect the urgency of the need for regeneration, which is applicable to an area of market failure and widespread vacancy and dereliction, but which could be regarded as too heavy-handed in respect of other areas.

The Task Force wishes to see the creation of designated Urban Priority Areas, to provide a focus for the application of packages of special measures to help achieve physical regeneration, and to provide a basis for integrating physical regeneration with economic and social objectives. The designated areas would constitute a mix of areas with large tracts of derelict, vacant and under-used land and buildings, and relatively built-up areas with a proliferation of infill sites and empty buildings. They could include run-down industrial and commercial districts, tertiary retail areas, neighbourhoods with poor housing stock, secondary town centres and so on.

In the past, the process of designation has been largely a top-down exercise. Local authorities made the case for how their areas met the funding criteria in competition with other areas, but the decisions were taken by national government which then handed out a standard package of measures. We conceive of designation in a different way. The case for designation of one or more areas within a local district would be constructed entirely by the local authority and its local partners. They would not only need to make the basic case to government for designation but also a full social and economic case for each of the measures which they would seek to apply within the designated area. The Secretary of State would take decisions on a case-by-case basis on the package of measures under consideration.

The importance of this approach is two-fold. First, it allows for a much more fine-grained approach to determining the most effective set of measures for any given area, hopefully avoiding wasted expenditure and duplicate provision. But second, and perhaps more importantly, it makes the Urban Priority Areas a potential means of rationalising other area-based initiatives. If we are to promote a targeted approach to area regeneration, then the introduction of Urban Priority Areas should, at the very least, be used to hoover up the various existing area designations for physical regeneration purposes. In the longer term, it could also, however, provide a framework for some of the social programme area designations as well.

Our recommendation is:

- **Create designated Urban Priority Areas, enabling local authorities and their partners in regeneration, including local people, to apply for special packages of powers and incentives to assist neighbourhood renewal. (31)**

How would the designations work?

We envisage a long term rolling programme of designations, with regional or national ceilings on different measures, e.g. taxation costs, being reached over a number of years. We are not suggesting that a new public expenditure line should be created for the Urban Priority Areas. The process of designation should be a means for local authorities and their partners to identify priorities for existing regeneration funding, particularly the funding previously received from English Partnerships. The UPAs would therefore be reliant on attracting existing funding

COMMUNITY-BASED REGENERATION IN HOLLY STREET, HACKNEY

The 1970s high rise towers and decks of Holly Street habitually occupied the lower end of Hackney's fortunes. 45% of young men aged 16 to 24 were unemployed. Crime and vandalism were rife. Community morale was also low. Before redevelopment started, and residents were decamped, only 2% of residents thought that they would ever want to return there.

In 1992 the Comprehensive Estates Initiative (CEI) was set in motion. Its priorities were: to create a competitive economy by attracting, keeping and creating jobs, to get people into jobs, to improve the physical environment, and to promote sustainable development by building a stable, mixed community.

There was substantial physical regeneration, with over 1000 units replaced by new housing. But the most significant shift was in economic and social regeneration. Employment and training projects were developed by a range of organisations in conjunction with residents. Community facilities were also constructed and fostered. Contrary to their original expectations, 50% of previous residents voted with their feet by choosing to come back to the area to take up the new housing.

Making the CEI into an integrated regeneration programme has relied on a series of partnerships – between the council, local residents and the private sector, and with the large number of private and voluntary sector organisations who have worked to revitalise the area. What really stands out is the deep involvement of the community in the programme: in shaping its aims, guiding its implementation and in continuing its work.

sources, albeit, as we set out in Chapter 13, that we hope there would be significantly greater amounts of funding available. In addition, it is likely that UPA projects would be the main beneficiaries of the proposed land assembly fund(s) described in Chapter 9 and the institutional investment funds described in Chapter 12.

We do not envisage that all the available benefits would flow to all parts of an Urban Priority Area. Once there is a spatial masterplan for the area it may make sense to restrict some of the benefits – perhaps land assembly powers and some fiscal measures – to particular development sites.

There is, as we have stated, also a danger of creating divisions between a regeneration area and the surrounding districts. One means of avoiding this would be to create an outer ring to the designated area which would receive only some of the benefits, particularly resources for minor improvement schemes and enhanced revenue funding.

In determining how long any designation would last, the accent would be on flexibility. The initial designation should be long enough to give the area a good opportunity to reach self-sustaining market values. One is therefore probably looking for a period of 7 to 15 years. However, this would need to be subject to regular review within an agreed evaluation framework. Equally, there would need to be flexibility to extend the designation period.

Again, based upon a flexible approach, it is also not necessarily the case that the basket of benefits that would accrue to the area in year one would also last until the end of the designation. For example, it may be necessary for the fiscal benefits to be capped by government, so that once a certain amount of revenue has been foregone, the incentives are removed.

The special regeneration needs of council housing areas

People with least choice and lowest incomes inevitably occupy the areas that people with choice can escape from – areas of run-down property, poor conditions, negative reputations, weak services, low values. A majority of the poorest neighbourhoods are predominantly council owned. Many such neighbourhoods in declining cities have a majority of households out of work; more people leave than move in. There is chronic low demand, high turnover and some abandonment of housing within the large urban conurbations where population is declining.

Similar neighbourhoods, in more buoyant cities, particularly London, may be equally unpopular with better off people, but crowded with low income migrants from other parts of Britain and abroad, trying to find a foothold in the growing economy and the housing market. There too, large numbers are outside the formal economy and many leave as soon as they can afford to. But there is an inflow to match or outstrip the exodus.

The dynamics of the two types of urban neighbourhood are different and need different approaches. But the regeneration task in both types of area is immense. Since 1991, all government guidelines have spelt out the need for partnership between local authorities, private and voluntary bodies. The 2,000 or more unpopular council estates highlighted by the Social Exclusion Unit's report 'Bringing Britain Together', are almost all in need of serious reinvestment, covering social as well as physical aspects. So far the resources are only available for a few spectacular examples. New Deal for Communities is the latest such programme.

There is a menu of choices open to local authorities for these most difficult estates:

- retain council ownership, (as the Broadwater Farm model illustrates in Chapter 4);

- transfer an estate or groups of estates to an arm's length non-profit housing company with substantial private finance, as Hackney, Tower Hamlets, Manchester and Liverpool, among others, are doing;

- break up the social structure and tenure of the estate through major demolition and intense restructuring with housing association and private developer involvement, as the Holly Street case describes;

- demolish whole estates in low demand areas and leave land vacant until alternative development becomes viable. Many northern cities have large numbers of such sites;

- adopt the Scottish model of community based housing associations to create a new local landlord within the regenerated neighbourhood, involving community representation alongside other partners. This is increasingly attractive in rebuilt estates. Best practice examples include Waltham Forest Housing Action Trust, London, and the Eldonians in Liverpool.

But the vast majority of estates will not receive anything like the scale of funding these models require for the foreseeable future. Therefore we have to explore more flexible, more modest routes to reinvestment, coupled with the kind of joined up approach to neighbourhood problems that the Social Exclusion Unit advocates.

There are some promising changes underway. The proposed new financial regime for local authority housing proposes a retention of money for major repair; it encourages planned reinvestment; it rewards clear strong management; and it favours autonomous housing landlord structures, separate from strategic local authority roles. It leaves to local authorities the choice of retaining or transferring ownership. These changes could have far reaching effects on council housing renewal, leading to incremental localised regeneration, coupled with a growing separation of ownership and management issues from political intervention and leadership.

THE NEW DEAL FOR COMMUNITIES PROGRAMME

The New Deal for Communities initiative is the latest attempt to address the needs of the most deprived neighbourhoods. It combines:

- targeting the most precarious estates;

- renewing the physical fabric and environment;

- developing bottom-up approaches to social and community problems;

- joining together every local partner;

- concentrating resources;

- experimenting with neighbourhood management;

- giving residents a major stake in decisions;

- delivering multi-faceted regeneration over 10 or more years.

The 17 pathfinder authorities developing New Deal for Communities projects are among the most deprived areas of England. All bar three are in major cities. The programme is only just beginning and it is too early to say how far it will break new ground. It is a resource intensive approach and may only address the needs of between 30–50 of the 2,000 plus identified areas. Nevertheless, it is obviously an important part of the Government's armoury in tackling social and economic deprivation.

Prioritising aftercare

As we established in the previous Chapter, the management of urban space and local services within regeneration areas will, over time, dictate the perception and use of the neighbourhood by prospective residents, businesses and other organisations. The end of a regeneration project brings us full circle, back into an ongoing regime of preventative management and maintenance, and incremental improvement. Planning for the active management of the assets created by a regeneration project needs to be addressed as part of the design and inception of the projects.

The handover strategy should include plans for:

- identifying the end date of the project based upon clear indicators of whether the original objectives have been achieved;
- how the ongoing management and maintenance of the regeneration area is to be resourced;
- establishing a neighbourhood management body to take on the day to day responsibility for the area from the regeneration body (if it does not exist already);
- the phased withdrawal of specialist regeneration staff and resources from the area, covering a period of at least 18 months after substantial completion of capital works;
- arrangements for the transfer of the residual assets, including to community-based organisations.

It is essential that the plans are accompanied by adequate funding, a subject we return to in more detail in Chapter 13 when we discuss public investment. Our recommendations are:

- **Require regeneration programmes to include a 'handover' strategy, agreed by the partners, as a condition of funding. The strategy should describe plans for continuity of staff and resources when the funding period is over. (32)**
- **Soften provisions requiring the 'clawback' by government of property sales and other receipts from regeneration programmes, so that a proportion can be re-invested in the long term management of the area. (33)**
- **Make it easier for regeneration bodies to endow cash and assets to local trusts and community organisations. (34)**

Wigan Investment Centre (Wigan MBC)

WIGAN CITY CHALLENGE: SUSTAINING THE CHALLENGE

Even before Wigan City Challenge received approval from government, the partners were planning how they could ensure that any new community facilities created by the initiative could still be funded after the five year programme ended. Once the programme got the go ahead, the City Challenge partners set up a unique dual company structure so that a specially created company, Douglas Valley Properties Company Ltd, owned and managed the programme's four principal assets, and then covenanted the surpluses to Douglas Valley Community Ltd, a charity, which owns four community centres and sublets these to local groups representing the four communities within the City Challenge area. The charity also used its covenanted funds to support local community and voluntary sector groups working throughout the City Challenge area.

The revenue generating assets which the Property Company owns are the Investment Centre, which includes a 370 seat conference centre and associated training rooms, a Business Centre, which forms part of a restored listed mill building, an Enterprise Centre for new community businesses created from a redundant school, and an industrial estate of eight small factories.

Extensive partnership has been the key to success. Community centres created by earlier initiatives had closed down because of vandalism and a lack of community activity. The City Challenge therefore handed over the development of the new centres to the communities themselves. The devolved management structures have been a considerable success and the Community Resource Centres, as they are known, have now formed their own network to share information and disseminate good practice.

WORKING IN PARTNERSHIP

There is a need for dedicated arms-length bodies to deliver area regeneration projects. Figure 5.2 sets out three main examples of current arms-length structures used in the context of existing funding programmes, and suggests the advantages and limitations of each option.

Urban Regeneration Companies

By bringing together the best features of past and present regeneration vehicles we can start to construct some model structures which we have called Urban Regeneration Companies (URCs) and Housing Regeneration Companies (HRCs). In doing so, we recognise that specific circumstances will require specific organisational structures, but nevertheless, the following roles, responsibilities and structures are likely to be relevant in many cases.

Most of the time, these company structures will be most relevant to intensive area regeneration projects. Some towns and cities may, however, consider that a company is better constructed with a borough-wide remit to tackle portfolios of development sites. This may be particularly appropriate where the area has only limited areas of significant derelict and vacant development land. Thus, for example, Nottingham has opted for a city-wide development company.

Fundamentally, an Urban Regeneration Company should be capable of acting swiftly, as a single purpose delivery body to lead and co-ordinate the regeneration of neighbourhoods in accordance with the objectives of a wider local strategy which has been developed by the local authority and its partners. The URC stakeholders are likely to comprise the local authority, perhaps a housing association, one or more development companies, local community representatives, and possibly major land owners and an RDA representative.

Figure 5.2: Delivering regeneration: different partnership structures

Type of partnership	Description	Advantages	Limitations
Informal project partnership with no legal status	This is an example of different organisations committed to working together, possibly backed up by a memorandum of understanding or service level agreements. There is, however, no separate legal entity.	Low establishment costs Not liable for VAT charges	Cannot employ staff directly Perception of lack of independent status Lack of clarity for outsiders about who they are dealing with
Company limited by guarantee without Accountable Body status	The regeneration body is a separate legal entity but is not ultimately responsible to government for the use of public funds. This responsibility would normally be adopted by one of the members of the company, usually the local authority.	Perceived to be independent Directors have limited legal liabilities Depending on degree of control of company, body may have more freedoms than local authority	Staff contracts have to be with the Accountable Body VAT liabilities and other costs incurred
Company limited by guarantee with Accountable Body functions	The regeneration body is a separate legal entity and is fully accountable to government for the use of public funds.	Independent Can employ staff directly Depending on degree of control of company, body may have more freedoms than local authority Long term presence, can take on other regeneration roles Directors have limited legal liabilities	Liable for VAT, employee costs, redundancy etc. Increased administrative costs, including costs of auditors

Source: Single Regeneration Budget guidance.

Each sector would contribute directors to the company, and in some cases, would also contribute staff expertise, resources and other assets. It may also be necessary for the local authority to pass some decision-making across to the company in accordance with an agreed strategy. This may include the powers to work up planning or development briefs, and negotiate with land owners, RDAs or Government Regional Offices. We do not, however, recommend that statutory planning powers should be devolved to such companies.

The main advantages of a legally registered company can be that:

- it establishes a legally accountable point of contact and corporate responsibility for local regeneration initiatives;
- it carries certain attractions from a private sector perspective, in terms of dealing with a fellow company with a dedicated remit;
- it entails clear responsibilities and obligations on partners through the company and board structure.

Such companies may hold land, buildings and other assets, although this is by no means necessary in every case. Indeed, some recent examples of joint venture regeneration companies have been effective precisely because they haven't been encumbered by such responsibilities. Instead they have been able to operate efficiently and effectively as single contact, leadership and co-ordinating bodies. In many cases, however, there may be compelling reasons for a company structure to undertake a more direct role in bringing forward regeneration activity, especially where the private sector is unwilling to take such steps unaided.

In England, local authorities face severe constraints on their involvement in companies. In particular, any local council stake of more than 20% in a company is deemed to be influential, and any expenditure incurred by the company necessarily counts against that local authority's credit approvals. We believe there is a compelling case to review this constraint, so as to encourage more effective partnership approaches to regeneration investment. At the least, there is a strong case for limiting any public expenditure penalties incurred on the

Communities informing the area regeneration process at Bold Street/Duke Street in Liverpool (English Partnerships)

part of the local authorities to only that proportion which applies to the public sector investment within the partnership company, rather than to the entirety as applies now.

We also wish to see a review of the current regulations governing the disposal of public assets at less than open market value, since there is a case for dedicated regeneration agencies having the benefit of such disposals where it makes possible the creation of an otherwise non-viable project, or where it can help create an asset base for such agencies to borrow, invest and so create longer term value. We welcome the recent relaxations in the 'set aside' rules for capital assets when applied for regeneration purposes, and we believe that the logic of this step should suggest a further relaxation along the lines outlined here.

There may also need to be greater incentives for private developers to contribute to the work of regeneration partnerships as the long term co-promoters of schemes.

Local regeneration companies should be locally visible, with a base in the area concerned, and with good accessibility for the local community to gain information. This kind of 'arms length', locally-based agency can prove effective in gaining the confidence of both communities and business.

Specific roles of Urban Regeneration Companies may involve:

- commissioning a spatial masterplan and development framework for the area and gaining its agreement between each of the company stakeholders;

Grainger Town Partnership, Newcastle: restoring former glories (English Partnerships)

- building the project partnership, undertaking feasibility work and attracting public and private funding, including block funding wherever possible;

- undertaking community consultation and engagement where appropriate;

- marketing and promoting the regeneration opportunities in the area concerned;

- assembling a dedicated team of professionals, working as a corporate executive, this may comprise seconded as well as specifically appointed staff;

- working closely with the local planning authority on the preparation of planning briefs, the management of development or design competitions, and the securing of site assembly, CPO notices etc.

In addition, it may be appropriate for the following functions to be incorporated into the role:

- acquiring public land and other assets, at discounted values in certain instances, in order to drive forward strategic area based renewal;

- raising private finance secured on this asset base, as well as through discrete project partnerships;

- undertaking direct site preparation, commissioning and providing certain key infrastructure, servicing and improvement works where this cannot or should not be undertaken by a private sector developer;

- undertaking direct development of certain commercial or quasi-commercial facilities where there is a proven need but little or no market appetite; e.g. managed workspace.

Our recommendation is:

- **Enable 'arms-length' Urban Regeneration Companies to co-ordinate or deliver area regeneration projects, by:**

– **ensuring that local authorities, Registered Social Landlords and the Regional Development Agencies have sufficient powers to participate fully as partners;**

– **making it as simple as possible for public bodies to transfer assets to the companies at less than market value, providing a demonstrable public benefit is served;**

– **enabling the companies to use their assets to raise additional private finance;**

– **ensuring that only the local authority's share of the investment counts against the companies' credit limits;**

– **encouraging private companies to become involved by providing some form of tax break for contributions made to running costs;**

– **enabling member organisations to extend any special VAT status they enjoy to the companies. (35)**

URBAN DEVELOPMENT SKILLS: WHERE DO THE GAPS LIE?

Core skills and employment needs

The scale and complexity of the urban renaissance agenda requires that we recognise where current gaps exist, both in terms of skills, and in relation to professional responsibilities. In some cases we need to get better at doing the current range of jobs more effectively. In other circumstances we actually need to establish new positions which bridge the areas of expertise previously segmented within existing employment structures.

A wide range of people will be needed to implement the urban vision – planners, designers, architects, landscape architects, engineers, environmental scientists, surveyors, developers, project managers, housing and neighbourhood managers. Operating within local government, regeneration agencies, private organisations, as well as a range of other institutions, they will require skills to take on the following tasks:

- production of design briefs prior to development of strategic design options;
- co-ordination of procurement methods and competitions to deliver high quality design alternatives;
- proactive use of the planning system to secure change;
- community involvement, in planning and implementation stages;
- integration of physical development programmes with urban management and maintenance, and other economic and social programmes;
- the assembly of land to create meaningful development opportunities;
- land remediation and reclamation, and ongoing environmental management;
- project appraisal, management and finance, including strategic planning, procurement, phasing, team working, and dealing with funding bodies and financial institutions;
- provision and financing of services and infrastructure, managing licensing and consents issues;
- creating and managing effective arm's length delivery bodies;

In some of these areas we are already strong. We are amongst the world leaders, for example, in developing land remediation technologies. But these in-depth skills are generally held by only narrow pockets of specialists. Public sector client organisations are often ill-equipped to procure and steer the skills they require to produce the best urban solutions.

Urban design, which combines architecture, planning and landscape design, is a core skill area which is almost totally ignored. Despite 15 different universities offering a range of over 27 courses which include components of urban design it is clear that more needs to be done to reach key audiences outside the design sector. There is the need for a clearer understanding of the role of design within development. Accessing a wider audience, including funding institution managers, elected members, housing association officers, managers of utilities, and urban regeneration partnership managers – as well as the more traditional list of architects, planners (including transport planners), highway engineers, landscape architects and conservation officers – is critical in this respect. This will mean both improving the range and quality of 'design' skills and the overall appreciation of a need for design quality.

The skills gap cannot be addressed in isolation from the employment structure within related industries. The scale of the change which is required to turn around our towns and cities will mean promoting new professional positions in central and local government, and the Regional Development Agencies, as well as within local regeneration partnerships, private practices and educational establishments. A growing requirement for multi-disciplinary teams will, for example, demand a new generation of project managers and independent co-ordinators who can bring together the professional abilities of their team members in what will be a continuous and complex process.

Strengthening the enabling role of government

The public sector's role in urban development has changed significantly over the last twenty years, both at the national and the local level. Many of the changes that have occurred over that period have provided public benefits. For example, much greater use is now made of outside experts and advice, in competitive processes and on limited-life partnerships. This has allowed access to parties with specialist knowledge and up-to-date experience that the public sector could not hope to replicate internally across the board.

This process of streamlining government's responsibilities in the urban development process was, however, distorted by the political priority, particularly during the 1980s, to reduce the influence and funding of local government, and to strip out many of the professionals across all government tiers. For example, over the last 15 years the number of qualified planners in the Department of the Environment, Transport and the Regions has fallen by 50% and architects by 95%.[1] Many local authorities have lost strategic planners, architects, landscape architects, urban designers and economic development staff, often reducing their planning departments down to little more than development control units who produce a development plan every now and then. It is indicative that in England, less than 10% of all our architects are employed by local authorities,[2] while the figure is 37% in Germany.[3]

The extent of the down-sizing, in scale and functional importance, of these professions within the public sector has caused serious problems. Funds for outside advice can be limited. And even an organisation which relies on consultancy for its expertise needs to retain enough knowledge to be an effective client. Similarly, whilst public-private partnerships can be seen as a valuable opportunity to make use of private sector skills as well as money, it is important that the public sector representatives retain credibility as effective partners and negotiators.

If the public sector is to act as strategic enabler, and local government is to lead the urban renaissance, then the Government must now take some steps to reverse the trend of running down the numbers of professional staff, by accepting the need to employ experts in certain key posts. It must also ensure that the ranks of generalist urban development decision-makers in national, regional and local government are exposed to an appropriate level of professional skills training and increased periods of sharp-end project management experience.

The changing needs of the development industry

As Sir John Egan's Construction Task Force recognised,[4] much of the development industry is heavily compartmentalised, encouraging career specialism in its recruitment, training and operation. There is a perceived lack of project management skills in the industry which detracts from overall confidence to take on complex mixed schemes that combine residential and commercial development, and related infrastructure provision. This again highlights the need for a wider range of skills to be held by any one person – so that they can, for example, operate as project managers on complex schemes, capable of understanding a range of issues from architecture and design, right across to development finance.

There are already some encouraging signs of change. For example, AMEC Developments, a major commercial developer, have recently formed a joint venture with the Berkeley Group, a major house builder, to take on mixed

1 Source: DETR

2 Source: RIBA

3 'Architecture and town planning education in the Netherlands: A European comparison'; University of York (1995)

4 'Re-thinking construction'; The Construction Task Force (1998)

development projects. Wimpey and Gleeson are two development companies now grappling much more actively with the potential for mixed use conversion projects. But good practice examples are more often found amongst smaller firms, operating more flexibly than the more traditional developers. Companies such as Urban Splash in the North West have led the way, directly employing multi-disciplinary teams of architects, surveyors and builders to manage projects in an integrated way from start to finish.

Building capacity to enable community participation

It is not just professionals who initiate and implement regeneration schemes. Community and voluntary sector representatives also play a key role in transforming their urban neighbourhoods. To maximise the contribution from these sectors means giving lay people the skills and the opportunity to participate at will on a number of different levels. This commitment to engage the community is enshrined in the 'Modernising Local Government White Paper', published in 1998, which highlights the importance of public participation right across the public sector. The drive for more active engagement with local communities will most effectively be realised by combining improvements in access to information, with a range of opportunities to influence the decision-making process. Developing the skills of local people is a crucial pre-requisite to making the most of these opportunities.

As well as a key role in long term urban management, area-based regeneration initiatives like the Single Regeneration Budget and New Deal for the Communities need local people to play a significant role. All too often when bidding for this kind of funding, an intensive participation requirement is thrust, too late, on a community ill-equipped to take it on, severely limiting their opportunity to influence properly the project in the crucial planning stage.

Regeneration as a basis for gaining work skills in Huddersfield

(Peter Addis Environmental Images)

It is important to invest in building capacity in local communities, both prior to and during the regeneration process to address this problem. The lead partner in any bid should acknowledge from the outset the need to map the possible involvement of all active voluntary and community groups within an area, as well as harder to reach groups who are often excluded from the more traditional approach to public participation.

To engage with the full range of stakeholders will require professionals themselves to become far more skilled in a range of participative mechanisms. At the most fundamental level it requires a jargon-free approach to consultation coupled with a flexible programme of engagement which allows different sectors within a community to participate on a range of different issues at different stages within the process. Some residents will take on a particularly active role in the regeneration partnership throughout its life. For these people in particular, specific investment needs to be made in terms of developing their skills to ensure that they have maximum input into the decision-making process.

At present, what is often termed public 'consultation' rarely allows people to participate in design and development in its essential early stages. Consultation can be abused as a means of rubber-stamping decisions and side-stepping a genuine debate and full local participation. The success of genuine participation exercises depends on the quality of independent facilitators who have the negotiating skills and understanding necessary to make projects happen. The educational and professional system must recognise the value of this emerging role and integrate these tasks and skills into new policies and academic initiatives.

EXISTING SKILLS PROVISION

Many of the organisational skills deficits flow from the types of education and training received by professionals, from undergraduate level onwards. Research undertaken by the Task Force demonstrates that there is a general and ongoing separation of career training amongst the various professions that militates against an appreciation of the wider urban development context and the role of the other professions.

We believe that there should be two main emphases of professional training: first, to increase the output of the relevant specialised skills, including retraining for those that have the right professional background but need to apply it to the task of urban regeneration; second, and critically important, to bring these skills to bear on team working in complex everyday situations. These needs should be addressed both by educational establishments as well as the various professional institutions involved in the accreditation of courses.

Academic and professional qualifications

We need to go beyond current perceptions of skills gaps if we are going to really address the problems. A recent survey highlighted some worrying aspects in terms of the perceptions of employers of planning graduates. Only 55% of employers considered that basic knowledge of urban planning was an important attribute for a graduate planner, and only 61% considered that appreciation of design was an important town planning skill.[5] Conversely, many private sector employers pointed to a need for specialists to have a greater knowledge of development finance and processes than is available within current courses.

In many cases, the teaching in basic professional technical skills is excellent. The main problem is a lack of cross-disciplinary learning with strong vocational relevance. We have estimated, based on analysis of a range of relevant undergraduate and post-graduate, professional and vocational courses, that even for students who went out of their way to maximise their knowledge of urban-related disciplines other than their primary area of study, by choosing subsidiary options, this would constitute little more than 10% of the course.[6]

Even at post-graduate level, there is a tendency for most training in this area, with only one or two exceptions, to focus on either specific professional disciplines or to opt only for the 'soft' end of the urban continuum – urban theory and policy courses – rather than the core skills of urban development such as design, planning, assembly, reclamation, servicing and management. Overall, only perhaps 3–4% of the graduates entering relevant urban professions each year will have undertaken the kind of hard-edged multi-disciplinary study on offer at universities like Sheffield Hallam.

While there will be a continuing role for the specialised one-year Masters programmes for particular interests, the main emphasis should be on broader-based courses that bring the skills together with a strong emphasis on problem-solving and multi-professional teamwork, such as the new Masters in City Design and Social Science at the London School of Economics. Such courses would have a strong core foundation in project management and finance, urban design and environmental planning, and be integrated through a pervasive emphasis on urban management. In some institutions they might be labelled an MBA, but in most we would envisage an extended (twelve-month) modular MSc in Urban Regeneration Management.

5 'Junior Employment in Town Planning – Review of Trends 1981-1993'; University of Central England (1994)

6 Source: PricewaterhouseCoopers (1999)

MULTI-DISCIPLINARY LEARNING AT SHEFFIELD HALLAM UNIVERSITY

Sheffield Hallam's MSc in Urban Regeneration is an example of one of the handful of vocational urban development courses to bring together business-like teaching from several relevant disciplines to equip practitioners with a genuine package of skills to take forward successful urban development projects. The curriculum is as follows:

Core
Urban policy
Housing policy
National and global economic context
Urban labour market strategies
Achieving local economic development
Community development and involvement
Securing funding
Development appraisal – financial viability/cost and value
Programme management
Site redevelopment and project management
Place marketing strategies
International comparisons

Optional
Assessing area-based regeneration
European approaches to urban regeneration
Practical mechanisms for integrating environmental objectives
Transport strategies and investment
Conservation of historic areas and buildings
Property law

[Source: Abridged from Sheffield Hallam University Prospectus 1998]

Continuing professional development

It is a characteristic of a professional in any field that they pursue Continuing Professional Development throughout their career. However, in some of the urban professions there is no requirement to do so, and where there is a requirement, the minimum level is set relatively low, and there is uneven monitoring of compliance. Further, much of the training currently offered is of a technical nature, tending to largely exclude the opportunity to gain wider urban development skills.

Our review of the Continuing Professional Development currently on offer reveals that over 80% of it is single discipline. If this is reflected in its take up, as suggested by the professional institutions themselves, then the average professional might spend only an average of two hours per year training outside of their primary discipline.

Accreditation by professional institutions of graduate courses and Continuing Professional Development has generally served to reinforce this introspective view, allowing education providers very little freedom to address a wider agenda. Furthermore, the very structure of single profession institutions could be seen as unhelpful in promoting more multi-disciplinary training. There have been some efforts to bring professions together to broaden each of their agendas. The creation of the Urban Design Alliance by a number of the main institutions to promote an integrated urban design agenda, is one example, but it remains a rare exception to the general rule.

Continuing Professional Development could be provided in various ways: through a part-time Masters course that could be taken on day or block week release, by evening courses, by distance learning, (though this will not be adequate in itself for the hands-on expertise that will be needed), by summer schools, through a variety of short courses and day-long or weekend seminars and workshops, and through supervised professional placements. These should be formally recognised through the award of appropriate diplomas.

These courses should be staffed by a core of permanent staff, preferably recruited for their professional expertise as much as their academic qualifications, but additionally, there should be a strong emphasis on the recruitment of part-time staff from the relevant professions, and on specialised seminars led by hands-on professionals.

Figure 6.1: Professional institutions: provision of Continuing Professional Development

Institution	**Membership**	**CPD requirement**	**Average amount of CPD purchased**	**Monitoring**
Royal Institute of British Architects	23,000	35 hours p.a.	15 hours p.a.	Sample
Chartered Institute of Housing	14,000	20 hours p.a. (not obligatory)	6 hours p.a.	No
Royal Town Planning Institute	14,000	25 hours p.a.	10 hours p.a.	Sample
Institution of Civil Engineers	80,000 (all categories)	30 hours p.a.	15 hours p.a.	Sample
Royal Institution of Chartered Surveyors	95,000	20 hours p.a.	6 hours p.a.	Sample
Construction Industries	c.63,000	20 hours p.a.	6 hours p.a.	System to be introduced
Average		**Approx: 20 hours**	**Approx: 10 hours**	

Source: PricewaterhouseCoopers (1999)

CREATING A SKILLS IMPROVEMENT STRATEGY

The Government needs to work with academic and professional institutions to put in place a new package of measures for improving urban development skills over the next decade. The strategy must cover existing professionals in all sectors as well as ensuring that there is a sufficient flow of new high calibre professionals, with a growing understanding of multi-disciplinary working, coming into the urban development field, expecting to work creatively in integrated teams to deliver real change.

The role of education and professional institutions

There is no doubt that much of the long term improvement in levels of urban development skills must fall to education and professional institutions. We need to address all levels of the educational system from school through to professional development. In particular, we need:

- DfEE to consider how the importance of urban design and management can be incorporated within the National Curriculum alongside the broader concept of 'citizenship';
- the DETR and DfEE to work with the higher and further education sectors to improve the urban development content of undergraduate courses and to increase the number of specialist post-graduate urban development courses;
- each of the professional institutions to establish targets for increasing the amount of CPD provision for urban development skills and knowledge beyond the core professional discipline;
- the main professional institutions – the Royal Institute of British Architects, the Royal Institution of Chartered Surveyors, the Royal Town Planning Institute, the Landscape Institute, the Institution of Civil Engineers, the Chartered Institute of Housing and the Institute of Economic Development – to establish a joint review and subsequent plan of action for how, over the next ten years, they can contribute towards increasing our urban development skills-base.

Our recommendation:

- **Establish joint working between professional institutions, education providers and employers to develop a plan of action for improving the skills-base in urban development over the next five to seven years, including:**

- **injecting the basic principles of urban design, development and management into relevant school teaching subjects – history, geography, design and technology, art etc. – through the National Curriculum;**
- **increasing urban development content and inter-disciplinary linkage in undergraduate and postgraduate courses;**
- **setting targets for increased provision and take-up of Continuing Professional Development training in urban development. (38)**

Regional Resource Centres for Urban Development

There is therefore much that can be done within the existing institutional context. Our prognosis, however, is that more is needed. We need to take a fresh look at current provision, demand and labour market conditions. We have to put together innovative packages of multi-disciplinary training options and sell them hard. We also need the capacity to draw together and disseminate best practice; stimulating interest, debate and innovation in the urban development field.

We have thought carefully about the relevant institutional model to progress these improvements. Traditionally, courses of this kind have always been taught in professional schools of universities or in specialised higher education institutions.

These have the human and physical infrastructure to do the new job, and they could do it economically. It could be argued, however, that they may give too academic an emphasis, divorced from the real world. The key, therefore, is in the selection of the right institutions that have shown the capacity to deliver courses that are both academically well grounded and professionally relevant.

We consider that the creation of Regional Resource Centres for Urban Development would help the academic and professional institutions fulfil this requirement, stimulating and co-ordinating the provision and take up of cross-disciplinary training and providing mentoring and best practice advice. These Centres would act as a resource to the public, private and voluntary sector, to raise standards across the board and fill gaps in existing provision. They would play a key role in developing a skills framework that included central government initiatives, (such as the work of the new Commission for Architecture and the Built Environment), the work of academic and professional institutions, city initiatives and the contribution of the proposed network of Local Architecture Centres described in Chapter 2.

We commissioned PricewaterhouseCoopers to undertake an independent feasibility study of the idea. As well as analysing current provision and calculating the financial viability, they conducted a series of interviews with people from professional institutions, universities, training providers, local authorities and other public bodies. There emerged a clear acceptance of the need to develop more multi-disciplinary and cross-professional skills and expertise to achieve more successful urban development.

There was widespread acceptance of the concept that Centres dedicated to training and dissemination of expertise and best practice could be an effective method of further improving skills and expertise. Overall, 80% of consultees agreed that there was a need for a network of dedicated centres.

INTEGRATED LEARNING: THE INSTITUTION OF CIVIL ENGINEERS' BUILD-A-BUILDING COMPETITION

The Institution of Civil Engineers, on behalf of the Construction Industry Council, promotes an annual competition for young professionals to stimulate multi-disciplinary thinking and working.

The challenge set is real. Past projects have included designing plans for redeveloping the ex-Ministry of Defence Gunwharf site in Portsmouth and Newcastle's Quayside. The common theme is defining urban space for effective mixed use development through the provision of infrastructure, services and buildings.

Teams include a civil engineer, architect, chartered surveyor and building services engineer, and often a landscape architect, structural engineer and planner as well. Taking the project from conceptual design and masterplanning through to the contract negotiation strategy, (virtual) construction, completion and occupation, participants consider the full range of local economic, social and environmental needs and impacts.

A key aim is that professionals learn early on in their careers a respect for and understanding of the role of wider disciplines in formulating innovative integrated solutions to today's regeneration challenges.

The feasibility study also showed that consultees were very clear about what they wanted such Centres to provide. The Centres should take a holistic approach to urban design and development, covering technical construction and development issues, non-technical partnership development and management issues and wider strategic and practical issues such as facilitating community participation. They also showed enthusiasm for an urban development MBA or similar, to increase the commercial viability of multi-disciplinary learning. The Centres would also need to work with and help strengthen existing initiatives such as the Centres for

PART THREE

MAKING THE MOST OF OUR URBAN ASSETS

TAKING STOCK OF THE HOUSING REQUIREMENT

The Government has set the challenge of raising the proportion of new homes to be provided on previously developed land or in existing buildings to 60% over the next ten years.[1] With projections that there are likely to be about 3.8 million additional households forming between 1996 and 2021, this target, if extended over the full 25 year period of the projections, could mean that about 2.3 million extra households would have to be accommodated on previously developed sites.

The target is important in focusing efforts on protecting the countryside, but the quality of development is as important if we are to attract people back into towns and cities. The priority is to achieve design excellence in the re-use of inner-urban land, thus reducing the need to build on greenfield sites in peripheral locations that pull investment away from our towns and cities.

One of the key tasks which the Task Force was given was to act as a sounding board for the creation of a National Land Use Database to help us identify how much previously developed land already exists and is suitable for housing, and how much is likely to become available in years to come.

In this Chapter we set out:

- the nature of the 60% target, how it could be refined, and the data that we have available to support the quantification of the target;
- the strengths and limitations of the National Land Use Database;
- the evidence on the availability of previously developed land and the potential for housing;
- a review of the factors that may impact on our ability to deliver the land and buildings for housing; and
- the results from a model designed to project whether we can achieve the 60% target based upon current policy assumptions.

Our overall aim has been to use the best available data, which are still limited, to establish a base case of how much housing is likely to be developed on previously developed land within the different English regions over the 25 year period of the current household projections.

1 'Planning for the Communities of the Future'; DETR (1998)

Figure 7.3: The National Land Use Database: strengths and weaknesses of data collection approach

Strengths	Weaknesses
Based upon a very large sample of planning authorities, sites and buildings.	It was a time-limited exercise.
Tight specification will have helped ensure consistent use of definitions and collection methods.	A national survey to compile consistent statistics will not cover the variety of local circumstances that can be addressed in a locally defined urban capacity study.
Teams of surveyors working alongside local authorities will have improved consistency of approach.	Given the difficulties of data collection over a short period of time, it is likely to under-estimate the potential contribution from the existing stock of buildings.
Independent validation of results.	It is a snapshot only of land supply which does not take into account the dynamics of brownfield development.
Combined expertise of DETR, Local Government Management Board, English Partnerships and Ordnance Survey co-ordinating the exercise.	There are some signs of inconsistencies with other data sources, for example the Derelict Land Survey (see below).
Work on supply availability is being counter-balanced by detailed demand studies.	There is likely to have been serious under-counting of small infill sites which, for example, form a very significant percentage of the recycled land potential in London.
	Windfall projections of local planning authorities over the next few years provide only a very limited basis for considering land availability over a 25 year period.

The National Land Use Database statistics are a welcome advance. But their real value will only become apparent over time as it is updated to reflect the actual experience in reclaiming land and buildings. If the Government continues with the initiative, the data collection exercise should be extended and refined, as follows:

- to monitor the type and density of housing being built according to location;
- to provide a statistical basis for measuring the impact of making different policy and market assumptions;
- to monitor the success rate, (or reasons for failure), of the redevelopment of sites which are identified as suitable for housing development in NLUD; and
- to provide a more accurate assessment of the contribution from the existing stock through conversions and refurbishments.

Given the factors outlined above, we have drawn together several data sources in assessing land availability and the feasibility of meeting the 60% target. This is still in many ways an incomplete picture but it is, we believe, the best that is currently available. The real value in creating a model is that it helps us to assess how changing different influences on land supply might affect the overall balance of development. A summary of the methodology employed is described in figure 7.4 and our use of the different data sources in figure 7.5.

Figure 7.4: Model map of how the Urban Task Force constructed its base case

To estimate the likely number of houses that will be built on previously developed sites (1996–2021)

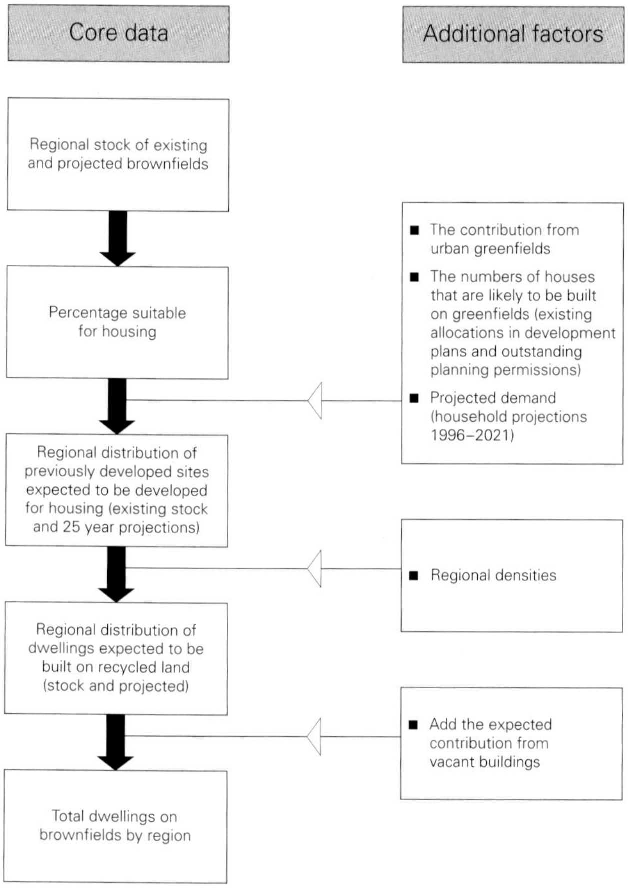

Delivering land for housing

We have pulled together the evidence on other trends that will dictate the rate at which the stock of brownfield land is redeveloped. To do this we have assimilated the data on:

- past trends in housebuilding;
- projected demand for new housing – we have taken the latest household projections as the base case;
- the contribution from urban greenfields, (those sites which would be classified as not previously developed but which fall within urban areas). These are typically formed as a result of urban expansion – for example, a road is built and formerly rural land is captured within the newly-defined urban area;
- the contribution from greenfields – there is a considerable amount of greenfield land in the development pipeline; and
- the density at which development has taken place in the past across the different regions; existing densities are assumed to be constant across the 25 year projection period for the purposes of creating this base case.

In the next section we present the overall results on availability of previously developed land together with an assessment of how much land is suitable for housing. The Task Force views these figures as the 'base case' from which it should be possible, in the light of all the report's recommendations and the supply of land and buildings that may not have been captured in the existing data sources, to improve on the numbers.

likely to be problems of low demand for land that has been vacant for some time. At a national level, and analysing the NLUD results, it would appear that about 40% of the total land stock is likely to be suitable for housing.

In our model we exclude land with planning or development constraints to give an estimate of about 5,300 hectares of vacant land for housing. When converted into actual numbers of dwellings, our analysis suggests that this would provide about 150,000 units.

Buildings

The NLUD results contain figures for the total land relating to vacant commercial buildings. It is slightly misleading to refer to this as 'land', since it is the capacity of the existing buildings – not the site area – which will be important in assessing total capacity. This figure should therefore be treated with caution. Nevertheless, the survey estimated that there are just over 4,500 hectares of land occupied by empty buildings. NLUD also estimated that there are a further 270 hectares of land in which there are 'vacant dwelling zones'. These are classified as areas with at least 25% vacancy rates. There is, however, evidence that this category had not been consistently recorded in the survey returns. In terms of overall units, the NLUD results suggest that existing vacant commercial buildings could provide about 95,000 new housing units.

Given that the NLUD results for 'vacant buildings' do not include single residential dwellings which would provide less than ten new units, we have also needed to add an estimate of the likely contribution from vacant residential dwellings. There are about 753,000 empty dwellings in England.[8] This represents 3.9% of the total housing stock. If we could implement the policy established in the 1995 Housing White Paper and reduce the total vacancy rates to nearer 3%, this would mean that a further 150,000 dwellings could be made available.

Re-thinking how we use urban space

8 Source: Empty Homes Agency, based on raw data from Housing Investment Programme returns (1998)

Some evidence that this may be achievable comes from the summary results in NLUD which suggest an additional contribution of about 11,000 dwellings from conversions of single residential dwellings. Over a 25 year period, this would equate to 275,000 units. Clearly, not all of these will come from the existing stock of vacant dwellings (and some will therefore form part of our 'projected supply' category (see below). Nevertheless, it does indicate that a target of creating about 150,000 net additional units from the existing stock of vacant dwellings should be achievable.

Taken together, the estimated contribution from residential and commercial vacant dwellings comes to just under 250,000 units.

Projected supply of land and buildings

The supply of previously developed land and buildings is not static. The above analysis is a snapshot of the stock of land and buildings at our disposal now. Over the period of the household growth projections to 2021, there will be new sources of vacant and derelict land and buildings. NLUD is a new survey and so does not give us any trend-based data. NLUD has tried to gauge this by estimating the likely contributions from buildings that are currently in use but which have redevelopment potential, looking at the next five year period only. This suggests that there will be a further 19,000 hectares of potential redevelopment land from two categories:

- land or buildings currently in non-residential use but with statutory land use plan allocation for redevelopment or planning permission for housing; and
- previously developed land or buildings currently in use with known redevelopment potential but without planning allocation or permission.

Clearly, this will only be a conservative estimate for the next five years of windfall sites, rather than a comprehensive picture of the potential for future brownfield housing.

From the NLUD returns, it has also been estimated that, on the basis of historic data, using the averages for the last five years, about 45,000 dwellings every year are currently provided for through windfall contributions, i.e. land and buildings that have become available which were not identified or earmarked for development through the formal planning process. If cast forward over the 25 years of the household projections, windfall contributions would amount to something over 1.1 million dwellings. Taken together with the two categories above, this would mean a total of over 1.5 million units over the period of the household projections.

To determine whether this is reasonable, and in particular whether the rates of windfall contributions will continue, we can also evaluate the likely rates at which new brownfield land and buildings will come on stream. It is clearly difficult to project land supply for 25 years. Looking at internal studies that were undertaken for English Partnerships by Ove Arup & Partners a couple of years ago, there is some evidence to suggest that some time over the next ten years, rates of dereliction will start to decline. Toughening environmental legislation will lead to fewer derelict legacies. But this may only have the effect of increasing the amount of new vacant land instead.

If this is correct, and previously developed land continues to come on stream at about the same rates as in the past, then there could be about 2,500 hectares of new derelict and vacant land per annum. This would give about 62,500 hectares of new vacant/derelict land over the period of the household projections (1996–2021).

We would need to add to this the future contribution from the existing stock of vacant residential and commercial buildings, and the incidence of new vacant buildings. When looking at existing stock, we know that the contribution from vacant buildings compared with vacant and derelict land is roughly 70–80% (i.e. 245,000 dwellings as against 315,000 provided for through vacant and derelict land). If we assume that vacant buildings will continue to contribute in line with this, a crude estimate would be that vacant buildings will generate a further 44,000 hectares of land (on the basis of a 70% ratio). Overall, this means about 106,500 hectares of land in total.

These figures on projected supply come attached with a large health warning. We are making our best estimate on the basis of the very limited data that are available. The estimates of windfall sites may be at the top end of the range. Types of derelict and vacant land are changing in nature, with a larger proportion of sites being made up of small ex-industrial sites and buildings which will often not be simple to translate into a meaningful development opportunity, particularly where the site is constrained by outdated or inadequate infrastructure, servicing and access. In other words, what may become available may increasingly fail to translate into what is deliverable. Even if present trends are maintained, the windfall sites may not come on stream in the right places. A number of housing associations are saying that fewer windfall opportunities for social housing are arising than even five years ago. The windfall figures will therefore need to be monitored very carefully in the years ahead.

If, consistent with the findings of NLUD, we assume 46% of the total projected stock is suitable for housing, this would give 49,000 hectares of land. At densities of about 30 units per hectare (i.e. roughly in line with existing densities on previously developed land), this would equate to just over 1.5 million dwellings.

DELIVERING LAND AND BUILDINGS FOR NEW HOUSING

There are assumptions in the previous set of figures which inform our estimates of how much of the total existing stock and the purported land and buildings supply will actually be developed for housing. Overall availability of land and buildings should never be confused with deliverability. The NLUD analysis gives us the local authorities' view on what is potentially available and suitable for housing. There will be a range of factors which should have gone into this analysis (albeit varying in consistency between local authorities) including:

- the quality of the land: heavy industrial sites may not be suitable for housing;
- the planning regime: although the respondents were asked to 'think freely' and not be constrained by this;
- political sensitivity: for example, over the loss of employment land for housing; and
- whether the sites are viable for redevelopment: some areas may have existing use values higher than those likely to be generated through housing development; or people may simply not want to live there.

Many of these constraints on recycling previously developed land should be overcome. Nevertheless, we need to be realistic about the amount of the overall resource that will be re-used for housing. We have considered a series of factors above and beyond what has been incorporated into the NLUD analysis. These relate to additional supply side factors and the likely demand for sites in different locations.

Housebuilding patterns

The development of new housing tends to follow trends in demand. The latest household projections from DETR suggest that there will be strong demand for additional new housing in London and the South East, with relatively low demand in regions such as the North West and the North East.

The results are set out in the graph opposite. We have then added a second column to compare these figures with the recent regional distribution of new housing, recognising that housebuilding comprises most but not all the supply of new housing.

The household figures relate to new additional households and not houses. Our model is based upon the projections. Nevertheless, we cannot ignore the likely market response in relation to these projections. There are some arguments to suggest that the correlation between household projections and supply of dwellings (particularly over the short term) is far from close. It can be seen from the above graph that there is the potential for a significant mismatch between the projections and rates of housebuilding in the different regions. While the market will obviously respond to a changing balance of regional requirements, it will take time for this to happen. As things stand, in the comparison of past trends and future projections, only the South West and the Eastern region seem reasonably balanced. London and the South East are projected to have significantly higher levels of household formation than the past trends in new dwellings could accommodate. At the other extreme, some of the northern and midlands regions would appear to have been producing a surplus of new housing relative to projected demand.

Figure 7.9: Comparing annual rates of projected household growth with past trends in housebuilding completions

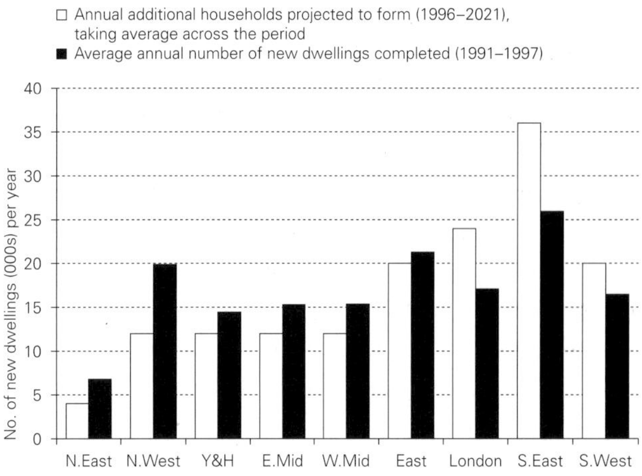

Source: DETR Housing Statistics; DETR press release (April 1998)

Reclaiming brownfield land but how much will the market deliver for housing? (English Partnerships)

Urban greenfields

One of the contributory sources to new housebuilding within urban areas in the past has been 'urban land not previously developed' – which we refer to as urban greenfields. This does not refer to parks, playing fields or allotments. The category is defined in the Land Use Change Statistics as "land in built-up areas which has not been developed previously and which is not currently used for agriculture, which is shown on the OS map as a 'white' area without annotation... if it was not in a built-up area, such land would be classified as agricultural land". It is typically created as a result of urban expansion. For example, where a new road bypass is created, the areas of former agricultural land that are caught within the new urban boundary will fall into the urban greenfield category.

Although there is no numerical evidence, our view is that this source of land for housing will decline over time. It is clearly a finite resource within urban areas that will increasingly be seen as a resource to be protected, in the same way as rural greenfield land. The effect of this will obviously be to push housing into other categories. If there is sufficient previously developed land, then clearly this can absorb the additional housing. However, given the overall scale of the land which can be recycled, the more likely consequence is that it increases the demand for new housing on rural greenfield sites.

Existing greenfield allocations

The capacity of the brownfield stock to absorb high levels of growth is not simply contingent on the factors outlined above. Given the dynamic nature of the land and property markets, we also need to know how much potential greenfield development is already in the pipeline.

The Task Force commissioned the Royal Town Planning Institute (RTPI) to undertake research into this issue through a questionnaire survey about the provision of housing on greenfield land. The questionnaires were distributed in October 1998 to all local authorities in England and 55% responded.

These responses were grossed up to provide a crude estimate of the full national picture. We know that the survey results must represent an under-estimate of the amount of recent development on greenfield sites. The survey reported that just over 400,000 new dwellings had been developed on greenfield sites between 1991 and 1998. However, this does not tally with the Land Use Change Statistics estimate of the proportion of new housing developed on greenfield land over most of this period. By using the Land Use Change Statistics and DETR housebuilding statistics, we estimate that just under 220,000 new dwellings were constructed on greenfield land in the three years 1996–1998 alone.[9]

Figure 7.10: Housing on greenfield sites

Category	I Developed (1996–1998)[10]	II Planning permission but not yet implemented	III Allocated for housing but no planning permission	IV Likely number of houses to be allocated in new plans	Total
Number of new dwellings	220,000	262,000	240,000	156,000	878,000
Land take (ha)	10,000[11]	10,200	9,750	6,600	–

Source: RTPI Survey, LUCS and DETR housing statistics

9 Sources: Land Use Change Statistics and DETR Housing Statistics
10 Sources: Land Use Change Statistics and DETR Housing Statistics
11 Assuming average greenfield densities

Even, however, taking the conservative estimates provided by the survey, it suggests that, as at 1998, as well as the dwellings completed on greenfield sites, at least:

- a further 262,000 have been granted planning permission but not yet implemented;
- 240,000 units have been allocated in local plans;
- a further 156,000 are likely to be built as a result of replacement plans.

In other words, looking at the period of the household projections, 1996–2021, at least 850,000 dwellings have either already been built, have already been granted planning permission or have been allocated for residential development in local plans. This represents just over 23% of the projected households to 2021 or over half of the 40% greenfield allocation that could be said to be assumed in the national target.

Such high levels of greenfield housing in the pipeline have important implications for the ability to ensure high levels of ongoing brownfield housing. They must influence the way targets are used to achieve more urban development on previously developed sites.

Density of new residential development

The overall densities at which new houses are built are relatively low. The evidence from the LUCS shows that overall average density on all residential developments (across both brownfields and greenfields) is about 25 units per hectare. There are also significant regional variations – from only 23 units per hectare in the South East to 47 units per hectare in London. With the exception of London, new housing in most regions tends to hover around 23–25 units per hectare.

The density figures that have been applied to our model are therefore based on past trends.

Figure 7.11: Average densities of housing development (units/ha)

Region	**Average brownfield density**	**Average greenfield density**	**Average overall density**
North East	27	21	24
North West and Merseyside	28	22	25
Yorkshire and Humber	26	21	24
East Midlands	24	22	24
West Midlands	31	23	27
Eastern	25	22	24
London	49	38	47
South East	23	22	23
South West	29	23	25
National	**28**	**22**	**25**

SUMMARISING THE RESULTS

We have set out in figure 7.12 the likely numbers of houses which will be built on previously developed land over the period of the projections across all categories.

Based on these results, over the period of the household projections (1996–2021), and assuming that each of the regions will have to accommodate the number of new households set out in the projections, we have estimated that, strictly on current policy assumptions, the regions will achieve the percentage figures set out in figure 7.13.

Assuming trends are reasonably stable over the 25 years, this implies that the target of 60% of new housing on recycled land, however defined, may not be achieved.

We do, however, attach a strong health warning to these percentages. They do not state what will actually happen. They give a good indication of what could happen if we are

Tackling outdated zoning

The concept of zoning is increasingly losing its meaning. With the barriers between home, work and leisure continuing to break down, the future emphasis of development plans should be on promoting flexible designations which enable mixing of uses and the ability to change the mix over time.

Too many local planning authorities are still practising rigid adherence to employment land allocations, for sites with no demand, and in some cases, no suitability, for modern employment uses. In many cases there is also evidence of authorities duplicating site provision; for example, neighbouring metropolitan districts all holding out for the same big inward investment opportunity.

We also recognise, however, that there are difficult political issues involved. For example, authorities, particularly in deprived areas, have to compete heavily to attract major employers, and are reluctant to reduce their chances by relaxing employment zones.

Careful co-ordination is required at the regional level to provide a rigorous analysis of commercial and industrial demand and potential. There needs to be an ongoing programme of regional research on changes in economic growth and land use within the region. In the shorter term, there needs to be rigorous testing of existing or allocated sites, to enable those with no likelihood of being used for employment purposes to be released for other uses, particularly housing-led mixed developments.

Our recommendation:

- **Review, at a regional level, the designations of employment sites in local development plans, taking into account economic needs, but avoiding over-provision, and accelerating the release of land for housing development. (48)**

The outcomes of this form of analysis and review should not only form part of the RPG and the Public Examination which informs it, it should also be addressed in each of the local planning authorities' next development plan reviews and examined specifically by the Planning Inspector.

Facilitating mixed uses

We wish to encourage a more flexible approach to planning and changing uses within urban areas:

- in changing mixes of uses within a single building; particularly flexibility in ground floor uses (residential, commercial and non-food retail), and the provision for conversions to live/work units;
- on defining areas in a development plan or spatial masterplan which will comprise a mix of uses, but without wishing to specify a static approach as to what combination of uses will prevail at any one time; in other words, giving an area freedom to evolve and change, with minimum need for planning intervention.

Ashbourne, Derbyshire: mixing uses at the centre of town (Martin Bond Environmental Images)

Kayes Walk, Nottingham Lace Market

(Technical Support, The Development Department, Nottingham City Council)

There are best practice examples of how to do this. In Sheffield, for example, the development plan defines mixed use areas where planning permissions can be granted that cover a broad range of use classes including potentially, small shops, offices, community facilities, businesses etc. In Birmingham, the authority grants mixed use consents which approve a range of floorspace allocations, specifying, where appropriate, relationships between one use and another. It establishes minimum and maximum figures for the quantity of space given over to each use.

There is a need for some best practice guidance, possibly on the basis of a new piece of research, demonstrating how flexible application of the Use Classes Order can create helpful conditions for undertaking mixed urban developments.

THE LACE MARKET, NOTTINGHAM

Situated in the heart of Nottingham City Centre, the Lace Market was the centre of an international lace trade which developed quickly during the 19th century as part of the mechanisation of local industry. The industry went into decline at the turn of the century and by the 1970s the area was characterised by blight and decay. Despite having some of the finest collections of Victorian industrial architecture in the country, there was pressure for wholesale clearance, with hundreds of thousands of square feet of vacant space and over 30 substantially derelict sites.

Over the last 20 years, the city has turned the Lace Market around so that today it is a fashionable address for residents and businesses. The majority of the buildings have been renovated, including all of the major problem sites. There is now a vibrant mixed use community, with over 200 homes, combining private and social housing, and with a very promising future.

The success factors include:

- long term political commitment to see through a series of integrated regeneration strategies;
- creative planning policies, flexibly applied, which continued to support the remaining lace and clothing businesses, and resisted blight by premature speculative acquisition and unnecessary building clearance and road widening proposals;
- promoting residential uses on derelict sites and through conversions;
- concentrated effort to tackle major problem buildings which were discouraging investment;
- establishing an arms length Development Company, combining local authorities and private sector interests to implement Investment Plans combining public and private funding.

Making better use of planning obligations and planning gain

Section 106 of the Town and Country Planning Act 1990 enables local authorities to enter into agreements which would remove barriers to development. Agreements can secure a number of positive and negative obligations from the developer or landowner. Although not formally acknowledged, these obligations can be used as a means of securing 'planning gain' – additional benefits provided by a developer to reflect additional costs to, or impacts on, the neighbouring locality arising from the development.

Our findings on planning agreements are based largely on a report completed for the Task Force by Lesley Punter of Reading Council.[5] Our main conclusion is that the use of planning obligations to secure planning gain is necessary and justified, but that the process is not currently being applied consistently. The problems can be summarised as follows:

- many of the agreements are taking too long to process;
- there is little or no standardisation in the drafting of Section 106 agreements;
- in using Section 106 agreements to secure planning gain, local planning authorities sometimes fail to evaluate the overall commercial viability of the scheme, often seeking to exact similar levels of gain in respect of marginal urban sites as with greenfield opportunities.

We would make the following recommendations:

- **Revise and relax national guidance on the use of planning agreements to:**

– **permit agreements where developers contribute revenue expenditure to help improve the quality and management of the urban environment;**

– **enable an extension of cross-subsidy of planning gain secured from development in one part of an urban area to assist the regeneration of other sites within the vicinity;**

– **provide more guidance on the drafting of Section 106 agreements, including model clauses to enable fairer and more consistent application;**

– **provide a guideline that Section 106 agreements should be settled within eight weeks of a resolution to grant planning permission. (49)**

- **Establish a 'fast-track' independent arbitration process for the conclusion of Section 106 agreements, which can be triggered by either party after a set period, at their cost. (50)**

- **Replace the negotiation of planning gain for smaller urban development schemes, (for example, an end value of less than £1 million), with a standardised system of impact fees. The fees collected should be spent on local environmental improvements and community facilities that reflect the priorities of local people. (51)**

Securing mixed income housing

The use of planning obligations to secure affordable housing is a particularly vexed issue. Current planning advice on this issue, contained in Circular 13/98, needs to be reviewed. In some urban areas, there is strong evidence of an over-provision of social housing, and in such places it is important to use planning gain for purposes other than additional rented housing. In other urban neighbourhoods, particularly parts of London and the South East, there may be a shortage of affordable housing. Such areas frequently offer little low to mid-priced housing for sale or for rent. Planning obligations can be used as one device to try to deal with this situation.

At present, we often face an unhappy stalemate where developers are required to provide substantial numbers of

5 Copies of the report, 'The future role of planning agreements in facilitating urban regeneration' are available from DETR

affordable homes to meet planning obligations, whilst frequently either buying themselves out of the obligation through cash payments, or else designing their way out through site layouts which separate low cost from market housing. As we established at the start of the report, mixing households is an important factor in creating more balanced and sustainable urban communities. This requires genuinely mixed cost housing for mixed income neighbourhoods. Therefore, in places with high land values present, there should be a presumption that a finer gradation of house prices and types are made available than is currently the case.

We would like to see a range of measures to address this issue. These include the promotion of shared equity housing on appropriate sites and more creative use of planning briefs to encourage, or even insist upon, a wider range of house prices and types within developments. We also consider that more creative solutions could be found, such as 'shared appreciation' homes, where prices are discounted through the use of restricted covenants in favour of lower income households.

Recommendations:

- **Review the mechanisms by which local planning authorities use planning gain to secure affordable 'social' housing to ensure that:**

- **developers have less scope to buy their way out of obligations to provide mixed tenure neighbourhoods;**

- **local authorities are not obliged to require social housing in contexts where there is already over-provision in that neighbourhood. (52)**

- **Enable more mixed income housing projects to proceed, including use of more challenging planning briefs and discounted equity stakes for low to middle income households in areas where property values are high. (53)**

THE PIGGERIES, FROME: PLANNING NEW HOMES IN OLD PLACES

The Piggeries housing scheme close to Frome town centre, recent winner of the special award for urban design in the 1998 Royal Town Planning Institute Achievement Awards, is an example of a quality finished product in a historic environment that has been achieved despite a prolonged and risk-laden process.

The Piggeries was a small derelict site. It was blighted by a long running County Council proposal to build a road through the area, by the multiple ownership of the land and the unwillingness of the landowners to co-operate with redevelopment.

The first step in the rebirth of the Piggeries came in 1985 when Mendip District Council persuaded the County Council to drop the road building proposal and allocated the site for housing. Site assembly was a much more lengthy and difficult process, but after ten years of effort, marked by the real risk of failure, the whole site was assembled.

When redevelopment eventually started in 1996, care was taken to work closely with the local community, and to attract housing associations to become financially involved. The main design principle that evolved from consultation was the scheme should be modern, but one that contributed to the character of Frome and that blended in with the context. Other design issues included concern over insufficient car parking, and complaints about the overshadowing of other streets which had been accustomed to open views across the site.

All these issues were satisfactorily resolved and in February 1998 the completed scheme of 71 housing units was handed over to the client housing association. The Piggeries completes another piece of the regeneration jigsaw for a historic part of Frome.

overcome low demand for housing in their area is to build on the surrounding greenfields, rather than tackling the regeneration of their urban heartlands. The release of such land will simply exacerbate their long term problems.

As a general principle, we consider that, subject to any constraints on land availability, recycling targets in low demand inner urban areas should be set very high indeed, and in some cases, there will be no case for any additional greenfield development at all. This places an onus on the local planning authority to work with neighbouring authorities in co-operation with the Government Regional Office and the Regional Planning Body to plan a joint strategy for housing provision which prioritises the regeneration of the urban core.

More generally, however, the revised PPG3 needs to provide local planning authorities with the ability to remove plan allocations for greenfield land and sites earmarked in housing land availability studies, as part of a plan revision process, where such releases will no longer be in accordance with national and regional policy objectives, and will therefore undermine regeneration efforts. There is, currently, uncertainty over the extent to which local authorities have powers to de-allocate land and how these powers vary according to the different level of certainty in any given allocations, depending on the description used. Some developers, who have bought up land on the basis of a plan allocation or inclusion in a housing availability study, may consider that they have a 'legitimate expectation' that consent will be granted. Government will need to provide clarification that no compensation is payable in these circumstances.

Our recommendations are:

- **Set ambitious targets for the proportion of new housing to be developed on recycled land in urban areas where there is a significant amount of previously developed land available and housing demand is currently low. (57)**
- **Require local authorities to remove allocations of greenfield land for housing from development plans where the allocations are no longer consistent with planning policy objectives. (58)**

The Green Belt and linking development

Green Belts have played a vital role over many decades in resisting urban decline and there should continue to be a strong presumption against amending Green Belt boundaries. There are, however, limited examples of where a case can be made for adjusting boundaries. This may represent the most sustainable option in extending an existing settlement, rather than allowing a 'leap-frog' of greenfield development into the surrounding open countryside. It would, however, have to be demonstrated that the sequential approach had been strictly followed, that the housing development was necessary and that the adjustment had clear environmental advantages over other options.

There is also a need for a more sophisticated approach in protecting and designating urban green space. There are important green buffer zones and strategic gaps both within and between our urban areas which could be given the same weight in development control terms as the Green Belt designation. This would help to protect urban biodiversity and ensure strong urban green space networks.

Planning guidance should also link future greenfield development to the re-use of previously used sites. We should explore further the scope for permitting some greenfield development where it would assist the strengthening of an edge-of-town neighbourhood, provided the developer returned a suitably located previously used site elsewhere in the town or city to green space, to strengthen the overall network. There would, however, need to be genuine environmental and social gains, not just the replacement of an equivalent amount of land. And this proposal would only be relevant where the greenfield location was considered acceptable for development during the development plan process.

Working to avoid sprawl: Tewkesbury in Gloucestershire (Skyscan Photolibrary)

Recommendation:

- **Retain the general presumption against development on designated Green Belt. Review whether there is a case for designating valuable urban green space in a similar way. (59)**

Releasing under-used public land assets

In recent years, there have been attempts to improve the operational use of public sector land and property holdings. The publication of the National Asset Register in 1998 went some way towards identifying targets for the re-use of public sector property, (covering, for example, Ministry of Defence, NHS estates and the coalfields). There is, however, still some way to go on this. The register itself needs to be expanded to identify urban regeneration potential, and under-utilisation of sites and buildings. In this way, the asset owners would be compelled to place in the public domain information on the amount of land and buildings they hold, the amount of land and buildings they classify as surplus and not essential for operational purposes, the location of the land and buildings, and the extent of contamination, in a useable and crosscutting format.

Part of the reason why public land is not fully utilised in respect of regeneration schemes is because of limitations on how those assets are disposed. In countries like the Netherlands and Denmark, the public authorities are more willing to reflect considerations in kind as part of the disposal price. In Rotterdam, for example, this was one of the main ways in which the municipality achieved high levels of private sector investment in design quality. These were regarded as 'over and above' costs and were therefore deducted from the sale price for the disposal of land from the municipality to the developer.

Second, received wisdom is that an acquiring authority must show that it has detailed plans for the development of an area, together with a proposed developer and funding solution, (as set out in statute and supported by DETR Circular 14/94). Most developers are reluctant to commit time, effort and resources to a scheme until there is sufficient certainty over land ownership. Therefore, authorities are faced with a vicious circle.

Urban Development Corporations were given a clear right to acquire land compulsorily without the need to provide an economically viable scheme. There is a case for extending this same freedom to local authorities in respect of Urban Priority Areas where they can demonstrate that this additional flexibility is required to make headway in regenerating sites. In doing so, there would, however, need to be some safeguards. Local authorities should not be free to buy up land with little or no potential for early development, or worse still, start competing with private developers. The area designation process should therefore test whether there is the prospect of long term value creation through an enhanced acquisition power.

Our recommendations:

- **Streamline and consolidate Compulsory Purchase Order (CPO) legislation. In the meantime, reinforce positive legal decisions on the powers of local authorities by amending the relevant government guidance. (69)**

- **Assist the land assembly process in Urban Priority Areas by removing the obligation for authorities to prove a specific and economically viable scheme when making Compulsory Purchase Orders. They should, however, still be required to prove the potential for creating long term development value in the site. (70)**

USING COMPULSORY PURCHASE WITH CONFIDENCE: THE CASE OF ROCHESTER RIVERSIDE

Local authorities contemplating getting involved in regeneration CPOs should be heartened by Medway Council's recent experience. In September 1998, the Secretary of State confirmed a CPO for the regeneration of a 35 hectare site on the Medway Riverside between Rochester and Chatham.

The area suffers from vacant and derelict sites, low value uses, poor access, contamination and a multiplicity of some 30 different ownerships. Despite an ambitious programme of land acquisition, the Council were always aware that CPO powers would probably be needed to bring the site together for regeneration purposes.

However, the scale of intervention contemplated through the compulsory purchase process was almost unheard of – certainly outside the Urban Development Corporations – for regeneration projects. The successful outcome demonstrated to the Council that CPO can be used as a tool to assist in regeneration. But success has only come about through political commitment, broad public support and by having a strategy in place to help the existing occupiers. It has also been critically important to have expert legal and property advisers on board together with sufficient resources to be able to see the process through.

In confirming the CPO, the Secretary of State agreed with the Inspector that the private sector in its own right would not invest in major new development. The local authority was seen as being the party best able to manage and co-ordinate the regeneration and land assembly process.

Skills

Many local authorities have not had to use their powers of CPO since the Comprehensive Development Areas of the 1960s. Where CPO is used today, it is generally in connection with the development of new highways.

There are a number of key measures which would assist in helping overcome the skills gap which has arisen through lack of use. One is the production of a good practice manual, which DETR is currently drawing up, In addition, we consider that there would be some merit in establishing some small teams of land assembly experts, possibly as regionally appointed panels of consultants or as an employed team, who can be called in to assist where and when required by a local authority.

Compensation

One of the major stumbling blocks with compulsory purchase arises out of the way in which owners of land are compensated for the loss of their property. We have been advised that it is not legally possible to have separate compensatory regimes for different areas, e.g. in designated Urban Priority Areas. Neither is it possible to distinguish between property speculators/absentee landlords and bona fide property owners.

Valuation is an inexact science and actions taken by public authorities with CPO powers to redevelop, or those planning to redevelop areas, can result in sharp increases in land and property values. We need to secure an equitable balance between the instigator of a CPO and the property owner. The basis of compensation should be prevailing market value at the time immediately before the announcement of any plans to regenerate an areas. A code of practice will be required to help administer these valuation decisions.

We also recognise that, if we are to lubricate the system, we should allow an additional payment for compensatory loss. Residential property owners are entitled to an additional 'home loss payment' to reflect "the distress and inconvenience which people suffer when they are required to move house at a time not of their own choosing". Such factors, however, may also be significant for business premises. Indeed, businesses who have premises with a low rateable value already benefit from an equivalent to the 'home loss' payment. So there seems little case to discriminate against larger businesses.

Our recommendation:

- **Allow an additional 10% above market value to be payable as compensation for the compulsory purchase of all properties. Payment of the extra compensation should be tapered according to a timetable to encourage early settlement. (71)**

In bringing forward this recommendation, we are aware of the dangers of speculative private acquisitions, simply to benefit financially from the process of CPO. There may be a case for enabling the determining authority to set aside the additional compensation provision in cases where it is clear that a business is not going to be materially affected by the acquisition process, or where the acquisition has taken place shortly after the announcement of the proposed redevelopment.

IN SUMMARY

We must do all we can to encourage developers to recycle previously developed land for housing and other essential uses wherever this represents the most sustainable option. In considering how best to achieve this objective, the planning system is the key tool in controlling land supply. We therefore advocate future management of our land supply based upon a plan-led sequential approach to identifying and releasing land for development. To support the sequential approach, we need better resourced Regional Planning Bodies co-ordinating a 'plan, monitor and manage' approach to housing allocations, delivered through regional planning guidance with stronger statutory status.

We have to tread carefully in respect of the use of economic instruments as a tool for constraining greenfield development. The focus of any charging mechanisms should be to ensure that external environment costs of development are properly attributed to the developer, and there are powerful arguments that such a mechanism should be delivered through the land use planning system, in support of its primary strategic management and control functions.

Land assembly is a crucial part of the regeneration armoury. The pattern of land ownership within our urban areas is highly complex. If we are to achieve redevelopment and rehabilitation of urban areas that are suffering from vacancy, dereliction and under-use of land and buildings, then it is essential that we facilitate the process. In many circumstances, the market will solve this conundrum itself. In other circumstances, the public sector will play a key role in facilitating private acquisition. And finally, there will be occasions where public acquisition is the best, or perhaps, the only option.

SUMMARY OF RECOMMENDATIONS	Responsibility	Timing
Key recommendations		
Formally adopt a sequential approach to the release of land and buildings for housing, supported by a system of regional and sub-regional reconciliation of housing needs and demand. Planning guidance should specify monitoring procedures for every local planning authority to apply.	DETR, local planning authorities	End of 1999
Require local authorities to remove allocations of greenfield land for housing from development plans where the allocations are no longer consistent with planning policy objectives.	DETR, local planning authorities	Development plan review timetable
Assist the land assembly process in Urban Priority Areas by removing the obligation for authorities to prove a specific and economically viable scheme when making Compulsory Purchase Orders. They should, however, still be required to prove the potential for creating long term development value in the site.	DETR	By 2000 (if primary legislation not required)
Other recommendations		
Establish clear procedures under the proposed 'plan, monitor and manage' system for assessing future housing demand, to ensure the early correction of an emerging undersupply or oversupply of housing.	DETR, Regional Planning Bodies	By 2000
Oblige all local planning authorities to carry out regular urban capacity studies on a consistent basis, as part of their development plan-making process, where necessary working together across borough boundaries.	DETR, local planning authorities	From 2000
Set ambitious targets for the proportion of new housing to be developed on recycled land in urban areas where housing demand is currently low.	DETR, Regional Planning Bodies, local planning authorities	By 2001

	Responsibility	Timing
Retain the general presumption against development on designated Green Belt. Review whether there is a case for designating valuable urban green space in a similar way.	DETR	Ongoing
Provide information on the regeneration potential of land and building assets in future editions of the National Asset Register.	National government, Regional Planning Bodies	As updated
Introduce a statutory duty for public bodies and utilities with significant urban landholdings to release redundant land and buildings for regeneration. Regional Planning Bodies could monitor compliance with the new duty and whether targets for land release are being met.	DETR, Regional Planning Bodies, public land owners	By 2002
Require organisations such as the Ministry of Defence and NHS Estates to negotiate the transfer of portfolios of development land to Regional Development Agencies and local authorities to secure locally-determined regeneration objectives.	National government	First tranches to transfer by 2001, then ongoing reviews
Consider options for reflecting the full environmental costs of new development through the use of economic instruments. Particular attention should be given to the feasibility of introducing a system of environmental impact fees through the planning system.	DETR, HM Treasury	Proposals by 2001
Prepare a scheme for taxing vacant land, which does not penalise genuine developers, but which deters owners holding onto land unnecessarily.	DETR, HM Treasury	Proposals by 2001
Strengthen and increase local authority powers of foreclosure and enforced sale to provide speedy mechanisms for dealing with abandoned and dilapidated sites or buildings.	DETR	By 2001
Modify the General Development Order so that advertising, car parking and other low-grade temporary uses no longer have deemed planning permission on derelict and vacant land.	DETR	By 2000

	Responsibility	Timing
Allow local authorities and other public bodies flexibility to pay disturbance payments over and above market value in reaching negotiated settlements for the acquisition of land. They should also be able to make greater use of purchase options and deferred acquisition payments.	DETR, HM Treasury	By 2001
Create revolving funds for land assembly, so that public investment in the initial costs of site purchase can be off-set by a share of subsequent gains achieved through regeneration and disposal.	DETR, Regional Development Agencies	By end of 2000
Streamline and consolidate Compulsory Purchase Order (CPO) legislation. In the meantime, reinforce positive legal decisions on the powers of local authorities by amending the relevant Government guidance.	DETR	Legislation by 2003
The current compensatory element for residential properties is expanded to allow an additional 10% to be payable as part of any compensation provision. The compensatory element should be tapered to encourage early settlement.	DETR, HM Treasury	By 2002

10

CLEANING UP THE LAND

There are significant amounts of land within our towns and cities that are contaminated as a result of previous uses. Urban regeneration can help to restore this land to a state fit for new purposes, whether it be to accommodate new buildings or create new areas of open space.

Widespread land contamination is a legacy of the UK being the first country in the world to industrialise. The development of industrial processes and the use of noxious and toxic chemicals preceded understanding of the environmental and health implications of their uncontrolled use. Industrialisation tended to take place on the edge of existing towns and cities, or in entirely new locations adjacent to places of extraction of natural resources, such as mines, quarries and rivers. However, industrialisation also occurred hand in hand with huge demographic shifts of population, from rural habitation to the expanding towns and cities or the new industrial locations. As a consequence, the cities and settlements enveloped the mills, power stations, processing plants and factories.

In the post-industrial age, most of these industries have now moved on, to edge-of-town or greenfield locations, or disappeared completely. They have tended to leave behind tracts of contamination, often arising from a mix of historic uses and resulting from decades, if not centuries, of mishandling and spillage of materials.

No-one really knows how much of our land is contaminated. Current estimates range from 50,000 to 200,000 hectares, somewhere between a city the size of Manchester and one bigger than Greater London. Much of this land is still in use. Where contamination does exist, it is often perceived to be a significant barrier to redevelopment. It is also a barrier in respect of people's willingness to live on previously developed land. In this Chapter, we seek to understand why contamination is a serious problem and what can be done to ease the process of reclaiming and developing contaminated sites. We conclude that:

- most contaminated land is capable of safe remediation using modern technology at reasonable cost;
- the present barriers to redevelopment are largely to do with the perception of risk;
- we have to simplify and consolidate the regulatory systems which seek to protect the environment from the consequences of contamination;
- we should promote greater standardisation in the way we manage the risks involved in redeveloping contaminated sites, and thereby promote a better and consistent understanding of the situation.

UNDERSTANDING THE PROBLEM

A barrier to development

A recent survey carried out by the University of Ulster on behalf of the Royal Institution of Chartered Surveyors[1] revealed that the process of remediating contaminated sites was the most significant adverse factor for investors in making investment decisions in respect of brownfield locations. Some 58% of investors cited contamination remediation as a major negative factor in making their investment decisions.

With the obvious exception of nuclear waste, the problem of land contamination is not primarily technical, although more research is undoubtedly required to make the remediation process more efficient and affordable. In almost all cases it is essentially a problem of finance and/or perceived legal risk. The reasons why contamination is perceived to be such a problem can be broken down as follows:

- there is an institutional view which regards land contamination as a difficult liability which, in turn, depresses land values and thus reduces the economic viability of regeneration projects;
- there is a lack of confidence in the outcomes of the remediation processes, fuelled by a lack of consistency in the quality of advice provided about the risks involved, and the way in which that advice is presented;
- we do not have a consistent statutory regulatory regime and, to date, the process of introducing such a system has been undermined by delay; this creates uncertainty for developers over future potential legal liabilities and potential additional costs resulting from future changes in statutory clean-up requirements;
- there is a lack of promotion of good practice and success stories in regenerating contaminated sites; this includes a lack of consistent data-sets on successful schemes to inform assessments of financial risk;
- not all risks can be accurately predicted and that fuels public fears about living on reclaimed land;
- there is no legal or financial comfort given to the developer or investor who takes on a difficult site; indeed, our current regulatory systems make life difficult, uncertain and costly for the urban entrepreneur.

Learning from abroad

Other countries share the same contamination legacy as ourselves, albeit often not on the same scale. We have looked at some of the policies and practices in the United States and elsewhere in Europe to see whether we can identify new ideas which would fit with our own management systems.

Looking within Europe, many countries have introduced systems covering information, risk assessment, remediation, allocation of liabilities and funding for contaminated sites. Examples of other countries' approaches which are of interest include Germany, which has enacted a new Soil Protection Act providing a single permitting regime for dealing with soil-based contamination when clean-up enforcement action is taken. We were also impressed by the Norwegian approach which uses a mix of standard guidance and simple numeric values to help establish site-based clean-up standards. They also use a 'ground book' land register to track the current state of any remaining pollution when land is transferred.

In the United States, there are some clear signs of a positive market response to taking on contaminated sites:

- a competitive insurance market has developed products that reduce risk to project investors;

1 'Accessing private finance: The availability and effectiveness of private finance in urban regeneration'; University of Ulster; RICS (1998)

- mainstream lenders in some States and larger urban areas are overcoming their nervousness about contaminated sites and providing new forms of venture capital for redeveloping the land;

- there has been growth in the number of specialist developers acquiring and redeveloping contaminated sites.

Measures to support this include:

- many US States have some form of 'sign-off assurance', which means that if certain remediation approaches are followed then the regulating bodies will usually signal their intent not to take future regulatory action;

- in most States, it is the development or regeneration agencies who take the lead in helping prospective developers through the regulatory maze of possible liability actions and licensing requirements;

- the public agencies, including the US Environmental Protection Agency, are becoming more proactive in accumulating and disseminating information to support investor decision-making. This has included the provision of technical education programmes for lenders.

Reclaiming industrial heritage in the Ruhr

PARK LIFE: THE INTERNATIONAL BUILDING EXHIBITION, EMSCHER, GERMANY

Once Europe's industrial heartland, the Emscher region now finds itself economically weakened and with a landscape of industrial dereliction, contamination and oversized, outdated infrastructure. The Emscher Park project is a regional structural programme, aimed at securing the ecological and urban renewal of the northern Ruhr district. The central element of this project is to create a Landscape Park comprising some 300 square kilometres of land running from west to east through the Emscher region.

This Park is intended to provide the central core of new infrastructure for the region. By remediating large swathes of contaminated land, connecting isolated open spaces, cleaning up the river Emscher (which served as an open sewer for the Ruhr area for about 100 years), restoring the landscape and upgrading the ecological and aesthetic quality of the countryside, the idea is to achieve a lasting improvement in the living and working environment for the 2 million inhabitants of the region.

All the 17 towns and cities in the region have undertaken to create north-south links into the Park, with seven regional green corridors. In each of these corridors landmark projects are being created to exemplify the themes and approaches adopted for the area making up an International Building Exhibition.

There are a total of 26 housing schemes which form the housing and urban development part of the Emscher Park Exhibition. At present there are some 3,000 flats in the planning or construction stages, and a further 3,000 existing ones are to be refurbished. Some 75% of the new housing will be public sector rented accommodation.

The scale of the Emscher Park project and the innovative approach of its Exhibition make it an important example of how industrial contamination need not be a barrier to reclaiming land on a large scale for eclectic and productive uses.

CLEANING UP OREGON

The Oregon Voluntary Clean up Programme (VCP) in the United States offers developers who fully implement a State approved remediation plan a No Further Action letter, which declares the State's intention to forego any future action to pursue legal action on the site according to data available at the time of the remediation letter. Upon receipt of an application to the programme, and an agreement to pay a fee charged by the State, the programme team assigns a project manager to manage the State's role in project implementation. Although the State's letter does not offer hard protection against Federal action, it virtually precludes a re-opening of the case by declaring the State's disinterest in further action on the site.

In summary, we found four main types of positive policy measures in use overseas which we could make more use of in England:

- measures to clarify the nature and extent of regulator involvement in relation to given sites; through comfort letters, memoranda of understanding and 'sign-off' letters;
- measures to simplify, standardise and make transparent the work required to determine whether land is potentially contaminated and the process that is required to clean it up;
- measures to require legal disclosure of the amount of clean-up carried out and the state of the land at the point of transfer;
- measures to increase the involvement of the private sector, in terms of their skills, expertise and financial muscle.

MANAGING THE RISK

Establishing the priorities

In England the bottom line is to ensure more clean-up and redevelopment of contaminated or potentially contaminated sites by attracting more private finance and investment into such development.

The two key barriers we have identified to this are:

- the complex nature of the current and the proposed regulatory systems covering statutory environmental protection requirements;
- a lack of common understanding of the real risk associated with development of contaminated sites.

We therefore propose tackling the problem from two perspectives:

- simplify and consolidate the regulatory systems which seek to protect the environment, including providing land owners with greater certainty over the adequacy of their clean-up strategies;
- promote greater standardisation of the risk management approaches adopted by funders, land owners and developers.

Regulating environmental protection in respect of contaminated sites

It is imperative that we protect our urban environment from the harm that can be caused by contaminated materials carried in soil, air and water. We must have a strong regulatory system for contaminated land to facilitate environmental protection. It is also, however, important that we have a regulatory system which promotes land regeneration.

In England our industrial legacy suggests that we should be some way ahead of most of our global competitors in the way that we regulate our contaminated land to protect our environment, but somehow we have managed to fall behind. The last Government issued a consultation document called 'Paying for our Past'.[2] This embraced two core principles – that our regulatory system for dealing with contamination should be constructed on the basis that the polluter pays for clean-up. Only if the polluter cannot be found or liability has transferred, should attention turn to third parties such as the current land owner. Second, that the remediation of contaminated land required by a regulator should be to a standard suitable for the use of the land in its environmental setting.

Five years on, this approach is still seen as having many advantages over apparently more stringent approaches which many of our European and North American neighbours manage. However our own development industry has not yet benefited because despite the enactment of the new UK regime in 1995, the system is not expected to come into force until later this year, some four and a half years on. At the same time, there are clear inconsistencies between the new regime governing contaminated land, and existing regulatory systems managing water and waste.

Given the delay in introducing the new system, there should be no excuse for the enforcement bodies not to be ready to take on their new roles. And yet local authorities and the Environment Agency still appear to lack the resources and the training necessary to fulfil their new statutory duties properly.

The European Commission is now considering in some detail whether they should seek to impose common rules on environmental liability for contaminated land management. The difficulty for the UK will be that most other European countries do not have the scale of problem which we face as a result of our industrial past. We therefore need to retain considerable flexibility for the public and private sector to work together in dealing with past contamination. As the condition of land has few cross-border implications, it would seem sensible if most responsibility remained with the Member States on clear grounds of subsidiarity.

2 'Paying for our Past'; DETR (1994)

Recommendation:

- **Resolve conflicts and inconsistencies between the different environmental regulation systems, covering contaminated land, water and waste at the first legislative opportunity. Site owners should only have one set of standards to work to when resolving problems of site contamination. (72)**

Where the Environment Agency is going to be responsible for regulating reclamation schemes within difficult regeneration areas – through a combination of contaminated land, waste and water regulation – it has to recognise that it has responsibilities to help promote regeneration as a part of the public interest. It is a direct stakeholder in that regeneration process. The onus should therefore always be on finding workable solutions and not placing undue obligations upon those seeking to bring about regeneration.

Our recommendations:

- **Establish an Environment Agency 'one-stop shop' service for regulatory and licensing requirements, moving quickly to a position where a single regeneration licence is available, covering all the regulatory requirements for cleaning up a site. (73)**

- **Give land owners greater assurances that the regulators are unlikely to take future action over contaminated sites once remediation schemes have been carried out to an agreed standard. (74)**

The realities of site reclamation (English Partnerships)

Managing development risk: the case for a new national framework

Regulation is not the only issue in managing contaminated sites. Over the last few years, there has a been a growth in initiatives which seek to standardise the process of investigating and managing the risks associated with cleaning up and developing contaminated land. The Royal Institution of Chartered Surveyors (RICS) has introduced a Land Quality Statement for use by both housebuilders and the commercial sector alike. These Statements summarise the status of the site and present the information on the site in a standard format. Organisations like the RICS recognise that the work prepared by technical specialists is often not user friendly to the market which needs a clear and concise synopsis of the issues.

The National House Builders Council (NHBC) has also introduced land quality assessment procedures as part of the standard terms of reference which housebuilders have to follow to gain kitemark recognition for the quality of their housing. At the same time, the insurance industry in the United Kingdom is slowly developing comprehensive management systems which will enable land owners to draw down environmental insurance to cover the possibility of claims from future damage caused by residual pollution, selecting from a wider range of policies than is currently available.

Overall, however, land remediation remains a young science. While the technical approaches required to provide safe clean-up are generally available, we are much more hazy about how we collect and present the information that relates to the risk associated with use of these technologies. The lack of consistency over the measurement and management of risk is one of the main reasons why many developers and investors are not willing to take on contaminated sites, and the public are sometimes unwilling to live on them.

Our recommendation is:

- **Establish a national framework for identifying, managing and communicating the risks that arise throughout the assessment, treatment and after-care of contaminated and previously contaminated sites. (75)**

The framework would look to establish a minimum basis for managing and presenting risk throughout the assessment, treatment and after-care of sites. It would not be prescriptive, in terms of trying to set standard numeric standards or even indicative numeric ranges for assessing different types of risk. Rather, it would provide a quality management approach to dealing with contaminated sites. There is already a considerable amount of guidance in the public domain that could facilitate the rapid delivery of a single coherent framework. The framework must then carry enough weight to incentivise its use.

Once this framework was in place, there would be a strong case for securing even greater consistency in the handling of site information by introducing a form of standardised documentation. More work would be required to test the market appetite, but building on the work of the RICS, the British Standards Institute and private industry, the idea would be to introduce a standard form of Land Condition Statement. The purpose of the Statement would be to ensure that during the sale, purchase and redevelopment of land, all concerned parties had access to the same data-sets and could therefore develop some general agreement between them on the levels of risk associated with that particular site and that particular use. The Statement would travel with the land and, as such, would be dynamic, reflecting the risk at each stage of redevelopment.

Our recommendation:

- **Pilot standardised Land Condition Statements, to provide more certainty and consistency in the management and sale of contaminated and previously contaminated sites. (76)**

The benefits of establishing a national framework for managing and documenting the risks involved in developing contaminated sites would include:

- providing greater confidence to the market-place on the basis of greater consistency and transparency of information;
- easing conveyance of previously contaminated land;
- enabling the insurance market to better assess risks and hence set realistic premiums for cover;
- helping the institutional investor establish some investment risk benchmarks;
- enabling consistent dialogue with the regulators.

Covering the development risk

Once a national risk management framework is in place, other possibilities arise. In our view it is never going to be possible for the Government to provide an absolute assurance that a remediation process has been carried out to a given standard. To do so would open the public sector to all sorts of contingent liabilities which it is totally inappropriate for it to carry. They are the risks which the insurance industry should be carrying and what we need to focus on is ensuring that insurance companies have the confidence to provide suitable products.

NORDHORN, GERMANY: PUTTING THE PAST TO WORK

Nordhorn, a medium sized town in north west Germany, straddling the Dutch border, had been shaped by the textile industry for more than 100 years. But the bankruptcy and closure of two of the three textile factories in the 1970s, and the poisonous legacy of job losses and derelict contaminated land has led the town to diversify and change.

The City of Nordhorn purchased the site of the Povel-van Delden textile factory in 1985. They immediately embarked on an ecological renovation of the central site. In designing their masterplan, the City considered the site's central location as an economic asset rather than a problem. The neighbouring polluted river and canals, which could have been seen as problematic, when cleaned up, also added to the attractiveness of the site. The City has further revitalised the canals and water gardens by connecting the area with colourful bridges, paths and unusually designed green areas. Now nearing completion, the 15 hectare site provides homes within a tranquil and open environment for a successful mixed use, high density (over 200 homes per hectare) neighbourhood of more than 1,000 people, many of whom have been attracted back into the centre from the suburbs.

It should be possible, however, for Government to provide a certification system for the management process. Individual site owners or developers, or, better still, representative bodies for entire sectors, could submit their standard methodological approach. This would then be tested to see that it accorded with the national framework and that all the necessary safeguards were in place. Once the Government was satisfied that this was the case, a kitemark could be given.

The benefits of this form of certification process are that:

- it should give additional confidence to the development and investment market;

- it can be self-financing;
- it need not open the Government up to potential liabilities; the essential difference is that they would be verifying a management method, not validating an end result in terms of the actual condition of a given site.

PROMOTING THE POSSIBILITIES

Our visits to the Ruhr region and Rotterdam, and, in this country, to Bede Island, Leicester and the Greenwich Peninsula, demonstrated that the availability of contaminated or ex-contaminated sites is a development opportunity which can help stitch back together the urban fabric and create value. This short section discusses how we can raise our sight levels.

Education

There are three main educational issues. First, there is education of the public and the end users. The recent creation of a public exhibition in Manchester to celebrate reclaiming land for new uses, shows that contamination can be tackled and made safe, even for residential uses. When presented in the context of the importance of clean land as a limited, finite resource, it is possible to engage public attention, whether it be the schoolchild in the school science laboratory or the prospective house-buyer.

Recommendation:

- **Launch a national campaign to 'clean up our land'. Targets should be set:**

- **for the net reduction of derelict land over the next 5, 10 and 15 years;**
- **to bring all contaminated land back into beneficial use by 2030. (77)**

Second, there is the education of the professional. Although there has been a significant increase in relevant course provision over the last five years, the Government should continue to work with the relevant professional and academic institutions to ensure that skills availability keeps pace with policy development.

Third, there is the education of developers, investors and insurers. There needs to be a regular and accessible national programme of Government backed seminars to increase the knowledge and confidence of these key players in the remediation process.

Research

Our investigations suggest that there is currently a critical gap in the UK research effort to promote innovative sustainable remediation technologies for cleaning up contaminated sites. The lack of adequate field scale research means that too many possible technologies never make it off the laboratory bench. We therefore applaud the recent Government decision to join forces with industry and the UK Research Councils to form a new company, CLAIRE – 'Contaminated Land: Applications in Real Environments' – to bring together site owners, researchers and technology vendors to test out new technologies in the ground.

We believe that, over time, this initiative will prove a major breakthrough for the UK remediation industry. To ensure that CLAIRE is successful, it must be provided with sufficient core funding to enable it to be a serious player. The Research Councils will also need to make commitments to provide significant funding – perhaps £2–3 million per year – for CLAIRE research projects.

A strong commitment to developing innovative technologies is a must; however, taxation rules are limiting progress on innovative regeneration. There is currently an exemption from the landfill tax for waste arising from the reclamation of contaminated land. In an ideal world, this exemption would not need to exist. It is obviously better that waste is not disposed to landfill but is treated on site, for example, through bio-remediation, or through washing and similar technologies. It is also possible that the existence of the exemption is handicapping those companies selling innovative remediation technologies.

The long term goal should be that the exemption from the landfill tax is removed. However, this should not occur until sufficient economic, innovative remediation technologies have been developed. In the interim, the Government should ensure that a higher proportion of landfill tax receipts are directed towards researching these technologies. A tax advantage could also be provided for those owners who make use of these methods.

Prevention

Achieving a target of bringing all contaminated land back into beneficial use by 2030 clearly depends heavily on our ability to prevent new stocks of contaminated land coming on stream in the years ahead. Unfortunately, we know that there are still sites and buildings with contaminating uses dating back to at least the middle of the last century, which are still in use and have not yet come on to the market for reclamation and redevelopment. The new regulatory system will capture those sites which have the potential to cause significant harm but many will remain contaminated for the time being.

We do, however, have a much stronger control over new ground contamination. Other than the necessary disposal of waste to properly managed site areas, there should now be no excuses for allowing the deposit or leakage of contaminated substances into the ground.

Our recommendation is:

- **Enforce a regime of strict liability on site owners who add to the problem of contaminated land, drawing on Integrated Pollution Control and Integrated Pollution Prevention Control regulations. (78)**

IN SUMMARY

Most contaminated land can be turned from liability into asset. It need not be a millstone around the nation's neck. We have the technical expertise to tackle the problems which contamination causes. We now need to ally that expertise with sufficient skilled professionals and adequate public and private resources to start making serious inroads into our unwanted industrial legacy. This will require a clear national political will – in prioritising resources and ensuring all the relevant agencies adopt a proactive approach to securing clean-up. It will also require a stronger commitment from research councils and industry to promote innovative remediation technologies which, in cleaning up our industrial legacy, do not leave an equally difficult legacy for the generations that follow. A twin-track approach to this problem – combining a simplified partnership approach to environmental regulation with a new risk management framework – will unlock the potential of many of our contaminated sites.

SUMMARY OF RECOMMENDATIONS	Responsibility	Timing
Key recommendation		
Establish a national framework for identifying, managing and communicating the risks that arise throughout the assessment, treatment and after-care of contaminated and previously contaminated sites.	DETR and selected partners	By 2001
Other recommendations		
Resolve conflicts and inconsistencies between the different environmental regulation systems, covering contaminated land, water and waste at the first legislative opportunity. Site owners should only have one set of standards to work to when resolving problems of site contamination.	DETR, Environment Agency, local government	By 2002
Establish an Environment Agency 'one-stop shop' service for regulatory and licensing requirements, moving quickly to a position where a single regeneration licence is available, covering all the regulatory requirements for cleaning up a site.	DETR, Environment Agency	By 2001
Give land owners greater assurances that the regulators are unlikely to take future action over contaminated sites once remediation schemes have been carried out to an agreed standard.	Environment Agency, local government	Ongoing
Pilot standardised Land Condition Statements, to provide more certainty and consistency in the management and sale of contaminated and previously contaminated land.	DETR	By 2002

	Responsibility	Timing
Launch a national campaign to 'clean up our land'. Targets should be set: • for the net reduction of derelict land over the next 5, 10 and 15 years; • to bring all contaminated land back into beneficial use by 2030.	DETR	By 2000
Enforce a regime of strict liability on site owners who add to the problem of contaminated land, drawing on Integrated Pollution Control and Integrated Pollution Prevention Control regulations.	Environment Agency, local government	Ongoing

TAKING THE STRATEGIC OPPORTUNITIES

Empty property strategies

We need to place the importance of recycling our existing buildings onto a clear statutory footing. Every local authority should therefore be required to produce and maintain a comprehensive empty property strategy for their area. Although many authorities currently have strategies, these often only relate to local authority housing stock. The strategies need to be comprehensive, covering all market sectors and prioritising the most important opportunities and challenges. Authorities like Southampton and Dundee are already pioneering a proactive approach to tackling empty properties, and we need to bring all authorities up to the standards of the best. This will include creating publicly accessible local database systems for maintaining details of empty and vacant properties.

Recommendation:

- **Give local authorities a statutory duty to maintain an empty property strategy that sets clear targets for reducing levels of vacant stock. There should be firm commitments to take action against owners who refuse to sell their properties or restore them to beneficial use. (79)**

Unpopular areas and low housing demand

In spite of virtually continuous housing shortages from World War II to the mid-1970s, particularly in low income urban communities, there is now clear evidence of housing abandonment within some towns and cities. This can threaten the long term viability of the urban neighbourhoods most affected. The problem is most extensive in council estates in the north and midlands, but exists in inner cities more generally. All tenures are affected in the most acutely declining areas. We visited areas where shops and houses were boarded up and empty derelict sites had been abandoned. This development is occurring alongside a large predicted growth in households and the argued need to build on greenfields.

Social housing that nobody wants to live in (Raissa Page / Format)

A shift in approach could open up real potential for repopulating inner areas. We can:

- build on the best of the initiatives already in train in low income neighbourhoods;
- market social housing to a wide band of the population to raise its value and increase demand;
- give private owners more help in maintaining their property;
- use regeneration projects to attract 'urban pioneers' back into city centres and gradually spread into the surrounding emptying neighbourhoods;
- incentivise social housing tenants who are under-occupying properties to move into smaller properties, where possible, in the same neighbourhood, to free up larger housing to attract families back.

It is not inevitable that inner city areas will continue to lose people, lose control, and lose viability.[4] We suggest a combination of strong management, open access and ongoing reinvestment as the best ways to keep estates working to preserve their value and to maximise their use as affordable housing.

4 'The Slow Death of Great Cities? Urban Abandonment or Urban Renaissance'; Power A. and Mumford K.; Joseph Rowntree Foundation (1999)

Our recommendation:

- **Allocate social housing by a more open system than just demonstrating a strict need to be accommodated. In unpopular areas, available housing should be marketed to other groups, including low to middle income working households and students. (80)**

Historic buildings and neighbourhoods

Historic buildings and townscapes are important assets. However, their full worth and contribution, and indeed their long term futures, can only be realised if the buildings are in productive use. Many developers are put off from undertaking development schemes in older building stock because of technical constraints and the number of regulatory hoops which they have to jump through. These can compound the additional technical, financial and skills barriers which these schemes often impose. It is a very specialist market with relatively few players. Persuading developers to enter the market-place comes down to a combination of skills, attitude, experience and knowledge on the part of those regulating the renewal process, coupled with significant resources.

The evidence we have collected suggests that early negotiation between a developer and conservation interests almost always leads to a higher quality solution. Success depends on the people involved in the process. Conservation bodies are playing an increasingly pivotal role as catalysts for urban regeneration. The expertise of these bodies needs to be exploited to the full, providing them with opportunities to contribute proactively to the renewal process, in partnership with the communities they seek to represent.

Georgetown, Washington D.C.: recycling the buildings and retaining economic prosperity (Martin Crookston)

PIONEERING URBAN LIVING IN THE NORTH WEST: SMITHFIELD BUILDINGS, MANCHESTER

Urban Splash is a young, property development company, specialising in the refurbishment of under-used buildings in the North West and with a commitment to urban regeneration. One of their latest ventures is the Smithfield Buildings in Manchester. This disused department store has been converted to 81 loft style apartments for sale and 21 retail units.

Smithfield is situated in the Northern Quarter of Manchester City Centre, an area historically associated with the textile industry. The development has been a catalyst for entrepreneurial and creative activity, attracting people to live in the area and locate new business.

The majority of the apartments were sold from the original plan. Purchasers were attracted by the open plan warehouse style; designed interior spaces accessed off an attractive central atrium.

The apartments offer a variety of different types of living space with the accent on flexibility. The purchasers are a mixture of all ages, including single professionals, young couples and families.

Smithfield Buildings has demonstrated the demand for this type of residential accommodation and commercial space, giving Urban Splash the confidence to progress with a dozen further schemes, most of them without the need for public subsidy.

Smithfield Buildings, Manchester (Urban Splash)

While over 80% of listed building consents are granted, the process is still felt to be a barrier to success. National and local conservation bodies must work together to find ways of reducing this deterrent effect whilst ensuring quality solutions. At the same time, local planning authorities must improve the quality of their decisions in respect of re-using historic buildings.

Regeneration and conservation policy should be developed in tandem. To this end, English Heritage will have to get much more involved in regeneration structures, particularly by creating a much clearer organisational relationship at a national level with the Department of the Environment, Transport and the Regions and, at a regional level, with the Regional Development Agencies. Heritage issues should also be explicitly covered in regional economic strategies and planning guidance.

There is a tendency for the planning system to treat historic districts as static, considering that the best way to retain the overall character of the historic district is to conserve as much as possible for as long as possible. In reality, blanket conservation can stifle urban regeneration and undermine the long term futures of our historic urban areas. Through the Planning Policy Guidance note which deals with historic buildings, PPG15, we need to build more flexibility into the system, recognising that in replacing some of the less valuable buildings of the past, we may be providing the opportunity for creating the heritage of the future.

Our recommendations are:

- **Introduce new measures to encourage the restoration and use of historic buildings left empty by their owners. These should include revised planning guidance (PPG15), inclusion of heritage issues in regional economic strategies, a review of building regulations and an end to the business rate exemption on empty listed buildings. (81)**
- **Review and enhance the role of civic amenity societies in planning the re-use of historic buildings and in securing regeneration objectives. (82)**

The derelict Hovis Mill in Macclesfield being converted into housing apartments

(Trevor Perry Environmental Images)

The upper rooms

In the past, shopkeepers used the upper floors of their shops to house themselves and their families. In more recent times, however, large numbers of these upstairs units have remained empty. The 1991 English House Condition Survey suggested that there were 26,000 vacant flats above shops, but this only measured the number of existing flats over shops that were currently empty. It is therefore a significant underestimate of the vacant space on upper floors of urban properties. A study produced for the London Planning Advisory Committee in 1998 estimated that some 73,000 additional residential units could be created in London alone from existing vacant and under-used shops and upper floors.[5] Bringing these properties back into use not only creates additional housing, it also attracts a mix of residents back into the commercial hearts of our urban neighbourhoods, creating the critical mass vital to economic and social regeneration. Bringing space back into use in this way actively enhances security by helping to protect against break-ins to commercial premises below.

Figure 11.1: Living over the shop: defining tenancy relationships

Freeholder/retailer

↓

Commercial lease

↓

Housing association

↓

Assured shorthold tenancy

↓

Occupier

Source: Living Over the Shop Project

5 'Dwellings over and in Shops in London'; London Planning Advisory Committee (1998)

Tapping the potential of flats over shops

During the early 1990s there was a succession of initiatives to bring these units back into use. When the Government's own Flats over Shops schemes were evaluated in 1995 they were found to offer good value for money in terms of the costs of conversion and the average level of grant required. The schemes were, however, very expensive when one took into account the amount of time required to negotiate suitable deals with the property owners, who often did not want the hassle of dealing with multiple leases.[6] The work of the Living Over the Shop Project, based at York University, resulted in the welcome introduction of a two-stage legal structure to enable an intermediary housing manager to deal directly with the residential leases. This meant that retailers could manage their relationship with the housing manager through a normal commercial lease, significantly reducing the management burden. Figure 11.1 describes this relationship. It is not, however, clear how many commercial operators are aware of this device or, even if they are aware, are choosing to use it.

CASE STUDY: STOCKTON TOWN CENTRE

At the end of 1997, Stockton City Challenge commissioned Living Over The Shop Ltd to carry out a survey of 286 commercial buildings in Stockton town centre to assess the extent and nature of the vacant space and to calculate the potential dwellings and persons who could realistically be housed in that space. The main outcomes of the survey were that 46% of the buildings had some vacant space and within these over 70% had space suitable for residential use. It was calculated that this space could house up to 500 people in the heart of the town.

Stockton is a free-standing market town with a broad high street and a fair number of well placed historic buildings reflecting its status as a Conservation Area. The town centre is busy during shopping hours, particularly on the days when there is an open market, but after business hours the centre is largely void of activity apart from pub and club life at the weekends. The Council's view, supported by the results of the survey, is that a targeted strategy to bring people back into the town centre as residents will offer vitality to the town.

It is estimated that as much as 80% of retail property is controlled by national companies, owning freeholds or leaseholds.[7] It is therefore critical that the Government works with these major retailers to ensure their properties are being put to beneficial use. Local authorities should be required explicitly to include flats over shops within their Empty Property Strategies and they should regularly survey the capacity that could be provided by flats over shops schemes in their main shopping areas.

Recommendation:

- **Facilitate the conversion of more empty space over shops into flats by providing additional public assistance, including public equity stakes and business rate reductions. (83)**

6 'Evaluation of Flats over Shops'; DETR (1997)

7 Source: Living Over the Shop (1999)

ADDRESSING THE CONSTRAINTS

Value Added Tax

Recent national statistics suggest that 87% of new housing is created through new build and only 13% through conversions.[8] This can at least in part be explained by the fact that people looking to bring existing empty dwellings back into beneficial use soon find themselves up against an odd anomaly. Refurbishment or conversion of existing residential properties carries full VAT at 17.5%. New housebuilding incurs no VAT, nor does conversion of commercial buildings for housing. There is therefore a strong case for harmonising the different rates, preferably by removing VAT on refurbishments or conversions of residential buildings, or introducing zero-rating.

Although this seems a sensible thing to do, constraints imposed by the European Commission may mean that harmonisation is only possible at the intermediate level of 5%. While harmonisation at 5% would increase the costs of developing new dwellings on greenfield sites, it would also affect brownfield development as well. Development schemes on recycled land are already more marginal in commercial terms. The imposition of VAT would therefore increase the costs and, in many cases, increase the need for public subsidy.

Therefore, while VAT harmonisation at 5% would create substantial revenue for the Treasury, a significant amount of that total might be required to increase regeneration funding to tackle the additional costs of development on previously used land.

It is essential that the UK presses the European Commission to enable harmonisation to occur without the need to impose VAT on new build housing development. Only if this is impossible should a 5% rate be considered. In those circumstances, there will need to be a significant lead-in time prior to the introduction of the tax on new build costs, so that developers are not hit by additional costs which they have not accounted for in acquiring land for development. There will also need to be careful consideration of how VAT would apply to new build – to the cost of materials, labour, sales etc., to avoid any unintended double imposition.

Our recommendation:

- **Harmonise VAT rates at a zero rate in respect of new building, and conversions and refurbishments. If harmonisation can only be achieved at a 5% rate, then a significant part of the proceeds should be reinvested in urban regeneration. (84)**

Local taxation

What can we do about the recalcitrant property owner sitting on a vacant property who will not sell the property or bring it back into beneficial use? The owner may well be using the property as collateral for other financial obligations, often perhaps based upon an inflated estimate of the property's value.

Nevertheless, we cannot allow these buildings to undermine the welfare of the wider urban environment. The local authority requires support in using its powers to ensure that such buildings, even if empty, remain in good repair.

Another option, as we explored in the last Chapter, is for the public sector to purchase the buildings and we have presented some options for easing that process.

We can also change the financial equation for the property owner. One means of doing this is through the local taxation system.

We would like to see a tightening of existing Council Tax rules. At present, with some targeted deconstruction or vandalism, owners can make their properties technically uninhabitable, and they then become exempt from Council Tax. We also consider that, in some cases, local authorities

8 'English House Condition Survey 1996'; DETR (1998)

should have the freedom to levy a higher Council Tax rate to reflect the adverse impact which the state of the empty properties is having upon the neighbouring environment. This additional resource would reflect the fact that local authorities are having to carry the cost of dealing with properties and manage the knock-on effects. Fire, vandalism, reduced values in surrounding properties, rubbish dumping, and environmental degradation are all associated impacts which local authorities have to tackle.

Our recommendation is:

- **Extend liability for full payment of Council Tax to all owners of empty homes. Where properties have been empty for over a year, the authority should have discretion to impose a higher charge. (85)**

THE RENAISSANCE FUND

One theme emerges clearly from this Chapter. We have to repair our existing urban fabric as a first priority of regeneration. As a theme, it is central to the principles of sustainability and resource efficiency which underpin our vision for the future of our towns and cities.

Some of the repair work which is required is on the grand scale. It requires large amounts of regeneration funding and the application of the best technical skills.

There are, however, many small gashes that render our urban texture spoilt. Some are buildings – the derelict empty chapel, the old car showroom site and the boarded up shop. Others are under-used spaces – the patch of wasteland on the edge of the housing estate and the disused railway line.

These are problems that members of a local community easily recognise themselves and can do something about. The success of organisations like Development Trusts, Building Preservation Trusts, Groundwork Trusts, Local Wildlife Trusts and the Priority Estates Project demonstrate that, given resources and training, many people care greatly and will give of their own time and effort to improve their own neighbourhoods. The impact of nurturing and encouraging such civic pride goes far beyond the physical results.

One of our key recommendations is therefore:

- **Establish a ten year national programme – The Renaissance Fund – to help repair our towns, whereby community groups and voluntary organisations can access the resources needed to tackle derelict buildings and other eyesores that are spoiling their neighbourhood. (86)**

The Fund would be targeted at 'places' – all sorts of buildings, and 'spaces' – the surrounding environment. Projects might include:

- bringing back into use some housing units over a shop;
- greening over a derelict eyesore or smartening up a decaying building;
- using an empty retail unit to create a community shop or cafe;
- turning a larger empty building into a community centre;
- reclaiming some land to create a new wildlife corridor;
- planting a new area of woodland or some street trees;
- creating a new pocket park with children's play facilities;
- buying some new street furniture;
- creating a new centrepiece for the neighbourhood such as a statue or a piece of civic art.

We propose that £500 million be provided over the next ten years to maintain this Fund. It may be that it could be created in partnership between national and local government and the National Lottery.

The scale of funding for an individual project might range from £1,000 to £250,000. It should provide a mix of capital and revenue funding that takes into account the long term management and maintenance needs of the assets created.

The great advantage of a community-based fund is that it can build links with other government programmes. For example, there could be an opportunity for unemployed people to learn new skills and undertake paid work. There would be opportunities for education, both for young people and under programmes such as the Department for Education and Employment's Adult Learning Programme. The Fund could also provide a good way of getting older people to recycle some of their knowledge and skills.

The Renaissance Fund could help turn the urban renaissance into a national endeavour.

Children ask residents what needs to be improved in Tower Hamlets

(Marcus Rose)

IN SUMMARY

Many valuable buildings – small and large – stand empty at the hearts of our urban communities, often having a disproportionate effect on the overall sense of economic and social decline. There are numerous opportunities to bring many of these properties back into beneficial use. In this Chapter we have focused on historic buildings, social housing and rooms over shops. Within the context of a statutory empty property strategy, local authorities should be equipped to facilitate private developers, and the voluntary and community sector, in recycling urban buildings.

To make the most of our urban assets, we propose a Renaissance Fund to enable community groups to make their own mark in transforming land and buildings from liabilities to urban assets.

SUMMARY OF RECOMMENDATIONS	Responsibility	Timing
Key recommendations		
Give local authorities a statutory duty to maintain an empty property strategy that sets clear targets for reducing levels of vacant stock. There should be firm commitments to take action against owners who refuse to sell their properties or restore them to beneficial use.	DETR, local government	By 2002
Establish a ten year national programme – The Renaissance Fund – to help repair our towns, whereby community groups and voluntary organisations can access the resources needed to tackle derelict buildings and other eyesores that are spoiling their neighbourhood.	DETR, DCMS, National Lottery, RDAs, local government	By 2000
Other recommendations		
Allocate social housing by a more open allocation system than just the strict need to be accommodated. In unpopular areas, available housing should be marketed to other groups, including low to middle income working households and students.	DETR, local authorities	From 2000 onwards
Introduce new measures to encourage the restoration and use of historic buildings left empty by their owners. These should include revised planning guidance (PPG15), inclusion of heritage issues in regional economic strategies, a review of building regulations and an end to the business rate exemption on empty listed buildings.	DETR, English Heritage	By 2000
Review and enhance the role of civic amenity societies in planning the re-use of historic buildings and in securing regeneration objectives.	DCMS, DETR, civic amenity societies	By 2000
Facilitate the conversion of more empty space over shops into flats by providing additional public assistance, including public equity stakes and business rate reductions.	DETR, HM Treasury, Housing Corporation, local authorities	By 2000

	Responsibility	Timing
Harmonise VAT rates at a zero rate in respect of new building, and conversions and refurbishments. If harmonisation can only be achieved at a 5% rate, then a significant part of the proceeds should be reinvested in urban regeneration.	DETR, HM Treasury, HM Customs & Excise	Budget 2000
Extend liability for full payment of Council Tax to all owners of empty homes. Where properties have been empty for over a year, the authority should have discretion to impose a higher charge.	DETR, local authorities	By 2001

PART FOUR

MAKING THE INVESTMENT

12

ATTRACTING PRIVATE INVESTMENT

Unless we can take private sector developers and investors with us, any urban vision will remain just that; an impressive concept with little prospect of leaving the draughtsman's board. Urban regeneration needs to demonstrate a positive return on investment. We will need to overcome two related and powerful obstacles – the well-established dispersed patterns of urban development, and a reluctance among parts of the property industry and the financial markets to develop on and invest in urban brownfield sites.

Public resources will be needed to pump-prime the provision of much larger sums of private investment. There are four main ways of doing this:

- public capital investment in land assembly, infrastructure provision, site clearance etc., delivered in the form of grants or direct expenditure;
- public revenue investment in the management, maintenance and general improvement of urban areas;
- partnering the private sector in joint venture structures by sharing investment costs, risks and rewards;
- the provision of fiscal incentives, whereby the cost to the public sector is usually in the form of revenue foregone.

This first financial chapter describes how the urban land and property investment markets currently work. It then suggests some innovative ways of attracting greater amounts of institutional finance into the development of our towns and cities. It also proposes a range of fiscal measures to stimulate the supply of, and demand for urban land and buildings.

We conclude that:

- an urban renaissance is not going to come cheaply; we have to increase the amount of institutional investment flowing into areas in need of regeneration;
- all public bodies involved in regeneration need to innovate more to achieve increased private investment in urban areas;
- we have to use our taxation system more creatively to increase the demand for and the supply of housing on urban sites.

URBAN PROPERTY INVESTMENT

Understanding existing patterns

The urban property market is made up of many different players, all with different objectives and reasons for developing, holding or investing in property. The majority of these players tend to operate independently from one another. Given the need to specialise in the corporate financial markets and to standardise products to compete in the financial services market, most banks and other lending institutions operate differently in terms of their respective lending to residential and commercial markets. Most surveying firms specialise either in commercial or residential, but rarely both. And most property developers do not tackle more than one sector. Taken together, these divisions tend to act against the interests of urban development, and certainly militate against the creation of mixed use, mixed tenure urban neighbourhoods, and the conversion of existing buildings.

There are two basic scenarios for residential development. The first, and by far the most common English scenario, sees a landowner selling land to a developer who develops homes and sells to owner-occupiers. Under the second scenario, much more typical on the Continent than in this country, a landowner sells land to investors who contract construction companies to build homes which are then held as part of an investment portfolio and let to tenants. There are many variations on both themes but this Chapter is concerned with maximising the flow of finance and the level of urban development activity under both scenarios.

Most residential development under the first scenario is financed through a combination of short term debt and the developer's own cash resources. The debt finance is usually in the form of revolving loans from clearing or merchant banks, repayable within five to seven years. Most volume house-builders want to be out of schemes as soon as possible after completion, making their money by realising profit on the back of gaining planning permission, a modest margin on construction costs and developing on a tide of rising property values.

Under the second scenario, investors are generally reliant on longer term sources of finance. The investor is concerned with the income stream over the entire holding period. Therefore, the quality of the building, the covenant of the tenants and the management costs, combined with the prospects for rental growth and capital appreciation, are the key investment criteria. Outside the M25 and, to a lesser extent, the major metropolitan centres, there has been little appetite among institutional investors for long term market residential investment holdings in urban areas. In the social housing sector, things are very different with housing associations having raised c. £13.5 billion of private money since 1988 to finance residential properties, often in very poor urban areas. This has been the product of well regulated stock management, substantial public funding which has created a subsidised asset base, and a guaranteed income stream, courtesy of housing benefit and demand from statutory entitlement for homeless families and vulnerable adults. The large public subsidy makes long term private investment attractive.

In the commercial property market, the story is a little more promising. Over the last ten years, the number of investors involved in urban regeneration activity has increased, but the market is still cautious in the wake of the property recession at the start of the decade. One survey published

The drive-in restaurant: one of the products of dispersed investment

last year showed that among the many companies not investing in urban regeneration schemes at all, the primary reasons were perceptions of low capital appreciation and low rental growth due to weak occupier demand.[1] These findings were recently backed up by work carried out for English Partnerships which suggested that only about 15% of total property investment each year could be classified as part of a regeneration scheme, highlighting the fact that most investors are choosing less problematic sites.

In general terms, excepting London, institutional investment in property, as a percentage of all investment assets has been declining for the last ten years, and returns are generally better in 'newer' edge-of-town locations. Therefore, relatively little institutional investment is flowing into the regeneration of our towns and cities. Where there is investment, it is concentrated in limited areas of Greater London and the centres of some of our more prosperous metropolitan cities. It is also principally focused on refinancing schemes once they have completed, with the developer having assumed the full development risk. There are therefore large parts of urban England that are off the map when it comes to attracting long term property investment.

Figure 12.1: Declining institutional investment in property

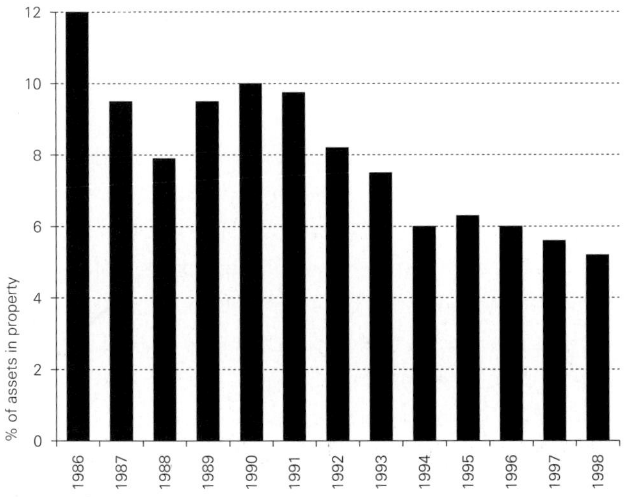

Source: Jones Lang Wootton Fund Management

Prospects for change

There are some encouraging signs of change in investment patterns. First, there is evidence to suggest that perception masks reality. Research by FPD Savills has suggested that residential property appears to have similar diversification potential, (i.e. it enables investors to spread their financial risks), within an investment portfolio, as commercial property. Their conclusion was that residential property had solid potential as part of a wider investment portfolio, with decent returns being achieved through a combination of rental income and increases in the worth of capital assets.[2]

Second, in the months leading up to the publication of our report, two major investment houses, Charterhouse Bank and Schroders, announced their intention to launch investment funds to tap into the private rented housing market. Analysts are predicting that more institutional investors are set to follow. In a context of lower returns from bonds, low interest rates and the availability of more reliable, professional management arrangements for rented properties, residential returns are looking increasingly attractive.

Third, developers and investors are becoming more willing to undertake mixed use development projects. Although to date this has tended to be in substantial projects in central city locations – Broadgate in London, Brindleyplace in Birmingham – once a few more success stories have been established, more providers of debt and equity finance are likely to enter the field.

These changes in investment behaviour are underwritten by the prospects of long term low interest rates and low inflation, combined with a steady increase in house prices in real terms, making property investment in general, and residential property in particular, a relatively attractive option.

These are encouraging signs but they represent only small incursions into the potential role of institutional investment, and the focus of those investors who are getting involved is still very much on wealthier parts of London.

1 'Accessing Private Finance'; University of Ulster on behalf of Royal Institution of Chartered Surveyors (1998)

2 'Beyond HITS: The prospects for further development of residential property investment vehicles'; FPD Savills (1996)

Our consideration now must be how to turn these small signs of change into widespread trends. We cannot secure an urban renaissance on the back of a combination of public investment and short term debt finance alone. We must have the longer term investors involved. Apart from the sheer weight of their potential resources, it is the long term investors who will retain the long term interest in the welfare of an area to protect their investment.

Criteria for intervention

In considering new investment structures and financial incentives for urban regeneration, we are not starting from first base. Over the last three years, English Partnerships has increased the amount of private finance it has leveraged through its regeneration programmes by over 100% to a figure of over £700 million last year. The Urban Development Corporations previously attracted £15.6 billion of private investment and the City Challenges, £4.5 billion. When added to the resources attracted by the social rented sector, these are not insignificant sums.

Ultimately, the financial markets will deliver significant funding for urban development projects provided:

- there is an appropriate balance between the security of their capital, the term of the investment and the rate of return on their investment;
- there is an acceptable spread of risk;
- there is sufficient confidence in the team managing the application of the funding to regeneration projects, and ongoing management costs are acceptable.

For the public sector to get involved, any new funding proposal will need to:

- supply proof of need, in that the proposed investment projects would not proceed without public support;
- attract new sources of private sector funding, thus avoiding displacement from other government investment priorities;
- bring forward regeneration outcomes substantially faster than would occur without government involvement through a different funding approach;
- provide an optimum public investment option, by involving less total investment from the public sector than other public funding options.

With these criteria in mind, we wish to bring forward two sets of proposals for increasing private investment in the process of urban regeneration. The first set of proposals is aimed at improving the flow and increasing the amount of institutional finance. The second set is a range of possible tax measures aimed at increasing both the demand for property in difficult urban locations and the supply of development and investment opportunities to meet that demand.

NEW FUNDING STRUCTURES

Joint public-private long term investment funds

We want to address the market's failure to provide the medium and long term risk capital required by complex area regeneration projects. At present, the public investment that is required to achieve regeneration in these areas tends to be in the form of short term development funding, aimed at tackling immediate project risks and abnormal site costs. The problem with this funding structure is that it does not reflect the real benefits of the total regeneration effort which should be worth a lot more to the private sector over the long term. Each area regeneration scheme is a unique mix of commercial, residential, industrial and public works improvements. These sorts of comprehensive schemes require a capital investment profile, typically over a three to ten year period, and sometimes even longer.

One of the roles which government can play to help attract longer term private investment is to help funders spread their property investment risk more effectively, particularly in respect of what may initially be marginal or high-risk investment opportunities. Our consultation with over 20 major banks, investors, investment groups and companies suggested that pooling public and private funding in long term investment funds could help overcome the following disincentives to regeneration investment:

- the relatively small size of some regeneration projects, which makes investment inefficient from a transaction cost and management perspective;
- lack of sophisticated public sector financial expertise at the local or project level;
- concentration of risk, in geographical terms and in respect of the timing of investment returns;
- perceived vulnerability to local policy changes.

We would like to propose a pooled approach to investment in mixed use schemes, so that investment from the same fund contributes to buildings with different uses within the same regeneration area. The majority of financial institutions are, however, still more comfortable with the concept of single use, as opposed to mixed use investment. Commercial (office, workspace, retail) and residential funds would therefore attract different types of investor and would need to be structured in somewhat different ways, but there are certain criteria which would be common to both:

- the institutional investors will normally expect to receive priority in repayment over any development partners, with the public sector partner taking the ultimate risk position;
- there may have to be some form of public underwriting of letting risk, through use of guarantees and an injection of public equity into the fund, in the form of cash or assets. The public sector would need to recoup this investment from a share in the eventual returns;
- investors will normally want a skilled and well financed private sector development manager involved, both as a significant financial partner and in driving the investment decisions;
- land assembly, land use planning and infrastructure issues must all be dealt with efficiently and up front;
- there would need to be a clearly defined exit route from the fund, for all partners.

With these conditions, joint investment funds could be set up specifically to target portfolios of individual projects across designated Urban Priority Areas, as defined in Chapter 5 of the report. This provides the following advantages:

- Urban Priority Areas will already have been tested and designated as areas of market potential;
- the Priority Areas will already be carrying other advantages – more streamlined planning process, stronger land assembly options, a clear long term masterplan and fiscal incentives, to make them more attractive to institutional funders;
- there will already be a dedicated project management structure in place on the ground in the locality, backed by the commitment of the local authority and other partners;
- it will give confidence of prolonged government investment and priority.

Our recommendation is:

- **Establish national public-private investment funds that can attract at least an additional £1 billion in private investment for area regeneration projects over three years. A minimum of 50% of the resources should be directed at residential portfolios. (87)**

Regional companies and debenture issues

Our second proposal is similar in type but focuses on the regions. We envisage the Regional Development Agencies establishing, probably as partially owned subsidiaries, Regional Investment Companies, structured in the following way:

- the companies would decide in which areas, most probably the Urban Priority Areas, to target their investment;
- they would attract 'subscriptions' in the form of debenture issues from regional institutions, (company and public authority pensions funds, businesses and individual investors), targeting those organisations with a direct interest in the regeneration of the localities likely to be in receipt of the company's investment;
- the RDA would seek an investment/development partner to help manage the fund.

There are some existing examples of locally based investment funds. Greater London Enterprise has recently established a pension fund-backed investment vehicle specifically to undertake development in the East London boroughs. The project is backed by the Newham Council Pension Fund. In Manchester, the Greater Manchester Property Venture Fund was set up by the local authority pension funds in Greater Manchester to invest in property in the region. These investments seek higher returns from greater risk with the added benefit of generating local investment and employment.

These types of initiative have real potential but need the full backing of the relevant Development Agency to create critical mass and momentum. There are also inevitable limitations in pursuing a regional approach:

- outside the south east, there is likely to be an upper size limit in establishing regional investment funds due to the limited financial capacity of the investment organisations which might participate in this sort of venture;
- there will be a limited ability in some of the regions to diversify risk; if the urban property markets go into recession, there are likely to be few places to hide;
- some of the RDAs do not yet have significant assets to contribute, and might thereby require additional central government funding;
- many of the investment opportunities are currently high risk, which means that there will be greater actuarial risk than with a national fund.

Nevertheless, if the Government's regional economic development policy is going to be successful, it will require private sector finance to start making more investment decisions within the regions. The creation of regional investment companies could be one means of achieving this shift.

Our recommendation:

- **Introduce regional regeneration investment companies and funds, to increase the amount of private finance flowing into the regeneration of all the English regions. (88)**

Private finance applications to deliver mixed development projects

The Government has placed a high priority on the need for Public Private Partnership (PPP) schemes and the Private Finance Initiative (PFI) to support capital spending priorities. Health, education, transport and social housing have all been targeted for consideration.

Up to now, there has been insufficient consideration of how these initiatives could be used to deliver more private investment into urban regeneration. It should be possible to structure a housing-based private finance scheme that incentivises the housing provider to take a long term role in meeting wider neighbourhood needs.

The scheme could have any or all of the following attributes:

- the transfer, renewal and subsequent management and maintenance of existing local authority housing stock;
- acquisition and renewal of derelict owner-occupied housing;
- provision of rented workspace and community facilities;
- provision of utilities (e.g. Combined Heat and Power (CHP) schemes, telecommunications etc.);
- other public private partnership financing options – including schools, transport and health facilities.

By insisting on more than just the provision of housing units, this type of scheme could provide scope for greater equity gains for private sector investors by, for example, creating a more desirable location out of a marginal housing estate. This could work particularly well where there is the need for partial redevelopment of the area. For example, if a local authority estate contains 1,000 houses with a 15% void rate, and a problem of low demand and social stigma, there may be scope to procure from a private sector provider a blend of refurbishment for affordable rent, private market rent and for sale, as well as demolition/new build for rent and for sale. The provider, who could be a private developer, local housing company or housing association, would need to manage the regenerated area in a way that makes it a desirable location, so that they gain from the demand and values generated. This approach has already worked in Rochdale, Liverpool, Newcastle and Manchester, in areas where the prospects of positive value were extremely limited.

In putting forward this approach we would stress that, to secure a return, standards would have to be at least as high as a more traditional public sector-led renewal process. The development companies or housing associations would have to comply with a well defined masterplan and design guidelines.

Our recommendation:

Pilot an estate renewal project and a more general area regeneration project through the Private Finance Initiative. (89)

The private rented housing sector: introducing the REIT-petite

A healthy private rented housing sector is a 'must have' for any ambitious European city wanting to benefit from the free flows of labour across the European Community. The UK private rented sector remains at a dangerously low ebb, at only 10% of the housing market, on a par with Ireland, half the provision of France and only a quarter of the United States.[3]

The case for and against public intervention in expanding the private rented market has been argued many times over. The principal problem is one of massive inertia. It is difficult to secure high enough rates of return for most private sector investors. In many areas, the required rents are higher than the rate suggested by market demand. The market ebbs and flows on a tide of small landlords but, in overall terms, it is pretty much stalled. Indeed, there is some evidence that, without public intervention, the market share of the private rented sector will soon move into renewed decline as landlords cash in their equity on the back of a rising property market.

To date, the private rental sector has not easily attracted large scale private investment without government assistance. There is heavy up-front investment, no certainty of long term equity growth in real terms, and outside London and the south east, relatively weak demand. Forty-eight per cent of landlords who own rented property only have one unit. Given the size of the housing market, and the low private rented sector share, government intervention is needed to make significant changes which could attract large scale investment from institutional investors.

3 'Hovels to High Rise'; Power A. (1993)

BOSTON GETS THE POINT: A PARTNERSHIP APPROACH TO REGENERATING HOUSING

Columbia Point was infamous: a poor public housing estate disrupted by drugs and violence, the buildings in disrepair, residents marginalised, and only 350 of the 1,500 units occupied. The estate was a huge burden on the Boston Housing Authority.

With residents' encouragement, the Authority took the unique step of transferring the ownership and management of the area to an innovative 50:50 joint venture partnership of private developer Corcoran Mullins Jennison Inc. and a residents' task force.

Development costs of $250 million were financed by a package of private and public loans, public grants and private equity, including tax credits. With the site went the condition that 400 units must remain as affordable housing. The partnership, not the public purse, would support affordable rent levels following the high public reinvestment.

A mixture of demolition, new build and restyling opened up the site up to the waterfront, improved layout creating a better community dynamic, and a complete change of image – even the trademark yellow bricks were dyed red to signify the change in fortunes. Boulevards, green spaces, shopping and leisure facilities, and high quality shared amenities were part of the radically upgraded and more professionally managed environment. A new name, Harbor Point, completed the rebranding.

Original Columbia Point residents were guaranteed a home in the new development, but a key goal was to establish a mixed community linked to the surroundings. The subsidised units are deliberately mixed throughout the site and are indistinguishable externally from those attracting full rents.

Harbor Point, Boston USA

The last Government was sufficiently convinced about the merits of intervention to introduce a special financial instrument for attracting institutional investment into the sector – the Housing Investment Trust (HIT). The proposal was for a company whose shares could be bought and sold on the Stock Exchange and which would distribute most of its income to private investors in rented housing.

A HIT was designed to solve a number of problems faced by putative investors investing in property.

- Improve liquidity: Property is an illiquid asset; by investing in a property unit investment fund, investors would not need to sell the underlying asset; rather, they could trade their shares in the HIT.
- Reduce overheads: Property management is perceived to be costly but costs per unit can be reduced within a large portfolio where disciplined control and administration processes are applied. Possibilities include outsourcing the management to specialist agencies or housing associations.
- Increase the potential return: The HIT was to be virtually tax transparent, aimed at levelling the playing field between owner occupation and private renting.

Unfortunately, changes to tax rules in 1997 inadvertently undermined the potential tax transparency of the HIT. Furthermore, a survey undertaken by Coopers and Lybrand in early 1998 indicated that other factors such as the onerous Stock Exchange rules and lack of past performance data also deterred investment.[4]

There is probably no point in attempting to resuscitate HITS. We need to clear the decks and start again. We would recommend a new instrument, based on a more limited version of the US Real Estate Investment Trust (REIT) model, offering sufficient yields to investors in private rented residential property, reasonable set-up and management costs for fund managers and reasonable rents for tenants.

4 'Housing Investment Trusts: Moving into the Millennium – the need for change'; Coopers and Lybrand (1998)

RE-INVIGORATING PRIVATE RENTING: CASPAR TO SHOW THE WAY

CASPAR (City-centre Apartments for Single People at Affordable Rents), is a pilot project sponsored by the Joseph Rowntree Foundation, designed to demonstrate to private investors and local authorities that private rented accommodation in city centre areas makes both economic and social sense.

The Joseph Rowntree Foundation believes that CASPAR will show that there is a pent-up market demand for affordable one and two bedroom rented apartments and further demonstrate that a satisfactory return can be achieved by institutional investors from residential property for rent. It is expected that the project will also act as an example of how inward movements of middle income, single people to the city centre can be facilitated, attracting people and money into areas that have lost both in recent years.

Forty-six CASPAR apartments are being built in central Birmingham on derelict land formerly used as a car park. A further 45 high quality flats for single people are being built as part of the redevelopment of a central car park on a half acre site in Leeds. Rents are expected to be about £100 per week.

The key feature of the new trusts will need to be full tax transparency. The trust itself should not pay tax, but tax liability should fall upon the owners, (investors or shareholders), at the point where the REIT shows a long term return. There should also be minimum limiting regulations in terms of the size of the trusts or the individual investments.

Recommendation:

- **Introduce a new financial instrument for attracting institutional investment into the residential private rented market. (90)**

FISCAL MEASURES

In comparison with countries such as the United States, Germany and Eire, the UK is very conservative in the way it uses its fiscal system to alter patterns of behaviour in respect of developing, investing in, owning and occupying property. In Chapter 9 we focused on use of economic instruments to discourage anti-urban development patterns. In this Chapter, the accent is on positive incentives to attract more urban development.

Recommendation:

- **Introduce a package of tax measures, providing incentives for developers, investors, small landlords, owner-occupiers and tenants to contribute to the regeneration of urban sites and buildings that would not otherwise be developed. (91)**

Chicago: pioneered the use of fiscal incentives in regeneration (Martin Crookston)

The Task Force has been working with KPMG and an expert advisory group to consider a full range of taxation options which might help kick-start our urban property market in areas where it is currently struggling. Over 50 different measures were subjected to tests in terms of their potential to influence market behaviour and their overall effectiveness, practicality and acceptability. The measures which survived these tests are presented in this section. None of them are without difficulties but they all have some merit. We hope that some of them can be introduced. We need a wider national debate about how our taxation system could be used to support government urban policy objectives.

Most of the tax measures we are proposing would have to be restricted to designated areas. This is the only way of sensibly controlling costs to the Treasury and avoiding too much free-riding. Nevertheless, in accordance with the designation of Urban Priority Areas set out in Chapter 5, the onus should be on local authorities and area regeneration partnerships to select which measures would be most appropriate for their regeneration areas and then make the economic case to government.

The principle of area differences in the application of national tax measures is not new, the Enterprise Zones being a case in point. We are, however, taking the concept further by extending the principle of differential rates to individual householders.

To test the potential impact of different measures, we selected some real case studies based upon the typical types of area where fiscal measures might be beneficial as part of a broader regeneration approach:

Inner-urban commercial area: Bold Street/Duke Street, Liverpool

Regional or satellite town centre: Batley City Challenge area

Peripheral town: Whitehaven, Cumbria

Inner-urban residential area: Blackburn City Challenge area

Tertiary retail/commercial area: Harlesden town centre, London

The outcomes of these case studies are reflected in the measures we propose below.

Stimulating supply

Developers

Incentivising developers through the taxation system to target their efforts at particular areas is not simple. First, we can provide whatever incentives we like but if there is insufficient demand for the end product, then the developer is not going to be interested. That is why we have placed so much emphasis in this report on addressing demand as well as supply. Second, developers are already able to obtain corporation tax deductions for practically all of their development costs regardless of where they develop, which reduces the scope for intervention.

Along with our proposal for harmonisation of VAT, covered in Chapter 10, we would put forward the following options.

First, we consider that there is scope for making it easier for developers to build up banks of brownfield land, so that they can phase their development activity with confidence. To assist this, we would advocate:

- The removal or reduction of stamp duty on property acquisitions within designated Urban Priority Areas.
- The introduction of a form of stock relief for developers by allowing them to defer corporation tax on brownfield site acquisitions for a period of up to five years.

Batley: a regenerating town that may benefit from fiscal incentives for developers (English Partnerships)

MAKING PUBLIC EXPENDITURE AND ASSETS WORK HARDER

Public investment is critical in attracting private investment into difficult urban areas. Through land assembly and the provision of infrastructure and services, it can carve out development opportunities that would not otherwise exist. Through the targeted application of funding to individual developers, it can make a project that would not otherwise stack up, a viable proposition. If the public sector does not use sufficient investment to maintain the value of all the previous investment, then the costs of dealing with the physical and social deterioration that will inevitably result, will fall to the public sector alone. The private sector will rarely find sound commercial reasons for picking up the pieces of under-investment.

The Chancellor of the Exchequer recognised the importance of this principle last summer in his statement, 'Fiscal Policy: current and capital spending'.[3] Reflecting on the fact that public investment had fallen as a percentage of government expenditure from 10% in the 1960s to just 3% towards the end of the 1990s, he spoke of, "...ending the discrimination against investment", which was inherent in the public finance system. Instead, to adopt the Chancellor's language, "we need to create the right incentives for public investment and for making the best use of public assets."

If, however, public and private investment are to work together to raise prevailing property values within declining areas, it means that the public investment must be used in a way which facilitates a positive market response. The accent

Investing in Civic Buildings: Reykjavik City Hall (Dennis Gilbert)

3 HM Treasury (1998)

should be on optimising the timing and targeting of public investment to hit points in the market cycle when private investors and developers can maximise their return. These sorts of decisions cannot be managed from Whitehall on the basis of a three year spending cycle. They can only be resolved within the context of long term area investment strategies.

There is a raft of government spending programmes which impact directly on urban life – crime prevention, educational achievement, health reform, welfare benefits – which will influence people's decisions about where they live, work and invest. Over the time we have been working, the Government has announced special urban initiatives in respect of education and crime. These are welcome. In addition, although they lack a proper sense of local integration, the resources bound up in Health Action Zones, Education Action Zones and Employment Zones will also benefit urban communities. To ensure this prioritisation happens more widely, all the relevant government expenditure departments need to be operating to the same set of priorities:

- testing their expenditure priorities and commitments to ensure that they are supporting urban regeneration objectives;
- making sure that revenue provision is supporting capital investment, and vice versa;
- maximising local flexibility over how public resources are spent in support of comprehensive local regeneration strategies;
- tailoring public investment programmes to make them attractive to the local partnerships, private developers and investors who will deliver regeneration.

In addition, all public bodies need to be considering the impact of their own asset management on the urban environment. In recent years, we have seen positive examples of government organisations – the Inland Revenue in Nottingham, Customs & Excise in Salford, and the Department for Education and Employment in Sheffield – using their own asset strength to facilitate the regeneration process. This needs to be extended to all tiers of government. A significant amount of public resource – perhaps as much as £5 billion each year – is spent on the development and management of public buildings. And yet the public sector is not giving a clear lead on the strategic significance and quality of these buildings, ranging from the town hall to the primary school. Too often, we are opting for the cheapest and least intelligent designs, and yet these buildings should be a source of civic pride.

Looking ahead, 'urban renaissance' needs to be considered as one of the Government-wide objectives on which the next comprehensive review of public spending is anchored. In the interim, we would like to see urban renaissance objectives included in the revisions of all the relevant Public Service Agreements (PSAs) between departments and the Treasury as the framework for their ongoing spending decisions. Certainly, following the next Comprehensive Spending Review, there is a strong case for introducing a cross-departmental Urban Renaissance Public Service Agreement, to operate as part of the new family of PSAs being developed for issues which require concerted Government-wide action.

Recommendations:

- **Include the objective of an urban renaissance in the terms of reference for the 2001 Comprehensive Spending Review which will determine public expenditure priorities for the following three years. (92)**
- **Amend the Public Service Agreements set for government departments to include urban renaissance objectives. A single 'Urban Renaissance Public Service Agreement' should be developed to operate across Whitehall following the 2001 Spending Review. (93)**
- **All significant public buildings should be subject to a design competition, adequately funded from the public purse. (94)**

LOCAL GOVERNMENT FINANCE

We have one of the most centralised systems of local government finance among Western democracies. In most European Union countries and under the federal systems of North America, the individual municipality enjoys much greater freedom over what money is raised in their area, through taxation and charges.

Local authorities in England spend about £50 billion each year on their main statutory services. Over 75% of the resources required to sustain this level of expenditure are allocated nationally.[4]

This degree of national control cuts both ways. On the one hand, it provides the potential for progressive redistribution, which is one of the ways of avoiding ghettoisation of our cities. Thus, for example, any proposal involving the total devolution of our non-domestic rating system to local authorities would be condemning some very deprived areas to a serious loss of resources. On the other hand, if we do not give local authorities some additional freedoms, then we undermine their democratic role and stifle local innovation to meet local needs.

Figure 13.1: Percentage of local government revenues raised through local taxation in 1995

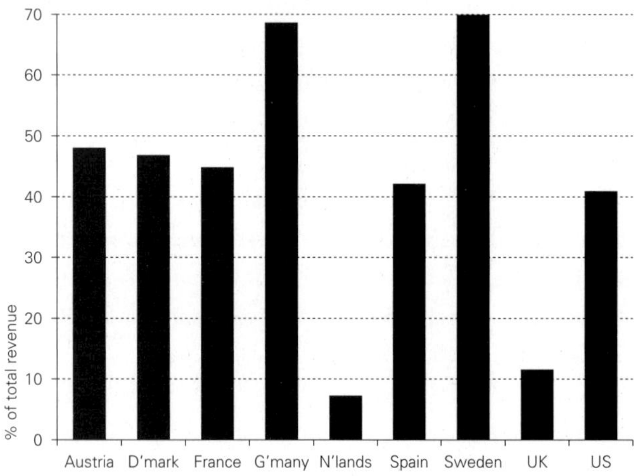

Source: OECD revenue statistics (1998)

We therefore need to recognise adequately the spending needs of local authorities in allocating national funding while at the same time giving local authorities some more flexibility to levy additional resources for specific urban regeneration and management purposes.

Revenue expenditure

The basic expenditure requirement of local authorities should be determined by a need to spend that reflects the whole basket of conditions that exist in their individual areas. The crucial question is whether the current approach to assessing need sufficiently reflects the expenditure requirements of our urban areas. We would suggest that there are a number of reasons why it does not:

- there is no explicit recognition of the management implications of maintaining declining urban areas where there are large tracts of derelict, vacant or under-used land and buildings and widespread neglect by land and property owners;
- the needs indicators used in the Standard Spending Assessment formula do not adequately reflect the poor 'quality of life' currently offered by many urban districts;
- while there is recognition of the service implications of sparse population within rural areas; there is arguably insufficient recognition of the inherent complexities of delivering services within denser, built-up areas with an intense mix of activities;
- larger numbers of low income households live in urban areas, involving greater reliance on public services; migration patterns reproduce this cycle, which leaves inner city authorities serving a disproportionate share of the poorest citizens.

The difficulties which many urban authorities face in meeting basic spending needs are reflected in their Council Tax rates. While some of this differential is explained by differences in local authority financial management performance and the costs of servicing debts, the overall

4 DETR Annual Report (1999)

message is clear. The average Council Tax for the six major central metropolitan districts is £947 for a Band D property, compared to an average of £878 across the metropolitan districts and £792 in the shire areas. London authorities generally manage to set lower rates, but authorities in some of the more deprived London areas such as Hackney, Haringey, Camden, Southwark and Islington are charging some of the highest rates within Greater London.

Although the Council Tax rates are highest in metropolitan areas, the average Council Tax is in general slightly lower, because over 85% of dwellings are in Bands A–C for valuation purposes. This means less revenue per household for the authorities in question. Although this lower tax yield is in part compensated for by the amount of Government grant these areas receive, it means that any problems with the funding formula, in failing fully to reflect urban spending needs, are exacerbated.

Having recently set three year Standard Spending Assessment totals for local authorities, the Government has announced a Revenue Grant Distribution Review, to re-consider the whole basis on which local authority revenue funding is allocated.

Recommendation:

- **Review the spending formula used to allocate central resources to local government so that it adequately reflects the financial needs of urban authorities in managing and maintaining their areas. (95)**

PUTTING MAINSTREAM FUNDING TO WORK: COMMUNITY-LED REGENERATION IN SANDTOWN AND WINCHESTER, WEST BALTIMORE

In Sandtown and Winchester, the neighbourhoods' vital statistics are hung in the community centre boardroom:

Population – 10,305.
Residents living in poverty – 49%.
Families with income below $5,000 – 27%.
Adults not in labour force – 50%.
Housing units in sub-standard condition – 79%.
Families paying greater than 30% of income in rent – 50%.
Owner-occupied homes – 20%.
Individuals without high-school diploma – 44%.
Women with no pre-natal care – 50%.
Residents with no health insurance – 50%.

But things are changing. In 1991, the residents of Sandtown and Winchester joined up with James Rouse's Enterprise Foundation and the City of Baltimore to 'transform the community and prove that inner-city communities can be saved'. Communities Building in Partnership (CBP) was born.

Physical regeneration has started with the housing. Six hundred vacant properties have been renovated to date. Seventy five per cent have been bought by Sandtown-Winchester residents; the remainder by ex-Sandtown residents attracted back by its now brighter prospects.

At community instigation, this has been coupled with a significant package of family-oriented social programmes, aiming to address education and heath needs from pre-school through to the elderly, as well as practical support for single-parent families and a tough approach to youth 'life skills' activity. Funded almost exclusively from re-packaging mainstream funding, resources are geared-up significantly by tapping into local skills, volunteers and a strong ethos of 'once you've gained, you give back to others'.

Investing in quality: a neighbourhood arcade in Slachthuisplein, The Hague

Capital funding

Following the Local Government White Paper, published last year, the Government is committed to providing the bulk of central government capital support through a single pot of funding which cuts across government departmental boundaries. This will not be implemented before the financial year 2001/02 although a single pot for housing capital resources will be provided sooner. This change to the capital finance system will allow local authorities to take greater responsibility for the internal allocation of their resources among services and, as a consequence, it will make it much easier for those same authorities to target expenditure on tackling particular regeneration priorities.

These measures should represent just the start of liberating local authorities from some of the restrictions that have been placed on them over the last two decades. We would also wish to see a continued increase in freedoms over the use of capital receipts, including for further housing disposals, and a greater ability for local authorities to use their remaining assets to raise additional finance. This could include, as we set out in Chapters 5 and 12, contributing their assets to joint public-private investment funds and companies.

To the extent that individual capital funding allocations will remain, it is essential that these support urban regeneration objectives. We need to move away from simplistic 'per capita' allocation systems which still underpin many individual capital funding programmes, and move to systems which more adequately reflect the scale of problems in deprived urban areas.

We must also escape funding formulae based on historic patterns, tying some of the poorest authorities to low capital and low revenue regimes.

In particular, given the extent to which the quality of education influences locational decisions for many households, the Department for Education and Employment must ensure that its capital programmes support inner urban schools in the following ways:

- adopting a more forward looking approach to new schools provision for new urban communities, so that the facilities come on stream early in the development process;
- not agreeing to new school provision or expansions in suburban locations without first undertaking a far reaching impact study of how the provision will affect the welfare of nearby inner schools;
- ensuring that the resources for new schools or school extensions are sufficient to ensure high quality, long lasting design.

Our recommendations are:

- **Extend government commitments to capital finance allocations against local spending strategies so they go beyond the definite plans of the three Public Expenditure Survey years. (96)**
- **Independently review the funding allocations, policies and formulas for school buildings, to produce proposals for accommodating future increases in pupil numbers in high quality facilities in regenerating urban areas. (97)**

Raising additional local revenue

The current Government has indicated a willingness to consider a degree of differentiation between local authorities in terms of their ability to levy additional revenue, most notably:

- by recycling traffic congestion and workspace parking charges;
- by enabling some authorities to levy up to an extra 5% on local business rates, phased over time, for local purposes.

Of equal interest, however, is enabling local authorities to retain and recycle revenue, rather than necessarily just raising more from existing residents and businesses. In Chapter 4, we advocated the Town Improvement Zone model for business and city centre districts. We were also impressed on our visit to the United States by a revenue retention scheme operated in a number of US cities in partnership with the Federal Government.

Under the Tax Increment Financing (TIF) scheme, these cities have designated a number of regeneration areas which are being redeveloped through a mix of housing and commercial facilities. The city authorities measured the local property tax take – from homes and businesses – being generated in these deprived areas prior to regeneration. They then agreed with Federal Government that this estimated revenue would be treated in the normal way, but that any increase in revenue generated by the regeneration process could, for a set period, be retained by the municipality and recycled for the benefit of the designated area. Some of the resource is also assigned back to private developers to use as security in raising further local capital to finance development in the regeneration area.

We believe that this approach has much to commend it, and could be applied to Urban Priority Areas, in particular to pay for management and maintenance of the regenerated area, and additional community facilities. The scheme would cost the Government only that increase in revenue which was a direct result of displacement of activities from outside the Priority Area.

Our recommendation:

- **Allow local authorities to retain a proportion of additional revenue generated from Council Tax and business rates as a result of regeneration in designated Urban Priority Areas. The retained resources should be recycled into the management and maintenance of the area. (98)**

THE GOVERNMENT'S REGENERATION PROGRAMMES

The big numbers

Following the Government's Comprehensive Spending Review, last year's public expenditure settlement heralded good news for the regeneration of our towns and cities. For the first time in many years, the Government promised to increase its regeneration expenditure over each of the next three years. In real terms, however, the increase in expenditure only means that by 2001/02 we will have just overtaken the amount that the previous Government was spending in 1993/94.

Figure 13.2: Government regeneration expenditure (1993–2002)

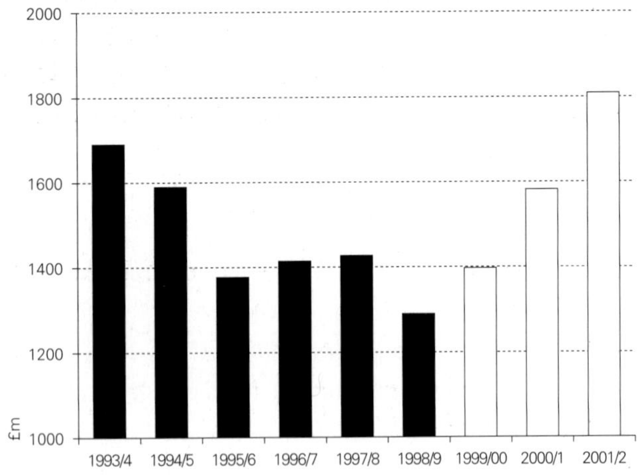

Source: DETR annual report (1999)

The Comprehensive Spending Review has set expenditure totals for the next three years. If we are to avoid a continuing deterioration of the value of our urban capital assets, then greater public investment in urban regeneration is going to be needed. As we argued in Chapter 5, the concentrated application of public resources to pay for integrated economic, social and physical renewal programmes in Priority Areas offers us the best chance of maximising private investment and securing lasting change which becomes self-sustaining. The Urban Development Corporations and City Challenges instigated this targeted approach. The Single Regeneration Budget has built on their precedent. It is therefore likely that an expanded, more integrated SRB programme will provide the main source of investment for the regeneration programmes operating within the Urban Priority Areas we described in earlier Chapters of the report.

An important question is how area regeneration funding will relate to the provision of new housing on recycled land. Over the last few years, scrutiny of the output figures of the different regeneration programmes suggests that around 30% of housing on recycled land has needed some form of public funding assistance. To secure an increase in the proportion of brownfield housing in circumstances where the complexity of redeveloping these sites is likely to increase as the easier sites are redeveloped, will require an increase in public funding coupled with fiscal incentives for greater public investment.

We estimate that there will be a need to fund approximately an additional 10,000 units per year if the Government is to meet a 60% target for accommodating new housing by recycling land and buildings over a 10, or even a 25 year period. Assuming that the amount of gap funding required follows historic trends of an average £15,000 per unit, this suggests an additional funding need of at least £150 million per annum.

Local authorities, private developers, housing associations and local regeneration partnerships must therefore be provided with sufficient additional regeneration funding to help the Government meet its brownfield housing target and to ensure that the housing is developed within well managed, high quality environments.

Programme management

Towards an integrated approach

Regional Development Agencies have inherited two main funding programmes – most of English Partnerships' Investment Fund, which covers the regeneration of land and buildings, and the Single Regeneration Budget Challenge Fund, which mainly funds area-based mixed economic, social and physical regeneration projects. With the advent of the RDAs there is little case for retaining two separate programmes. It causes headaches for local regeneration partnerships and private developers, in knowing how to obtain what resources. To facilitate the provision of block funding to local regeneration partnerships for integrated strategies, these two programmes need to be integrated as soon as possible.

Our recommendation is:

- **Combine the Single Regeneration Budget Challenge Fund and most of the land and property funding inherited from English Partnerships to create a single regional funding pot for area regeneration. (99)**

Restoring the Felaw Maltings, Ipswich Wet Dock (Ipswich Council)

ON THE WATERFRONT: IPSWICH WET DOCK

Built in the 1840s and at the time the biggest in Europe, Ipswich Wet Dock has been in continual use for more than 150 years. During the 1980s however, the Dock began to decline and by the end of the decade there were few traces of the Wet Dock's glory days as one of the international trading points of England.

Today, Ipswich Wet Dock has a future which may even exceed its past. The evolutionary change of the early 1990s, which saw offices, pubs, restaurants and a marina take up some of the slack from the contracting dock activities, has been given an added impetus by the allocation of first round funding from the Single Regeneration Budget and English Partnerships' subsequent investment in land purchase and preparation.

Today, there are four major schemes. The biggest is Felaw Street Maltings, a large listed building that visually dominates the waterfront. It has been refurbished to house the principal business centre for Suffolk. This includes Suffolk TEC, a local enterprise agency, a Higher Educational Business School, Suffolk Chamber of Commerce and a substantial private sector company in a 100,000 sq. ft. conversion.

Bellway Homes is currently building waterfront flats. There are also proposals to extend arts and waterfront exhibitions along the waterside. This summer, the Wet Dock is the venue for the third annual Maritime Ipswich Festival, which attracts over 30,000 visitors to a waterfront event.

By adopting a long term regeneration approach, the town should ensure occupancy and use of the dock area for at least another 150 years.

In terms of establishing long term commitments to area-based regeneration, as we stated in Chapter 5 we would like to see the Development Agencies move quickly towards establishing long term strategic regeneration plans with local authorities and regeneration partnerships. Greater amounts of regeneration funding should be flowing into local programmes on the basis of proactive strategies such as those being produced by New Commitment to Regeneration pathfinders, and less allocated reactively on the basis of unrelated project applications. This will mean a significant review of how programmes such as the Single Regeneration Budget operate, whereby an over-emphasis on ex-ante output estimates, individual project appraisal, match funding requirements and static, competitive application deadlines, rules out many opportunities for local innovation and risk-taking.

To reduce these obstacles, the Government will need to sign up to long term funding commitments for area-based strategies, with the funding to be delivered to local regeneration partnerships through the RDAs in the form of block funds, giving local partnerships maximum discretion over how and when resources are spent on different constituent projects. Some of the funding commitments will need to be for ten years or more.

Our recommendation is therefore:

- **Give Regional Development Agencies (RDAs) the freedom to establish flexible area regeneration funding programmes over ten years or more, with a clear funding bank established for the full period. (100)**

Getting the phasing right

Too many previous funding regimes – among them City Challenge, City Grant and, to a lesser extent, the more recent SRB Challenge Fund – have adopted funding timescales that have more to do with central government accounting requirements than with the optimum delivery requirements of a regeneration project. For example, City Challenge provided the same amount of money to each of the projects it funded, regardless of their funding needs. SRB projects are limited to a maximum time period of seven years. We consider that statutory funding should be tailored to fit the needs of a project, not the other way around.

The physical development components of urban regeneration projects tend to fall into three broad phases:

- start-up; which is about constructing the partnership, consulting local residents, building capacity amongst the partners, undertaking feasibility work, getting the masterplan right, appointing specialists, obtaining permissions and generally creating the conditions for investment; this phase might typically take up to two years;
- development works; the main phase of the project when the development is actually undertaken, including reclamation, infrastructure, servicing and building construction;
- managing the outcome; this is about avoiding a cliff-edge when the development team finish their work; ensuring that there is continuity of some staff and resources after the project to maintain the results.

In the past, most government programmes have tended to focus the timing of resources on the development phase with little regard for what needs to come before or after. For example, English Partnerships were statutorily bound only to provide capital funding for development despite the fact that many of their schemes placed long term additional management and maintenance burdens on local authorities.

The availability and timing of private finance and public funding streams must be planned to come together to guarantee a successful mixed use, mixed tenure development. Otherwise, the private housing will be developed in response to the market, and social housing when funding is allocated as part of grant programmes. Schools will only be built when pupil numbers provide justification. Commercial and retail facilities require sufficient spending power in the local area to sustain them. Each of these elements need to happen together, and public funding should be sufficiently flexible to subsidise the commercial activity and services until the population is in place.

All the statutory bodies responsible for funding regeneration schemes need to ensure:

- adequate provision for feasibility work and up-front design investment;
- funding timescales which are realistic and which have a phased exit strategy;
- sufficient resources to deliver the necessary aftercare of the regenerated area.

Increasing efficiency

There is a more general issue about efficiency in the regeneration funding process. The main way of improving efficiency is to reduce the number of ingredients in the project funding cocktail. We found projects where the project delivery team spends much of their time juggling the demands of English Partnerships, the SRB Challenge Fund, the Government Office European Structural Funds team, the Housing Corporation and several National Lottery bodies. There is therefore an urgent need to review the RDA inheritance of funding programmes, plus European funding, and bring forward a set of proposals to reduce the burdens which are placed on private sector applicants and others in seeking public funding.

Our recommendation:

- **Regional Development Agencies should offer a 'one-stop shop' project appraisal service for applicants that cuts across requirements of individual funding programmes. (101)**

GREENWICH WATERFRONT DEVELOPMENT PARTNERSHIP: RESOURCING AREA REGENERATION

The Greenwich Waterfront Development Partnership is an equal partnership of Council, community and business. Its aim is the regeneration of seven miles of Waterfront area in the northern part of the Borough of Greenwich.

Since its foundation in 1992, the Partnership has had to challenge a legacy of economic and industrial decline. Its area included a thousand acres of derelict land, much of it contaminated. Transport links were poor. There was heavy unemployment. The area needed public sector resources to improve its fitness to compete for private investment.

The Partnership has had to combine different sources of public funding. The area now benefits from five distinct Single Regeneration Budget (SRB) programmes, funding from the Government's Urban Regeneration Agency, English Partnerships, from the European Union's KONVER programme for areas suffering from the economic effects of loss of defence industry jobs, and successful Lottery bids.

The SRB programmes are managed by arms length agencies, each constituted from Council, community and business partners. In Woolwich, for example, the Woolwich Development Agency manages an integrated programme of business development, town centre improvement, housing renewal and provision of education, training and community support. Its £25 million of SRB resources has been used to lever a further £75 million, including significant private sector funding.

The Greenwich Waterside Development Partnership demonstrates the value of a long term strategic approach to area regeneration based on partnership and deploying all available resources to achieve clearly defined objectives.

PART FIVE

SUSTAINING THE RENAISSANCE

These objectives will have to be achieved in the context of a fast evolving global urban geography. We are now at least 25 years into the transition from a carbon-based industrial economy to a silicon-based information economy. We do not know how long this latest wave of global economic development will continue but we do know that our towns' and cities' ability to respond to the opportunities of the information era will determine the prosperity and quality of life enjoyed by their citizens.

Every English town and city will have a role in creating an urban renaissance. London's status as a world city must be protected and strengthened. Our major regional cities such as Newcastle, Birmingham, Manchester and Leeds must become genuine regional capitals, winning investment for themselves and their hinterlands. Smaller towns and cities must forge a clear economic identity, retaining and attracting population and workforce by the quality of life they offer.

How our own towns and cities fare will depend in part upon the success of national economic and social policy, and on the strength of local leadership and strategic thinking. It will also, however, crucially depend on the quality of the urban fabric. Every successful town or city will require a fluid and flexible land and property market, founded on access to institutional investment, and responding to a clear requirement to provide high quality developments within a clear design framework.

In the early years of the new Millennium, we will become increasingly aware of the fragile nature of the urban environment. Fifty per cent of the global population will soon be living in towns and cities and the numbers will continue to grow. Cities such as Beijing, Mexico City and Cairo are creating a dangerous scale of urbanism which could not have been conceived a century ago. We must lead by example – pioneering and exporting environmental technologies in the same way that we pioneered and exported our industrial prowess some 200 years ago.

We have the opportunity to establish and sustain a new and prosperous future for urban communities throughout England. There is no immediate panacea to at least 20 years of under-investment and urban decline. Nor can any one recommendation secure significant change. However, taken together, the proposals set out in this report, when combined with the right economic and social policies, will provide the necessary impetus. We can harness the driver of the information age to create new economic opportunities. We can harness changing life patterns to attract people to come back and take advantage of the facilities which our towns and cities can offer. And we can harness technology to respond to the environmental imperative to create more sustainable environments.

We can turn our towns and cities around. The humanist city is once more within our grasp. Our actions over the next 20 to 30 years will determine whether we succeed. As we look ahead, and as we develop our policies and strategies, our goal should be that the main beneficiaries of our efforts will be the next generation of urban inhabitants. For it is that aspiration which represents the true vision of a sustainable city.

'...our expectation should be that the main beneficiaries of our investment will be the next generation of urban inhabitants' (Development Trusts Association)

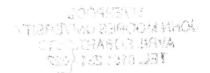

POSTSCRIPT

The Task Force invited different towns and cities across England to submit their vision of what their town would be like in 20 or 30 years time. Over 50 different towns put forward submissions. Perhaps not surprisingly, the most inspiring visions came from young people and we would like to present two of these in closing our report:

'Gravesend into the Millennium'

Class 11, Ifield School, Gravesend

We want to make Gravesend better for everybody.

We think the town will go all green and cars will be banned.

There will be a super fast ferry linking Gravesend to Essex run by a robot.

A force field will cover the town to regulate the environment. There will be no litter. There will be little robots who go around picking up litter and zapping it. There will be disintegrator bins that disintegrate rubbish and turn the rubbish into recycled materials.

We think there will be a virtual reality cinema where the audience walk through the sets and act with the characters in the film.

People shopping will not have carrier bags to carry but everyone will be able to have a hover trolley that uses magnets to hover.

The streets are to be lined with trees and pavements covered in Astroturf to make it look like one big country park.

The town will have big trees all around and millions of flowers in flower beds to make it look nice and give a nice smell.

'What I would like for Hartlepool'

Diane Jones, Class 11Y, Dyke House School, Hartlepool

I would like Hartlepool to stand out above each and every town and city in England.

I hope each individual in Hartlepool will have an occupation, a job to which these people belong.

We need to give each other respect – children, elderly, middle-aged and nature.

I think we should begin by tidying up the area. This will give jobs to people and a tidy area gives people personal pride.

The first thing that will help people get jobs is EDUCATION. How about opening a college for adults, just like children have school, to give them a second chance. With education, we can produce an intelligent, talented workforce.

When the majority of people work, then money goes back into the town, which in turn makes the town grow and prosper.

Stereotypes don't allow change. We will not be a stereotypical north east town, high in unemployment and crime. We need to work together to improve the town, which will hopefully make the people inside the town respect each other and become a team.

Let's build buildings on brownfield areas. Let's use derelict areas that can't be built upon and place grass there, which people can be employed to maintain. A clean healthy heart to the town, which doesn't get littered, in turn gives a clean healthy body.

A clean healthy Hartlepool can contribute to a clean healthy England.

ACKNOWLEDGEMENTS

ACKNOWLEDGEMENTS

URBAN TASK FORCE

Lord Rogers of Riverside	Chairman
Richard Burdett	Director, Cities Programme, London School of Economics
Tony Burton	Assistant Director (Policy), CPRE
Alan Cherry	Chairman, Countryside Properties plc.
Martin Crookston	Director, Llewelyn-Davies
Anthony Dunnett	Chief Executive, South East Economic Development Agency
Sir Peter Hall	Bartlett Professor of Planning, University College London
Phil Kirby	General Manager, BG Properties
David Lunts	Chief Executive, The Prince of Wales Foundation for Architecture & the Urban Environment
Anthony Mayer	Chief Executive, Housing Corporation
Anne Power	Professor of Social Housing, London School of Economics
Sir Crispin Tickell	Chairman, Government Panel on Sustainable Development
Wendy Thomson	Chief Executive, London Borough of Newham
Lorna Walker	Director, Arup

WORKING GROUP MEMBERS

Roger Aldridge	Director of Estates and Store Development, Marks and Spencers plc.
Mike Appleton	Director, AMEC Developments Limited
Tom Bloxham	Chairman, Urban Splash
Chris Brown	Director of Urban Renewal, AMEC Developments Limited
Ben Denton	Director, Abros
Clive Dutton	Head of Regeneration, Sandwell MBC
Peter Fanning	Chief Executive, Public Private Partnership Programme
Imtiaz Farookhi	Chief Executive, National House Building Council
Richard Feilden	Senior Partner, Feilden Clegg Architects
Nicky Gavron	Chair of LGA Planning Committee & Chair of the London Planning Advisory Committee
Professor Malcolm Grant	Head of Department of Land Economy, Cambridge University
Peter Headicar	Reader in Transport Planning, Oxford Brookes University
Maurice Hochschild	Director, European Capital Company Limited
Marie Hodgson	Head of Special Projects, English Partnerships
Doug Johnson	Director of Strategic Support, Newcastle-upon-Tyne City Council

Roger Levett	Director, CAG Consultants Limited
Richard MacCormac	Senior Partner, MacCormac, Jamieson and Prichard
David McKeith	Tax & Legal Services Partner, PricewaterhouseCoopers
Fred Manson	Director of Regeneration & Environment, London Borough of Southwark
Adrian Montague	Head of PFI Task Force, HM Treasury
Sam Richards	Policy Officer Planning, Local Government Association
Professor Tony M Ridley	Head of the Department of Civil & Environmental Engineering and Professor of Transport Engineering, Imperial College of Science, Technology & Medicine
Dickon Robinson	Director of Development & Technical Services, Peabody Trust
Brian Robson	School of Geography, Manchester University
Rosalind Rowe	Director, Real Estate Tax Group, PricewaterhouseCoopers
Tom Russell	Deputy Chief Executive, Manchester City Council
Les Sparks	Director of Planning & Architecture, Birmingham City Council
Bill Stevenson	Deputy Chairman, Bellway PLC
Tony Struthers	Director of Development Services & Deputy Chief Executive, Salford MBC
Tony Travers	Director, Greater London Group, London School of Economics
Michael Ward	Director, CLES
Roger Zogolovitch	Lake Estates
Sir Jack Zunz	Senior Consultant, Arup

We would also like to extend our thanks to all those people who worked and commented on each Chapter of the report.

SECRETARIAT

Jon Rouse (Secretary)	English Partnerships
Miffa Salter	Office for Public Management
Elizabeth Coles	Department of the Environment, Transport and the Regions
Charlie Fulford	KPMG
Emmet Bergin	London School of Economics
Brian Everett	Bellway Homes
Antonia Stacey	Abros

Ruth Phillips
Katrina Rizzolo
Maureen Smith
Peter Smith

LOCAL GOVERNMENT SECONDEES

Pauline De Silva	City Centre Manager, City Centre Management, Leeds
Trevor Howard	Manager, Portfolio Property Management, Coventry
Lesley Punter	Head of Planning and Transport, Reading Borough Council
Peter Yeomans	Senior Development Officer, Birmingham City Council

SPECIAL ACKNOWLEDGEMENTS FOR ONGOING SUPPORT

Laurie Abbot	Richard Rogers Partnership
Richard Best	Director, The Joseph Rowntree Foundation
Jonathan Blackie	Regional Director, North East Regional Development Agency
Richard Caborn MP	Minister for the Regions, Regeneration & Planning, DETR
David Child	Director, The Sheffield SRB Partnership Team
Roger De La Mare	Development Director, The Housing Corporation
Peter Drummond	Labour & Social Affairs Attaché (Benelux), British Embassy, The Hague, NL
Mike Dudman	Head of Investment, Housing Corporation
Paul Evans	Director of Regeneration, DETR
Herbert Giradet	Urban Futures
David Gibson & Michael Lenz	Draught
Paul Hackett	Special Adviser to the Deputy Prime Minister and Minister for the Regions, Regeneration & Planning DETR
Julian Hart	Senior Environmental Scientist, Arup
Maarten Hajer	Professor of Public Policy, University of Amsterdam
Josef Konvitz	Director, Urban Affairs Division, OECD, Paris, FR
Robert Lion	Director General, Energy 21
Stuart Lipton	Chief Executive, Stanhope Property Developers
Sebastian Loew	South Bank University
David Mackay	MBM Arquitectes S A
Duncan Maclennan	Director, ESRC Cities Programme, University of Glasgow
Gerard Maccreanor	Partner, Maccreanor Lavington Architects
Pasqual Maragall	Candidat – President de Generalitat de Catalonia
Clare Mason	Environmental Regeneration, DETR
Arlene McCarthy MEP	Labour's European Spokesperson on Regional Affairs
Seamus Munro	Construction Manager, BG plc
Lucy Musgrave	Director, Architecture Foundation
Greg Parston	Chief Executive, Office for Public Management
John Roberts	Divisional Manager, Regeneration, DETR
David Rock	President, Royal Institution of British Architects

David Rudlin	Director, URBED
Shirley Smith	Consultant, English Partnerships
Max Steinberg	Regional Director, The Housing Corporation North West
Jim Taylor	Former Director, Nottingham City Council
David Utting	Advisor to the Joseph Rowntree Foundation
Phil Walker	Principal Policy Officer, Sigoma
Andrew Wright	Principal, Andrew Wright Associates

INSTITUTIONAL SOUNDING BOARD

British Urban Regeneration Association
House Builders Federation
Institution of Civil Engineers
Local Government Association
National Housing Federation
Royal Town Planning Institute
Shelter
Civic Trust
Royal Institution of Chartered Surveyors
Friends of the Earth
SIGOMA
Royal Institute of British Architects
Institute of Housing
Urban Forum

CONSULTANTS

KPMG
PricewaterhouseCoopers
URBED, in association with MORI and the School for Policy Studies, Bristol University

STUDY TOURS

We would like to thank our hosts on visits to: Manchester, Salford, Sandwell, Sheffield, Liverpool, Hull, Leicester, Portsmouth, Plymouth, Stroud, East London, the Netherlands, Spain, Germany and the U.S.

SPECIAL THANKS TO THE FOLLOWING ORGANISATIONS FOR THEIR GENEROUS SUPPORT

Abros
DETR
English Partnerships
KPMG
PricewaterhouseCoopers
Bellway Homes
Empty Homes Agency
Housing Corporation
Arup
Royal Institution of Chartered Surveyors

INDEX

INDEX

Italics have been used for figures

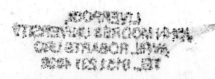